Cusp

Cusp

Recollections of Poetry in Transition

edited by

Geraldine Monk

Shearsman Books

Published in the United Kingdom in 2012 by
Shearsman Books Ltd
50 Westons Hill Drive
Emersons Green
BRISTOL
BS16 7DF

Shearsman Books Ltd Registered Office
30–31 St. James Place, Mangotsfield, Bristol BS16 9JB
(this address not for correspondence)

ISBN 978-1-84861-250-1
First Edition

Acknowledgements
Versions of some of these pieces have previously appeared as follows:
Connie Pickard's 'Basil Bunting and Me' first appeared in *Stand*;
Tom Pickard's 'Work Conchy' first appeared in *Northern Review*.

The editor and publisher are grateful to Thomas Meyer, executor of the Estate
of Jonathan Williams, for permission to quote the letter by Jonathan Williams
quoted at the end of Tom Pickard's 'Work Conchy', pp.93–95.

CONTENTS

Preface

This book is probably best described as a collective autobiography. With few exceptions the contributing poets write about their origins and influences and how they became involved in poetry. My main objective is to present the spirit of a brief era which, in retrospect, was exceptional in its momentum towards the democratisation and dissemination of poetry. The era or "cusp" I'm concentrating on is between World War II and the advent of the World Wide Web. Already extraordinary in its social, political and cultural upheaval, it seems even more heightened when set against the technological transformation which has since been unleashed.

As the next dazzling innovation presents its irresistible self to the world—iPads, Xboxes, Skype, Kindles, desktop publishing, email and the plethora of social networking sites, memory of a time before these inventions becomes increasingly distant, if not altogether alien. With the emergence of the second generation of children who are computer-savvy and to whom the new technology is second nature, it begins to seem inconceivable that none of this was available a couple of decades ago. We didn't realise it at the time but we were living out the last few years in a world to which there would be no return.

But why this collection when the web holds many pages of biographical information on the majority of poets here? Firstly, books still have a strong draw and contrary to popular belief not everyone is on the web. Secondly, the web, for all its wonders, can be very bitty and disjointed so building up connections and interconnections can be very hit and miss. This book brings poets together in one place where those connections can be made at a glance. As space on the printed page is finite and precious so I have limited my catchment area predominantly to poets living and writing in England & Wales. These two countries seemed to harbour the nerve centre of the poetic activity I was most aware of and which was such a formative part in the development of the poetic aesthetics of the late 20th Century.

I have also concentrated on poetry happening away from those two strongholds of poetic power, and sometimes clubbish exclusivity, London and Cambridge. I am not denying the huge impact both places have had on poetry, nor the fine poets that have been connected with them (many of them my good friends and colleagues) but there is a growing tendency of associates to write up these places as if they were the *only* centres of poetry. It is a paradoxical turning inwards towards insularity when the truth is much more complex, extensive and exciting. The poetic insurgence that began in the 1950s/60s was very much a provincial one emanating from the industrial cities of the North and Midlands such as Liverpool, Newcastle, Nottingham and Cardiff. To ignore this regional involvement and importance is to cut the heart and soul out of our poetic legacy. Not that this book is a total London/Cambridge-free zone, far from it, but my emphasis is most definitely *Elsewhere*.

*

The seemingly spontaneous outbreak of poetries and poetry communities which emerged out of the dreary ashes of post-war austerity was a phenomenon no one could have predicted. The uniformity of appearance and rigid conformity of thought was stifling. Behaviour, attitudes and emotions were in permanent check. It could be very lonely. Up until the 1970s few people owned a telephone. Communication was almost exclusively through the post which lacked the immediacy of email but had its own rhythm with copious writing of letters and two deliveries a day. But how did we all find each other in the first place? It seems highly improbable that such contacts should have happened at all. Jim Burns sets the scene in the opening essay as he remembers 1950s Lancashire; quoting the American poet Gary Snyder he begins, "you had to go a long way to find a friend in Fifties America". It was the same in Fifties Britain. Jim outlines the very real difficulty of finding kindred spirits in small provincial towns. Fortunately he did eventually find them and became one of our most enduring and valuable poets. It is worth noting that after all these years I still haven't met or had direct contact with many of the poets in this book. I've never met Jim Burns but I shared my very first review with him, courtesy of Jeff Nuttall in *Aquarius* in 1977.

Everyone has their own story of how they came to be involved in poetry at this time but the two main areas of contact were through the small press publishing network and the alternative or specialist bookshops. It is no coincidence that almost all contributors either ran a press or, in the case of Alan Halsey, Kris Hemensley, Peter Riley and Peter Finch ran a press *and* ran or owned a bookshop. Bookshops were the nerve centres of the poetry world. Since the advent of the World Wide Web both presses and bookshops have been in sharp decline.

The running order of the book is loosely chronological, starting with poets born before or during the war, it forms a very imperfect arc. Following Jim Burns comes another "scene setter" from Peter Riley with his more cheerful account of another cotton town, Stockport. Peter notes the communality of hymns and the phenomenon of both west gallery music and the textile workers' love of choral societies. Next comes a sweet and succinct contribution from the committed "provincialist" and esteemed poet, Roy Fisher. Roy also pays tribute to the inimitable Gael Turnbull, one of the great unsung influences on British poetry. Moving slightly south, Simon Cutts put me in contact with Hannah Neate who has conducted a superb survey on Nottingham in the 1960s and The Trent Bookshop. It has extensive interviews with Simon and Martin Parnell, recounting the excitement and difficulties of opening an alternative bookshop in this small Midland city.

Chris Torrance, another poet of considerable influence and founder of the famed Cabaret 246 in Cardiff, briefly worked as a London solicitor before scurrying to the hills of Wales with his beloved words. He has remained there ever since, still writing, and still in contact with the Carshalton "mob" pals of his youth. A stroke of good fortune was my chance encounter with Gillian Whiteley. She had been working on Jeff Nuttall's archives. "Have you heard of him?" she asked me. Heard of him! Jeff still works in mysterious ways. Gillian kindly penned a tribute for me about one of our most remarkable and colourful characters who was a tireless champion and generous supporter of the work of others, not least my own.

Nuttall is not the only dearly departed one to be remembered. Connie Pickard and Tony Baker both evoke touching memories of Basil Bunting, a man who obviously elicits great affection from those who knew him. In his beautifully woven piece from his time in the North East, Tony Baker also remembers his dear friend Ric Caddel. Staying in the North East, Tom Pickard, co-founder of the legendary Morden Tower with Connie, recounts his battle to be officially recognised as a poet. His extraordinary saga which entails civic and governmental involvement, from fawning acceptance to outright aggression was given a running commentary in the local press. It is a scenario inconceivable today.

Kris Hemensley is your man if you want a roll call of who was there, where and when. A resident of Australia since the '60s, he remembers his formative years in Southampton and his meetings with F.T. Prince. Kris also alludes to the strange disconnect of living in Australia, both part of, and apart from, the UK poetry world. Over in Cardiff the tireless experimenter Peter Finch was shaking foundations and managing Wales' flagship bookshop, Oriel. John Freeman would also end up in Cardiff via many places, including a stint in Sheffield. It was here he met David Tipton, whose Rivelin Press gave "a public presence to a swathe of mostly northern or northern-based writers". Like others in this book he also recounts that awful day he heard of the death of his friend, the poet John Riley, who was so mindlessly murdered in Leeds.

Peter Hodgkiss is a rare creature indeed, someone who was deeply involved and central to the poetry world but wasn't actually a poet. Having no vested interest other than a love of contemporary poetry, Peter produced the essential *Poetry Information* with its invaluable listings sections (a feat that Hercules would have balked at) followed by the wittily titled *Not Poetry* and if that's not enough he ran Galloping Dog Press. Why? Read on. Alan Halsey and David Annwn opted to join forces and present their contributions through the momentum of conversation. It develops into an organic and energetic exploration of poetry and poetics, place, displacement and passions with amusing insights and serious observation.

Fred Beake, whom I always associate with the West Country, was born in Cheshire and spent much of his childhood in rural Yorkshire. Here he tells how he founded *The Poet's Voice,* which eventually become *Poetry Salzburg Review.* It would be hard to find a bigger contrast between *The Poet's Voice* and Paul Buck and Glenda George's *Curtains.* Paul and Glenda were digging into corners that, at the time, no one else dared to dig, bringing writers like Bataille, Blanchot and Jabès (Rosmarie Waldrop being a major translator of Jabès and a *Curtains* contributor) to a small but hungry English-speaking audience. The unashamed erotic contents of *Curtains* would eventually see them fall foul of the authorities, with dispiriting consequences.

At roughly the same time I was staring out the window of a St Joseph's Roman Catholic school in Lancashire, John Seed was staring out the window of a St Joseph's Roman Catholic School in Co. Durham. Both of us experiencing the harshness, and at times brutality, of a Catholic education soothed by ritualistic spectacle and the dulcet tones of Latin. My own contribution tells the bittersweet tale of escaping the factory to live the life of a poet whilst John tells how he came across new worlds of poetry in the 'Ultima Thule' bookshop in Newcastle upon Tyne.

Back in the West Country we find poets Tilla Brading, Frances Presley and Tim Allen. Tilla, along with Derrick Woolf, working out of Coleridge Cottage, had a trio of magazine titles to their names: *Quorum, Odyssey* and *PRQ.* Frances Presley talks about her time and travels in America and her involvement with the collective publishing venture, North and South. Tim Allen, editor of *Terrible Work,* muses and amuses on the highs and lows of running poetry series such as the Poetry Exchange and The Language Club. He demonstrates the difficulties of running poetry events outside the comfort zone of colleges and universities.

Ian Davidson gives a thumbnail sketch of life at Essex University with classes from Douglas Oliver and Ralph Hawkins, and fellow alumni such as Kelvin Corcoran, John Muckle and Anna Mendelssohn a.k.a. Grace Lake. Nicholas Johnson could set up a reading on Ascension Island at 3 in the morning and still get a packed house. Here he tells how he founded the Six Towns Poetry Festival in Stoke-on-Trent and made it a runaway success. Lastly, one thing that struck me in these accounts was how few people cited pop music as an influence. Even someone as massive as Bob Dylan gets relatively little mention which I found surprising. So it was with some delight I received Anthony Mellors' piece which is almost exclusively about the influence of pop music—and when Pink Floyd gives way to The Smiths and The Fall, with perfect symmetry we end back in the North West of England where this book began.

*

It is hoped that through the recollections of these poets a fair and comprehensive picture emerges of the nature and interconnectedness of the poetry world with its bookshops, pioneering reading series and primitive self-publishing techniques. Without a doubt there are many more poets I would have loved to invite but, due to lack of space, it wasn't possible. Everyone will cite someone who "should" have been included and I'll be the first to agree. However, the generosity of the contributors does amount to a fair reflection of the people, poets and events of the time.

It would take a social historian to explain why so many young, working-class people took to poetry at this time, especially the more experimental areas of expression. The uninspiring life on offer at the time, with few having the opportunity to go to university, was enough to spur us on to search for something else. With the after-effects of two world wars still palpable and the Cold War hotting up with the ever-present spectre of nuclear warfare forming a permanent, doom-ridden backdrop, keeping calm and carrying on until World War III was not an option.

It is evident that there have been many cultural changes since the "cusp" and I shall pick up on three aspects which I found of particular note. The first is the insidious policing and civic opprobrium which was prevalent at the time. The famous *Oz* obscenity trials were just one amongst many instances of censorship. Dave Cunliffe found himself before Blackburn magistrates court when an issue of his magazine *Poetmeat* was deemed obscene. He narrowly missed a prison sentence but the fine incurred all but ruined him financially. In Yorkshire, Jay Jeff Jones fell foul of the authorities when he published 6 short stories by Jeff Nuttall in *New Yorkshire Writing*. The fallout from this brought attention to Paul Buck and Glenda George's *Curtains*. Glenda outlines the vindictive nature of the times when benefits towards their son's school meals and uniform were withdrawn.

Not only the poetry police but the moral police were still a force to be reckoned with; when Connie Pickard left her first husband for Tom she got the sack from her job as a teacher and was advised to leave the village. Indeed, Tom's whole piece demonstrates how poetry, outside the shelter of universities, was very susceptible to the vagaries of community approval. The present trend amongst some young poets to spout expletives every other line or shout obscenities is all well and good but they do it in the full knowledge that they're not going to be arrested or face potential imprisonment or a hefty fine.

Secondly, we come to the inevitable question of where all the women were. Their absence from poetry events in the 1960s and '70s seems shocking now (see Hannah Neate's list of participants at the Nottingham Poetry Festival in 1966). By 1985 David Tipton had mustered 33 of us women poets together for his Rivelin Grapheme Press anthology *Purple & Green*, and that same year Glenda George had gathered a dozen more women for her guest-edited edition of *Reality Studios*. The situation was getting better but it was by no means overwhelming. I have written about this elsewhere as have others (see the online magazine *Jacket* 34, October 2007, a debate moderated by the marvellous American poet Cathy Wagner) so I will keep this brief.

As with the policing of poetry mentioned above it has to be remembered that it was a very different world then. National Service was still compulsory for men until 1960, corporal punishment was still administered in schools, the contraceptive pill wasn't yet commonplace. Gender rôles were still very much prescribed and segregation of the sexes much more pronounced. Men didn't push prams and women weren't supposed to smoke in the street. So it wasn't just women who had to find their voices: men also had to find theirs. Reading and writing poetry certainly wasn't expected of "real" men. However, because of social constraints and stunted attitudes, it was always going to be immensely more difficult for women. The way forward was not just to write poetry but to start running presses, become editors and run poetry events, as Carmen Callil realised in 1973 when she started Virago Press. Ultimately, women's rôle in poetry wasn't men's to give but women's to take and this is now happening with a determined confidence and exceptional poetry.

Thirdly, it is noticeable how little theory and theorists are referred to, with most contributors citing other poets as their main inspiration or influence. It is now almost obligatory for poets to trot out a litany of theorists as their main source of influence with other poets taking a very poor second place. I find this an extremely sad failure of belief in one's chosen genre. It is an attitude that has emerged from the universities, not the streets. John Freeman sums it up perceptively in his book *The*

Less Received (Stride Publications 2000): "…Critical Theory, or simply Theory, now dominates university English departments in Britain, the rest of Europe and America… one effect of the dominance of Theory has been to make its adherents less receptive to the prophecy of poetry. Poets, and writers in general, tend to be regarded by theorists less as seers than as impostors or dupes to be seen through, to be caught out, unconsciously reinforcing a dominant and malign ideology". He continues with the chilling anecdote, "One professor announced, in a short lecture that he saw it as 'his mission' to try the writers of the past and find them guilty."

That "mission" fills me with dread and foreboding as it demonstrates the success of the theorists' gambit to destroy the "author" and usurp the crown of creativity. I can see why some academics might endorse this, but to see poets buying into it is disheartening. Maybe it is a passing fashion but it is a fashion that is also infecting the art colleges. If there was any evidence that this love-in with theory was producing better poetry or visual art I'd be all for it but I don't see that evidence anywhere.

As Creative Writing courses become more prevalent in our universities and colleges the "lives of poets" are changing beyond all recognition, maybe for better, maybe worse, maybe neither, maybe just differently. The post-war, pre-Web "cusp" was certainly very different from what had gone before and what came after, as can be seen in the diversity of the lives of the poets gathered here.

Geraldine Monk
2012

The Left Bank of the Ribble

Jim Burns

Gary Snyder once remarked that "you had to go a long way to find a friend in Fifties America" and it always seemed to me that the same was generally true of this country in the late 1950s and early 1960s. I take it that Snyder was referring to the scarcity of kindred spirits in terms of poetry, or the sort of poetry he was interested in and wanted to write, and I'm certainly not talking about local friends of the kind you meet at work or through an interest like sport or music. It's the literary aspect that concerns me here. In Preston, Lancashire, in the late 1950s, there was the kind of mini-Bohemia revolving around a few jazz musicians and folk-singers, and some students and staff from the art school, and it had the atmosphere of provincial non-conformity so well evoked in Philip Callow's novel *The Hosanna Man*. But I couldn't find anyone who was seriously interested in what was happening in poetry.

I'd left the army in 1957 and soon after began to pick up on the new writing that was starting to filter through from the United States, with the Beats obviously to the fore. They were the first ones to make an impact, though, as other books became available and little magazines spread the word, I became aware of the Black Mountain poets, the New York writers, and various individuals who didn't necessarily fit into any particular group. I think it's essential to say that the little magazines were of key importance and without them it would have been much harder to find out what was happening and who the most interesting poets were. Publications like *Evergreen Review, Big Table, Yugen,* and *The Outsider* in America and *Migrant, Satis, Outburst,* and *New Departures* in Britain, had an important role to play and as they usually weren't easy to obtain, even in London, I subscribed to them. I've written about all these magazines elsewhere, so I won't go into detail about their contents, but they all provided informative leads to the new, even if it sometimes didn't appeal to me. It seemed necessary to read it, though.

It took me a little while to find my own feet as a poet and in 1962 I had my first published poems in a little magazine called *New Voice* which, in true little magazine fashion, never appeared again after that first issue. It at least placed me alongside one or two poets I'd read in other magazines and who were writing in a way I found stimulating. I'm thinking in particular of Anselm Hollo, a Finnish poet then living in London and in touch with Gael Turnbull, Michael Shayer, Roy Fisher and others clustered around Migrant Press, as well as with American poets.

In a way receiving all these magazines was a means of finding friends, or at least realising that there were people who might be on a similar literary wavelength to myself. I still needed to know other poets in person and it was coming across a copy of Dave Cunliffe's *Poetmeat* that gave me the opportunity to do just that. Dave lived in Blackburn, not too far from Preston, and after getting in touch with him we arranged to meet. I can't remember whether that first meeting took place when Dave and Tina Morris came to Preston or when I visited them in Blackburn. We got along and, among other things, I have a memory of a poetry reading in Manchester with Dave, Tina, David Chaloner, and myself participating and a small audience listening to us. I also recall that when most of the people involved, poets and audience, went to a nearby pub after the reading some of them were refused service by the landlord on the grounds that he didn't want beatniks in his bar. Narrow attitudes still prevailed in the provinces in the early 1960s. And perhaps I could be guilty of them. In 1964 I wrote an article called *Blackburn Beats* for *The Guardian* in which I expressed surprise at finding someone like Dave Cunliffe in the town and that *Poetmeat* was published there. The BBC picked up on it and we were interviewed for a radio programme.

Dave and Tina Morris never received the recognition they deserved for the work they did with *Poetmeat*. I'm not going to claim it was an outstanding publication. The contents were often variable in quality, with the early issues perhaps overloaded with would-be Beat writing. And, inevitably, many of the contributors failed to develop as poets. What did happen to them? Kenneth Rexroth once said: "The world is full of sea captains who used to play trombone". Those who published a poem or two in little magazines were for a time just as much a part of the scene as those poets who went on to publish books. Returning to the contents of *Poetmeat* it's useful to quote something that Denise Levertov said when writing about some British magazines in *Kulchur*: "A lot of the poems in them are not especially good, perhaps, but any kind of 'outburst' after more than a decade of unrelieved propriety is a healthy symptom."

Poetmeat did improve and in 1965 devoted a full issue to what it described as "The New British Poetry" which tended to invite an unfair comparison with Donald Allen's famous anthology *The New American Poetry 1945–60*. The *Poetmeat* selection wasn't perfect and some poets who should have been there (Edwin Morgan and Andrew Crozier, to name a couple) were missing while others could well have been omitted without any great effect on the overall contents. But it was a reasonable attempt to present a broad survey of some of the activity taking place around the country in the early 1960s. It's an indication of the growing interest in what was referred to as the "underground" poetry scene that this issue of *Poetmeat* was launched with a reading at the ICA in London with many of the contributors taking part. Looking back to 1965 I seem to remember Roy Fisher, Gael Turnbull, Anselm Hollo, Michael Shayer and Michael Horovitz being there. Interestingly, they were all also present, along with Jeff Nuttall, Adrian Mitchell, and many others, at the large weekend gathering organised by the Trent Bookshop in Nottingham in 1966 which was another example of how something new was happening in poetry.

Before leaving *Poetmeat* it's worth adding that, along with the poems it published, the magazine provided a service with its coverage of other similar publications, including books and pamphlets from small presses which often couldn't be found in bookshops. It's also relevant to note that being active as a poet and publisher, particularly of what could be seen as radical or offbeat writing, was almost guaranteed to invite attention from the police and others suspicious of any unusual activity in a place like Blackburn. Dave Cunliffe was eventually accused of obscenity when he published *The Golden Convolvulus*, a textual collage of limericks, toilet-wall rhymes, and the like. He was found guilty at Blackburn Magistrates Court of the lesser charge of indecency, and escaped imprisonment but the hefty fine put *Poetmeat* out of business.

To cover all the magazines coming from around the country in the 1960s would be impossible, but a couple I remember were *Origins Diversions* from Carshalton and *Iconolatre* from Hartlepool. One magazine led to another because the need to communicate meant that editors exchanged publications and listed what they'd received. Budding poets could then easily obtain the addresses of magazines likely to be interested in their work. Personal contact was important, too, and among those who paid visits to me in Preston were Chris Torrance, Andrew Crozier (his *The English Intelligencer* worksheets were invaluable at the time), Tim Longville, editor of the excellent *Grosseteste Review*, and many others. One visitor I remember was the American poet George Dowden. He had some links to the "deep image" poets in America, though I have to admit that I was never really sure what that term meant. In any case, a tour around the pubs of Preston with some friends tended to distract from theories about poetry and ended with George and me unsuccessfully trying to board a Russian ship berthed in Preston dock. I think George wanted to establish some sort of rapport with the Russians and so dispose of the Cold War. I wrote a humorous account of the events that *The Guardian* published under the title, *The Night of the Poet*.

A publication from this period that deserves attention was the *Anthology of Little Magazine Poets*, edited by Tony Dash and published by Asylum Publications, Bootle, in 1968. It had work by 27 poets, most of them regulars in little magazines, and included Paul Evans, Chris Torrance, David Chaloner, Pete Morgan and Dave Cunliffe. What also makes it of interest now is the front cover, which shows a map of Britain with the locations of over 40 magazines pinpointed. They're all long gone, of course, with the exception of *Ambit*.

Encouraged by the contacts I'd made, sometimes in person but more often by post, and aware that publishing a little magazine would be a good way to put me even more in touch, I decided to start *Move* in 1964. To put together a first issue I simply wrote to poets I'd read and liked in other publications. I think everyone I contacted responded and the magazine featured Dave Cunliffe, Tina Morris, Roy Fisher, Lee Harwood, Kirby Congdon (an American I was in touch with), Anselm Hollo, Ian Vine, George Dowden, and Lionel Kearns, a Canadian then living in England. Later issues had Gael Turnbull, John James, Tom Clark, Gill Vickers, Daphne Buckle, Max Finstein, Larry Eigner, Joan Gilbert, Pamela Millward and many others. Andrew Crozier guest-edited one issue and had work from Jack Spicer, Robin Blaser, and Richard Duerden. And there was a supplement to *Move* called *Thirteen*

American Poets which included Charles Bukowski, Taylor Mead, Jack Micheline, and Carol Bergé.

Move was economically produced. It was duplicated, had 20 pages in each issue, and either pink or blue paper covers with a printed sticker saying MOVE in large letters. I typed the stencils and briefly had a small hand duplicator on which I ran off the required number of sheets. We (my wife Audrey helped) produced 200 copies of each issue. When the duplicator proved unsuitable I shopped around for help. Dave Cunliffe did at least one issue on his better machine. I remember going to Blackburn to collect all the loose sheets and bring them back in a large suitcase on the bus. Another issue was duplicated courtesy of the local branch of a large union, though I don't think the branch secretary ever knew about it. And one appeared from the Town Hall, thanks to an amiable oddball who worked there. By today's standards it no doubt all seems very primitive and time-consuming, but the interest and energy pushed me along and it seemed important to get the magazine distributed, with perhaps a third of the copies going to America and Canada and a few to Mexico, Australia, and one or two other places. Did I really think that 200 copies of a tiny duplicated magazine were likely to change things? I think I did at the time and it did work in terms of putting me in touch with other poets and editors.

It has been suggested that almost all the editors were poets and that we were merrily printing each other. There is some truth in that idea, but it was a small world and we possibly thought that supporting our fellow editor-poets was a kind of defence against the indifference of the literary establishment and the general public. The limited audience for little magazines and small-press books was where the interest was and, at that stage, not too many people were thinking in terms of popular success, large sales, and being noticed in mass-circulation newspapers and magazines. It wasn't likely to happen, though the Liverpool Poets, primarily Roger McGough, Adrian Henri, and Brian Patten, did attract attention for a time, perhaps because they functioned in a setting that journalists could manipulate. This isn't a comment on the quality of their work, some of which I liked, but has more to do with social factors. Liverpool lent itself to being written about, as for example in Sean Hignett's 1966 novel, *A Picture to Hang on the Wall*.

As well as placing poems in many of the little magazines of the day I was writing articles and reviews for various publications, and in 1965 I was asked to write a quarterly column on little magazines for *Tribune*, the left-wing weekly paper. In time the column was extended to cover small-press pamphlets and books and it ran until 1984. I'd also edited another magazine, *Palantir*, for several years. It had been born in 1974 but only two issues had appeared and in 1976 I was asked to take over. I was conscious of the fact that things had changed since I terminated *Move* in 1968. There were far more poetry readings, many of them arranged by groups or organisations so that poets were paid and didn't have to rely on a few free drinks and a makeshift bed on someone's floor. Even on a local level there was more activity. In the early 1960s I was very much a lone voice in Preston but by 1976 there were several other poets in town (Alan Dent, Philip Pacey, Michael Curtis), a poetry workshop met regularly in a pub, occasional readings by established poets took place, and Preston Polytechnic had an evening creative writing course. Duncan Glen's magazine *Akros*, though mostly devoted to Scottish poetry, was also published in Preston, and in 1970 he had asked me to write an article about what he termed "English-English" poetry and select a small group of English poets (Andrew Crozier, David Tipton, Wes Magee, among them) to accompany it.

It didn't seem as necessary to use *Palantir* as a platform for promoting a specific kind of poetry, not that I'd ever done that with *Move* beyond perhaps favouring a few poets I found particularly interesting. A natural suspicion about cliques, manifestos, and theories, always inclined me to look at poems on an individual basis and not as expressions of a specific approach. As a consequence I just published what appealed to me.

Move had been financed out of my own pocket and had been cheap enough to give away. I did ask anyone wanting a copy to send a stamp to cover postage and a few people did, but on the whole most copies were sent out free. *Palantir*, however, had some support from Preston Poly and, at their insistence, I applied for a grant from North West Arts. They did provide some small sums for a few years and those enabled me to publish a bigger and tidier magazine than *Move* had ever been. I have to acknowledge that neither the Poly nor North West Arts ever tried to influence the contents of *Palantir* and I always had complete editorial control. My notion was that I didn't want to edit something focusing solely on poetry so I tried to vary the contents by using some short stories and reviews of books about art, politics, films, the social and literary history of bohemianism, and other subjects. There were reviews of contemporary poetry, and I have to admit to indulging myself by printing work by and about writers with Beat associations, that being a particular area of interest for me. I don't think everyone approved of what I was doing with the magazine and I got the impression that certain poets had little or no interest in anything other than their own work and that of a few of their literary acquaintances. Other people, though, seemed to find the mixture of prose and poetry entertaining.

Palantir ran for 23 issues, 21 of them with me as editor, and just a few of the contributors were Edwin Morgan, Roy Fisher, Edwin Brock, Gavin Ewart, Michael Hamburger, Lee Harwood, Douglas Dunn, Martin Stannard, John Ash, Robert Sheppard, David Chaloner, Christopher Middleton, Alan Halsey, and Barry MacSweeney. There were also Americans like Seymour Krim, Carl Solomon, Fielding Dawson and John Clellon Holmes. I was sometimes accused of not publishing enough women writers but a quick survey showed that they were quite well represented in the magazine. I won't name them all but they included Tina Morris, Fleur Adcock, Diana Hallett, Corinne Howells, Marguerite Prisk (a satirical poem about several male editors-poets, including myself, at a symposium in Cardiff), Patricia Pogson, Farida Majid, Rosemary Maxwell, Valerie Sinason, Judith Kazantsis, Elizabeth Bartlett, Vivienne Finch, Jane Deverson and several more. There was also prose from Joy Walsh and Suzanne Stern-Gillet, and an interview with Carolyn Cassady. The reason for using the work, whether by males or females, was because I found it interesting and not because it represented a particular ideology or literary theory.

I decided to end *Palantir* when I left Preston in 1983, partly due to the difficulties I'd encountered with printing and distribution, but also because I felt that I'd done enough with it. It was only a short time later that *Tribune* thought that my little magazines and small presses column had served its purpose and no longer had the relevance it once had. They were probably right in that the social situation was different in 1984 to what had existed in 1965. In any case, I wanted to do something different, though I carried on reviewing for *Tribune* for another ten or so years. And I wrote quite a few short histories of various little magazines so that their contributions to literature would be remembered and a correct historical record established.

Looking back it strikes me that if anyone wants to understand what was happening outside London, and away from the literary establishment, in the 1960s then a study of the little magazines is essential. The problem may be that tracking down many of the flimsy, small circulation publications could be difficult. If that's the case then an argument can be made for looking at three anthologies: the *New British Poetry* issue of *Poetmeat*; the *Anthology of Little Magazine Poets*; and *Children of Albion: Poetry of the 'Underground' in Britain*. Michael Horovitz's selection is the key one, but the others supplement it, and his long afterword, written in his typically idiosyncratic manner, provides useful information about activities in the provinces and some obscure publications.

There were several other anthologies, all of them published as Corgi paperbacks, which can also be referred to: *Love Love Love* (1967), edited by Pete Roche; *Doves for the Seventies* (1969), edited by Peter Robins; *C'Mon Everybody: Poetry of Dance* (1971) edited by Pete Morgan. Not all of the work in these collections, and the ones mentioned above, has stood the test of time. But that's true of any period of poetry. It's a fact that very little poetry is truly memorable, but that doesn't mean to say that it should be dismissed easily, especially when we're looking back. What does come through from reading the publications concerned is the openness of the era in terms of the kind of poems that were written and published and the range of contributors they came from. It was an openness often decried by many academics and established critics, and I wouldn't want to deny that it could lead to untidy writing and sometimes silliness. But some interesting work was produced and I've always thought that the flawed but interesting might be of more value than the worthy but dull.

Whenceforth

Peter Riley

1

We had nothing to complain about. We were not underprivileged, or economically disadvantaged, or in any way disregarded. We could do or get anything we wanted, as far as we knew, within the norms we inhabited, which were not restrictive in what mattered. Our sociality was as good as anyone else's, and maybe held relict performances long lost to the four-wheel-drive Surrey boys playing at estate management. Long, long gone. Before the coldness and boredom of modernity crept in we gathered at each others' houses and made music. It wasn't "tradition"—the solos were from sheet music and together we sang any old thing. My "Uncle" (who was not even related) Walter was a very good pianist, adept at some kind of 1940s swing, also community singing and hymns for the local Sunday-school of which he was the superintendent. Otherwise he supervised the local marshalling yards. His wife, Jessie, a tiny woman from Oldham with a piercing voice and thick accent, was a brilliant comic actress. Given a good script she could have an audience helpless. My Uncle (who was related) Norman was also a good swing (or kind of half-jazz) pianist who sometimes sat in on professional bands. My father was also a good pianist, indeed gave lessons, but stuck to amateur classical on account of a sense of family exceptionality. These people were not unrecognised flowers in a provincial desert. We recognised them. The school plays were more effective than most things I've seen on a stage since, and included rarities such as Milton's *Samson Agonistes,* which the school did in about 1956. So it was with many things: choral societies, amateur theatricals, and The Stockport Amateur Operatic Society which did musicals and whose *Show Boat*, circa 1955, was a triumph; I still remember that the rendition of *Ol' Man River* stopped the show. These performances succeeded because they were not subverted by an alien professionalism. They were for us and of us, there where we were. We didn't go to London to see if it was being done any better there, why should we? We weren't trying to copy something seen on TV. It had been like this for centuries. The Lancashire hand-loom weavers had their own unique and active musical culture in the 18th Century based on Handel. I only recently discovered that traditions of west gallery music have persisted aurally in moorland villages of the southern Pennines to this day. Such practices were progressively eroded, with a core persistence which was remarkably resilient. If we but knew it, Thomas Hardy was our spokesman. I only caught the edge of this musical sociality before it withered. I later learned that if I'd been around fifty years earlier I would have known something richer, and more specific to the locality, but I would probably never have got out of it.

We got a good education, in my case by scholarship to a direct grant school at eleven, but that wasn't the only way. We left the school with no excuse for not knowing the rudiments of science, the content of European history and English literature, the musical classics, the situations and conditions of most countries on the globe, at least one foreign language, and the whereabouts of the hole in the hedge between us and the girls' school. We were also, in spite of ourselves, kept physically fit. We were privileged, but didn't feel it because we'd gotten there by work, passing examinations and doing our homework. Others paid for the privileges, and others were dumped in low-grade schools.

The culture we absorbed didn't deal in "attitudes" but knowledge, and nobody ever suggested that we or anybody else had such a thing as an "identity" to be safeguarded, personal or group. We learned what we were as we went along, from within and from without. There were inspirational teachers: the remarkable John Stanley, arts master, not so much for the art but for leading troupes of boys out on excursions: to archaeological excavation at Bakewell, to the Dolomites and the Pyrenees and around Italy and Spain... at a sufficiently slow pace and condition of venture for it never to be forgotten. And William Johnson, head of English, a Leavisite and admirer of T.S. Eliot, which was more-or-less what you needed at that stage of things. I leapt ahead of him and wrote the minutes of the school debating and literary society in the manner of Pound's early Cantos. Pound became my aerial, the songs and the satire, the extraordinary "floating" of words into the mental air. Fifty years later I'm informed by some smart tabloid poet-pundit that it was all a big mistake. It wasn't a mistake, not at that stage. Later it was a disaster but that didn't invalidate the first lessons.

At sixth-form parties in our house when my parents were out, to which a few young women luckily gained access because of school contacts with local drama groups, I sometimes at the end of the evening turned the lights low and put Varèse's *Poème Electronique* on the stereo. It usually went down very well. Those sonorous booms and a disappearing choir intoning what sounded very like "Ongar"… People sat and lay around, sipped their drinks and listened intently, and were interested. How was this possible? (a) Sexual activity of any kind was so unlikely as to be not worth thinking about, so proceedings didn't splinter. We all stayed together. (b) Economic constraints on alcohol supply were such that we all still knew who and where we were. (c) There was no pop. What did we use the stereo for through the evening prior to Varèse? I don't know, maybe some jazz or folk, or it was silent and we talked. The Beatles hadn't yet struck, nobody was very interested in American Skiffle, R&B, C&W, or whatever interest there was it didn't become a necessity, key to personal advance, exclusivity, volume to the top. If maybe Lonnie Donegan was OK, or Mozart for that matter, you could also turn to, or accept when offered, Varèse, not having been primed to be repelled. (d) Something greater than any of these, something now out of the question, which meant that we had and needed no leverage onto Varèse, no position under threat, no programme, no correctness—Varèse was not part of some campaign. And our ears were free in the same way that our thought was free—to pursue the narrow confines normally available compared with the scope of the rich, but pursued in such an unthreatened and openly debated manner that an arrival from another world, like Varèse, wasn't any kind of problem. It arrived, and you gave it ear. If you can listen to Varèse now without experiencing repulsion, you're assumed to be a member of some élite force of revolutionary heavies. It was a form of innocence.

2

I was born in Stockport in 1940, during an air-raid. From the hospital window you could see Manchester burning in the distance. Stockport is an industrial market town now absorbed into Greater Manchester, formerly a mill town specialising in men's felt hats, the dampness of the climate being considered particularly favourable to the felt-making processes. It certainly seemed to rain an awful lot. Around mid-century most men stopped wearing hats, except for the perennial northern peaked caps, which are mostly not made of felt. This left Stockport as the nondescript block of urban spread which I was brought up in. But the hills of the Peak District were visible on the horizon from the town centre and the cultural facilities of Manchester, which were not negligible in those days, were within easy reach. We inhabited this town as very much the normal and median stratum of society: office workers, shop assistants, nursing staff… The grandparent generation had been mill workers. Your fathers, and usually your mothers, went to work; you went to school, and came back in the late afternoon, and all this daily rhythmic to-and-fro took place through streets, big streets and little streets, streets leading to more streets, with areas of waste ground and parklands here and there, surrounded by streets. When not walking from A to B you mostly sat at desks or tables, or larked around in the various corners of free space which were to hand, and slept. Most people lived in standard three-bedroom brick houses, in semi-detached rows, most streets resembling most others, but with an awareness of older and poorer zones of cottage rows, and of better off, possibly even middle-class, larger detached houses, not far away. To all outward appearances it was a dull place.

So how did I, coming from this environment, become involved in a career in poetry which, whether it works or not, sees itself as positioned centrally and has a modicum of success which agrees with this: that it is "high culture", the very contrary of "provincial". Was this done by removal and disaffection from Stockport, by insertion in a very different milieu? Even if so, were there forces in operation within Stockport all those years ago which impelled me to this particular form of ambition? Was something carried over from one to the other, was there a continuity? Perhaps none of it is surprising, or needs explaining. Perhaps the University of Cambridge and all that followed was no more culturally rich, sophisticated, better informed or in touch with modernity, than Stockport was, and the lives lived there no more fulfilled or creative.

In that case it is all one, and those northern streets are where I still am, the country, the condition, the dialect, that I inhabit. Nothing has changed. The poetry arises from the entire history, the knowledge and the ignorance hand in hand. I write as a ten-year-old and as a 70-year-old and as everything in-between. This is individuality itself, the this-ness of a person's being. The streets are the same streets: cobbled streets with barely a car touching them all week, and the car-inferno I now have to face every time I go to buy a loaf of bread. I go to places like Transylvania and the earthen village streets there are the ones I was brought up in, they have just been moved to the other side of Europe; the present tense includes the entire history. This simultaneity produces, of course, perceptual suffusion, the art of being both this and that, here and there, inevitably touched by melancholy for the loss of the singular. The 1939-1945 war dominated my first seven years and subsequently disrupted everyone's sense of where and what they were.

North was not a problem. We knew of nothing that was denied us by being northern, nothing at any rate that we missed. We weren't aware of "southerners" as a category. There was not the aggressive northernness I usually find when I go back there these days. Listen to the great northern comedians, some of whom I was lucky enough to see live—Arthur Askey, Stan Laurel, Frankie Howerd, Les Dawson… The northern accent is there, but it's not stressed, it's not pushed in your face. It's more musical, an ironic counterpoint, a knowing wink of the servant class, and the tone is liable to be self-deprecating. And no Lawrentian dark animality either, or no more than you'd expect when the light is turned off.

It was also important to fill the lungs and shout out the hymns. It was a powerful insight into how the lyrical text works. We didn't believe a word of it—well, some of us did, and one of my friends was to become a vicar, but he never seemed less ecclesiastical than when he was shouting the hymns. And many other things: carols, anthems, the Biblical readings, the occasional glimpses of further reaches in Latin. They weren't belief structures, they were magnificent participatory architecture. The great slow Victorian hymns arched over us and confirmed the vast extent of our breath, with all the doors open. The terms (God, Lord, faith, etc.) were linguistic abstracts of great power which lived on the surface of the text like magnificent frescoes, magnificent narratives. "And there were shepherds abiding in the fields…" None of us had more than the vaguest notion what kind of thing a shepherd was, or why it was abiding, it was as fictive as the storks that brought the babies. The babies arrived, the mutton was in the shops (not yet re-labelled "lamb"). "Angels" were not involved in the commerce that surrounded us, they were in "realms of glory" singing creation; they were winged words. It wasn't just that we were momentarily enclosed in a mythology, it was also that the arena which lay open to the imagination stood revealed. The big songs and their occasions were like a theatrical illumination which was the epiphany of where and what we were, and would never desert us whatever we did or wherever we went. Some of us rejoiced in it and shrugged it off, forgot it completely; some of us rejoiced in it and took a message and then a refuge out of it which stuck to them; some of us rejoiced in it for ever after and took to poetry. We were never going to do any better than "The earth in solemn stillness lay To hear the angels sing."

3

Poetry moved to a central position when I was about 17, though I don't know exactly how it happened. It was rather suddenly there, at the focus of hope for the future. What did I know about it, how did I find out its potential? School got us as far as Eliot and omitted almost everybody, as academics have continued to do ever since. Things learned at the ages of ten to twelve left a deeper impression: Masefield, Belloc, Davies, Stevenson… songs by Vaughan Williams and others. The open road, the steady trade winds blowing, do you remember an inn, Miranda, with fireflies, the apple-tree doth lean down low… and all that. For modernity, or as much as we needed of it, we had a stronger and more generous informant than the partialising edicts of professional critics and self-advancing poets; it was called second-hand bookshops. Does anyone remember them? Stockport was obviously not the artistic and intellectual centre of anything, but it had a big second-hand bookshop called the Garrick, occupying a floor of a former mill or warehouse building, a strange space with irregularly shaped wooden-floored rooms on different levels. A lot of talking went on there. The man usually in charge, a small man with big glasses, enormous nose and a thick local accent, had strong opinions on literary merit and would recommend and disrecommend with conviction. If you took a late Henry James novel up to the counter he would sniff and say quite emphatically, "Ay, yes, late James—the *great pretender*." But he had no strong opinions on poetry, perhaps fortunately. Before I went to university, with cash set aside from a modest weekly pocket money, I was able to get the basis of a contemporary poetry collection together from the Garrick, plus later the Manchester shops and an open-air book market there, with careful use of new bookshops for things which failed to crop up second-hand. Thus easily, straight off the shelf: Yeats, Eliot, Lawrence, Auden, Day Lewis, Spender, Sitwell, Owen, Graves, Masefield, Sassoon, Dylan Thomas, Housman, Frost, Crane, Masters, H.D., Stevens (I got my Collected Stevens for two shillings from a sale in the basement of Boots the Chemist in Manchester)… Pound was more difficult, I had to put in a special order. *Ulysses* was bought with much hesitation and fear of detection from a porn bookshop next door to Manchester Cathedral. Also Lorca, Rilke, Mayakovsky, Pasternak… but not many translated, and not so many Americans, our culture was more native, without being in any way regional.

For current poetry, which mainly meant the 1940s, there were no instructions to follow, no propaganda. There were no big poetry prizes or National Poetry Days or any other marketing campaigns to tell you what you had to buy, and no poetry festivals to back up the publicity, and no poets going around doing stand-up promotional tours. And we didn't have people shouting at us about what we must under no account buy or read or have anything to do with, at our peril. The most we had were book reviews, which were expected to argue cogently and remain civilised, and which I rarely saw anyway. My method was to take a book from the shelf, open it, read a poem, if not repelled read another poem, and if still not repelled, buy it. Thus I collected, for a few pence each, books by such poets as Nicholas Moore, W.S. Graham, Sidney Keyes, Wrey Gardiner, Henry Treece, Alun Lewis, Lawrence Durrell, Rayner Heppenstall, Ruthven Todd, many more. Such books had not yet been withdrawn into a *de luxe* market called "First Editions" by which the dust jacket was worth ten times the book and monstrous prices were transmitted electronically to every back-street bookshop in the land. We also shared our finds with each other and discussed them—schoolboys this is, meeting together in the evenings at home or in pubs.

There was no reason to believe, from outside comment or from what was in the books, that some of these poets were in violent conflict with each other. The Cambridge academics hadn't yet made partisan intervention in the production and reception of new poetry, or if they had the noise hadn't reached Stockport. The first I remember of that kind of thing was Donald Davie on the radio about 1960 blasting Ginsberg, which quite shocked me. The destruction of most 1940s poetry careers by the 1950s poetry police was a thing we knew nothing about; we could take seriously Thomas, Moore, New Apocalypse, anything we liked, without feeling we were violating national virginity. And, interestingly, what we were collecting as new poetry was about ten years old, because we relied so much on the second-hand market, and this is perhaps a quite healthy situation. The roaring and the clearances of its production were over—those noises young poets and others so often have to make to clear a space for themselves, the methodical trashing whether from left or right, the poetical missionaries setting up instant canons. What we had in our hands was the product, for what it was worth. This included, as I remember, Ted Hughes' first book (1957) as the forward edge of our modernity. It seemed quite in accord with what we were already reading, or had read (the open road etcetera). Larkin never happened in Stockport; I don't know why (unless it was that I read a poem and put the book back on the shelf).

Of course poetry wars had been going on all century but they didn't concern us. What we entered was a landscape, of which in retrospect the ups and downs, hardness and softness, bleakness and pastoral, of the Peak District were a figure. Nobody was standing in the middle of Edale declaring the top of Kinder Scout to be difficult or obscure or undemocratic (though difficult it certainly was). I particularly remember 'Landscape', a drawing or etching by Lucian Freud, opposite page 60 of *Atlantic Anthology* (1945) (another Garrick find, in fact there were two copies there) as seeming to signal what there was to look forward to, since there was something very slightly and delicately unreal about it, and it was an opening-out which was also incisive. Everything was open to us; we supplied the constraints ourselves. The way was clear and straight; we supplied the torsions ourselves.

That anyway was it, that was the way in. Whatever happened next, which was mostly confusion, division and coercion, poetry was established in its place, somehow, out of all that jumble and a lot more—out of the generational tensions, the pull of the past against all the post-war ambitions of the families, the drive to exceptionality, the tension between a northern superstition that says "Here we call a spade a spade", and literary mystification… And it happened before there was access to the American poets who opened up new avenues in the 1960s. Possibly the particular interpretation of poetry I was drawn towards involved the need to multiply the perceiving self, to no longer be the one thing in one place I had been led to think I was, however variegated and contradictory the place was. But I have come to think that the equanimity which distinguished that early episode, depending on a sense of an entire, intact and expansive culture, is still there, if you can reach it, and still a creative incentive. Innovative too, if you need that. It would be a matter of inhabiting, in the work, what you actually do inhabit.

NOTE

This text is redacted from a longer and more circumstantial memoir of my early years, which can be found on my website www.aprileye.co.uk/

My miscellaneous collection *The Day's Final Balance* (Shearsman 2007) contains two relevant pieces: 'St Albans' which is a meditation on the territorial reach of childhood and the abrasion on its edges, and 'Manchester' which is concerned with my gap-year spent working in a department store, first encounters with professional poets, the forthcoming revision of the "city", and a confirmation that an interest in what was later called modernism didn't necessarily separate you from the society in which you worked selling kitchen furniture or lampshades. Only the ticket to Cambridge did that.

Meanwhile

Roy Fisher

An easily bewildered child, I nevertheless had no problem in hanging on to the idea that sewn like a lining inside the customary world there was another with tones and imperatives of its own. A shadowy synaesthesia, I suppose, it has been with me lifelong. It visits most days. It arrived without language, for it never came up in conversation, so throughout childhood I drew and painted obsessively, eventually acquiring an identity as the official artist of Wattville Road Junior Elementary School, Handsworth, Birmingham.

A few sharp incursions of language. At about nine, clear-eyed Edna Barnes who sat a few rows in front stood up to sing a song to the class: *Barbara Allen:* words that held beauty, life and death. Around the same time I wrote an epic, 'The Battle of Crécy', in eight thumping lines. Then at twelve, in the grip of a fervent undeclared adulation, I wrote a love poem, a bundle of clichés I was fortunately too timid to deliver. Instead I gave it to a friend to use as a valentine to a different girl, substituting her name, at some cost to the metre. I could have charged him a permission fee.

My painting ran out of road, just as I was suddenly hit hard by jazz music, first in the form of the recordings of Chicagoan blues and boogie pianists. Here were sounds from another world: a music in which I was not only permitted but *required* to invent material that resembled my inner existence. Starting from scratch I set myself to learn to play and within a few years had a new identity as a useful jazz club pianist. And alongside that there was a substance called Modern Poetry, which came partly by way of school, where I was studying poetry without any thought of writing it. Young masters back from the war, their tastes formed in the Thirties, would entertain us with oddities by MacNeice and Auden. Much of this poetry was freakish and permissive in a way that took my fancy—Edith Sitwell's obtuse 'Aubade', Pound, some imagists. On my own I'd seek out anthologies of translated poetry from many different ages and cultures; and constantly to hand there was D.B. Wyndham Lewis's *The Stuffed Owl*, a treasury of pretentious and ludicrous verse.

In 1948, in my first year reading English at Birmingham University I became aware that there was a scattering of people who were openly writing and circulating poetry, something I'd never encountered before. There was a staff-student Writers' Circle, and the university's little catch-all arts magazine *Mermaid* always carried a few poems. At the same time my piano-playing had struck a technical *impasse* I couldn't resolve, and the scene that had supported it was tired and in dispersal; so I gave up playing in public for several years. I had a hunch that poetry might hold the sort of energy and surprise I'd been used to finding in music and I began to try building my habitual verbal doodles into poems. My extra-curricular reading was heady and thrill-seeking— Rimbaud, Lautréamont, Dylan Thomas, Dalí, The New Apocalypse, any surrealism I could find—but my own writings turned out spurious, forced and lumpy. I was astonished and baffled by how inept I was. Having nothing to show I made no contacts with the Writers' Circle or the magazine for a couple of years. But I was being trained to write balanced and reasoned critical essays stiffened with whatever flashy-looking erudition I could cadge. I took some of this material, cast it into iambic pentameters and showed the results around. Riding the pentameters was fun though I could sense something hollow and showy; but I was immediately accorded a new identity, as a poet, and was given *Mermaid* to edit. My long hair and bow-tie were justified. At the same time I became fascinated by some, at least, of the ideas in Graves's *The White Goddess*, chiefly its archaic exoticism and the exalted qualities it attributed to poetry. This allegiance had one beneficial effect: it ensured that whatever I wrote during the next five or six years was automatically unpublishable. Meanwhile I learned to write.

*

A single grotesque fantasy found its way into print, a couple of years after I'd written it and it caught the eye of Gael Turnbull who was guest-editing a British number of the American magazine *Origin* and on the lookout for anything unusual. We met, and, although his work and mine had little in common, became fast friends for the rest of Gael's life, nearly fifty years. For the first ten of those years all the circulation and acceptance my work had was attributable directly or indirectly to

Gael. He opened things up and licensed me to go on writing. Trying to characterize the unique nature of his presence in the poetry scene I'm reminded of the stratified social system of Imperial Japan, where the rigid levels of aristocracy and peasantry held sandwiched between them the Floating World of administrators, artists and the like who had fewer obligations and more freedom. Having virtually no contact with the poetry establishment (particularly in England, though America and eventually his native Scotland found him easier to value) and instinctively staying clear of the activities of self-congratulatory but incurious amateurism, he could roam free in the floating world of little magazines and quixotic publications. He had a nose for what he considered honest work and had no preconceptions about where to go looking for it. He distrusted anything smooth, slick or subsidised: his predilection for issuing tiny editions, mostly of his own work, in booklets hand-sewn with covers of wallpaper offcuts, the texts on the poorest quality paper and made with obsolete basic technology, was proverbial. Some of these qualities were carried forward into the magazine *Migrant*, in fact more a serial anthology of the editors' finds than a conventional magazine, which he set up with Michael Shayer, and then into their Migrant Press, which was to publish my first pamphlet, *City*. Unobtrusively and with no thought of advantage to himself he was the enabler of countless fertile contacts. Stuart Mills, whose Tarasque Press generated several of my pamphlets, was sent to me by Gael as was Stuart Montgomery, founder of Fulcrum Press, which published my first four books.

Because the Trent Book Shop Is in Nottingham

Hannah Neate

In 1972 Stuart Mills, co-founder of the Tarasque Press, made the following comment in the catalogue for the exhibition 'Metaphor and Motif', held at Nottingham's Midland Group Gallery:

> This exhibition, in its own way, sets the balance straight. If it is seen, if the catalogue is read widely enough then it should be clear that something surprisingly consistent has been going on in Nottingham for the past few years.

This chapter is an attempt to explain some of the activities to which Mills was alluding. It is the story of an overlooked literary and artistic life in Nottingham from 1964 to 1972, which centred on the Trent Book Shop. This was a brief but significant period when avant-garde bookselling and the British Poetry Revival came to the East Midlands.

The Trent Book Shop

In his memoir of life in Nottingham in the sixties Ray Gosling describes how:

> There were books and magazines that you could only buy in special places, lots of little magazines from Greenwich Village, New York City, and all over the English-speaking world. Stuart and Martin who drank in Yate's Wine Lodge and listened to the trio with us were teachers. They went part-time and opened an avant-garde bookshop, the first of its kind in our town to sell these free-thinking books.[1]

The shop to which Gosling refers to is the Trent Book Shop, opened in 1964 by Stuart Mills and Martin Parnell on Pavilion Road, in the West Bridgford area of Nottingham. The bookshop remained open until 1972 when it closed following bankruptcy. According to Mills "this was probably no more than coincidence. It had done what it set out to do and run its course."[2]

The Trent Bookshop came into being when Stuart Mills "moved to Nottingham, ostensibly to teach" but "opened instead the Trent Bookshop and recklessly filled it with Art and Literature and any small-press publication that could be found."[3] At this time he made contact with Andrew Crozier's Ferry Press, Gael Turnbull of Migrant, Ian Hamilton Finlay's Wild Hawthorn Press, and Jonathan Williams' Jargon Society, all of whom were also exploring the poetic possibilities of the modernists.

The Trent Book Shop was a unique literary outcrop with aspirations to be "one of the main poetry holdings outside of London."[4] Well known London-based avant-garde bookshops like Better Books and Indica are often discussed in cultural histories of the 1960s and for Simon Cutts, Trent Book Shop employee and the other co-founder of the Tarasque Press, these were "seminal bookshops… in far more of a maelstrom type of situation than the isolation of the Trent Book Shop."[5] This isolation was reflected in both the location of the bookshop and its specialist nature. The Pavilion Road site was south of the River Trent, next to the Forest Football Ground, in the mainly residential West Bridgford—reputed at the time to be the land of "Cricket, Chrysanthemums and Conservatism."[6] As Parnell explains:

I moved to Nottingham in 1963 after I'd finished my degree in Leeds, although I actually come from London, and I taught for a year—or just over a year—in what would be described now as a bog standard comprehensive. Absolutely awful. And I met a guy called Stuart Mills who was as disenchanted as I was and we spent our breaks and lunchtimes talking about what should happen in Nottingham, what was missing in Nottingham. One of the things that we agreed on was the absence of what we thought would be a good bookshop… We were interested in looking at contemporary literature, not just in this country because both of us were interested in developments that were occurring in the States. My tutor at Leeds was Geoffrey Hill and he, well I wouldn't say that he turned me on to Beat literature but it is one of the areas that we spent a lot of time talking about, and the imagists, like Ezra Pound. So I came to Nottingham with, let's say, a more radical approach to the literary scene than was current outside of London. Stuart and I, we spent hours discussing what we could do and we came up with the idea of the bookshop, but we didn't want it to be just a bookshop, we wanted it to do other things other than just selling books. We thought of things like an art gallery, poetry readings, publications, and in 1964 we got it all together and we opened.

The location of the bookshop was explained more than anything by convenience—Parnell and Mills both lived and worked nearby. Never put off by the prospect of a select clientele Parnell and Mills reworked the interior, following some very clear aesthetic intentions:

> We actually got the lease on it during the summer and we started working on it, doing it up. Stuart brought in some of his friends from Birmingham [art college] who designed it, there was some fantastic shelving, unbelievably high quality wood, they created this amazing stuff obviously influenced by their ideas that they'd picked up at art college, Bauhaus, Scandinavian and new concepts. With the limited resources we had we thought we'd do something very radical and very, very modern.[7]

Not only did the Trent Book Shop have a visually appealing interior, it was also a place to become immersed in the stock, which was arranged in a way that meant you had to "delve to find stuff, current stuff was put on a kind of rostrum table in the middle."[8] This was not a bookshop to visit if you knew exactly what you wanted to buy. It was more important to browse and rummage. This was due in part to the founders' decision to "specialise in poetry though it would concentrate on the arts generally."[9] Their stock included publications from both the UK and the United States and this rare amassing of small press publications gained the bookshop an international reputation.

The Trent Book Shop formed part of a select community of booksellers in existence in the 1960s, most of which had similarly brief life-spans. What made these shops distinctive was a particular attention to contemporary and experimental poetry. For Simon Cutts, who began working at the Trent Book Shop on Saturdays, "it was one of the best poetry stocks that I have ever seen."[10] Contemporaries of the Trent Book Shop included Indica, Compendium and Better Books in London; Morden Tower in Newcastle; Unicorn in Brighton and The Paperback Book Shop in Edinburgh. Mills and Parnell made sure the Trent Book Shop was in touch with all of these because they "were all exchanging information, sending each other small magazines and books."[11] These links to other publishers and booksellers extended to the Olympia Press in Paris, New York's Gotham Book Bar and Lawrence Ferlinghetti's City Lights in San Francisco. Although it was only a minor feature within Nottingham, the Trent Book Shop formed part of much wider networks of booksellers intent on promoting contemporary writing.

From the outset, the Trent Book Shop intended to carry out wider activities other than just selling books. One such activity was the organisation of poetry readings. Initially, these were held within the shop itself. Martin Parnell explains that:

> Sometimes this was difficult because often the only way they [the poets] would come was if they were funded and we didn't have that sort of money, but in a few cases we did manage to get people, particularly Americans. We had connections with people like Mike Horovitz from New Departures, and once you'd hooked up with people like that you had connections with the Liverpool beat poets and it would just spread out because everyone was relying on somebody else to sell their publications. People used to hawk stuff around and I knew, for instance, Jon Silkin from Leeds who did *Stand* magazine… so they would come and read for us.

Eventually, because the shop was too small to cope with the audiences of between 20 and 50 who attended, readings were moved elsewhere. Pub venues were used, as well as the Workers Education Association Buildings, and on occasion, the Midland Group Gallery. These drew together people interested in the contemporary literary scene, and forged contacts within the overlapping book-selling and small press publishing circles. The poetry readings organised by the Trent Book Shop were therefore important in maintaining the vitality of the shop. An event that has been written about extensively in cultural histories of the 1960s is the International Poetry Incarnation that took place in the Royal Albert Hall on 11ᵗʰ June 1965. As members of the audience on that occasion, the staff of the Trent Book Shop were interested, although not entirely satisfied, participants. Simon Cutts remarks that "It was great fun and all but it was kind of narrow and showbiz."[12] Martin Parnell comments in a similar vein:

> We'd all been down to London, the big event at the Albert Hall where they were smoking pot whilst they were performing. I think that Stuart and myself… were quite unsympathetic to the self-centredness of all of them. Particularly Allen Ginsberg, because we weren't great admirers of beat poets, we actually preferred a different sort of poetry, and just to see these people thinking how great they were, it didn't matter basically—it reminds me of the worst way that Brits perform, taking your trousers down and showing your backside—that is the way they performed. Let it all hang out and we can do what we like. No respect for the audience… I thought it was a missed opportunity but that's the way they wanted to operate.[13]

Because they were unsatisfied by the poetry gatherings that took place at the Albert Hall (and another in Cardiff) in 1965, the staff of the Trent Book Shop decided to stage a poetry conference in Nottingham. It was titled 'Poetry 66' and took place on the 18ᵗʰ and 19ᵗʰ of February 1966 at Nottingham's Albert Hall and at the Midland Group Gallery. A circular sent to a long list of potential participants set out the intentions of the conference: to "trace the role and development of small magazines and presses in the country since the early fifties" thereby acknowledging "the role played by these mags during the last 15 years."[14] Poetry '66 was envisaged as something that would be "better" than the Albert Hall readings, notably because it would be "something more professional."[15] The desire to organise a large gathering of poets to discuss and reflect upon the development of poetry in Britain since the 1950s was explained in a circular sent out to participants:

One might hear the question "Why Nottingham?" Well basically the answer would be "Because the Trent Book Shop is in Nottingham." The shop, which has been open for just over a year now has been attempting to bring to the provinces an attitude to bookselling/bookbuying common at the moment only to a few specialist shops in London. For twelve months we have been pursuing a policy of monthly readings (many poets next month will already be acquainted with Nottingham, and the shop) and it is our hope that this larger event will draw attention to not so much the plight, but an intention to continue to exist as an independent outlet for good literature in all forms, whether we are recognized as being worthy of financial assistance or not.[16]

This was an attempt to look at a growing revival in British poetry in both the written and spoken form, and Poetry '66 attracted an impressive array of poets.

You can hardly name a poet who did not actually come to the festival, from the surreal ambience of people who we might loosely talk about, from George Macbeth to Robert Garioch to Turnbull... Spike Hawkins was there, I believe, to Patten to Roger McGough, Adrian Henri, the kind of people whose work I was not directly interested in, but I mean, as a festival these people came and it was a big affair.[17]

Poetry '66 also sought to gain representation for small press publishers, a community that, maybe intentionally, lacked a coherent voice. Nottingham's Albert Hall was nothing like London's namesake but to even attempt to fill a hall which could hold 1,500 people shows a certain confidence in the robust nature of the support for poetry at the time. Taking place over two days, the conference began on the Friday night with "A Concert of Poetry and Jazz with New Departures and Leading Poets," the evening being compèred by the American writer and publisher of the avant-garde, Jonathan Williams.[18] Of the event Williams recalled:

> I met "The Belper Belter" (aka "Lord Burner of the Questing Vole") [Stuart Mills] in 1966 at the Nottingham Poetry Festival, of which he was one of the organizers. I remember drinking beer with him in a Yates's Wine Lodge, where a trio of ancient female cellists were performing dangerously on the balcony. Some of the rest of the company included Ronald Johnson, Ray Gosling, and Dom Sylvester Houédard, OSB. I remember rather less clearly being the compere at an evening reading. Pete Brown was good; Spike Hawkins was very funny; Adrian Mitchell and Christopher Logue were very intense; and Michael Horovitz simply would not shut up.[19]

The Saturday was billed as "an informal day of readings and discussions" that started at 11.00 a.m. and carried on well into the night, the list of participants reading as a cross section of experimental and avant-garde poets.[20] However, these characters were hardly happy bedfellows, as correspondence from Jon Silkin, editor of *Stand* suggests: "I'd like to read but I do NOT want to read with the load of old crap New Dep." Such personal proclivities certainly added a frisson to the event.

For David Briers, who attended the Saturday events of Poetry '66, the lasting memory of the event reflects the cross-over between poetry and performance taking place in the mid-1960s, which extended beyond New Departures' jazz poetry of the Friday night and entered the realm of the experimental:

> I remember one man, a poet… who worked at Leeds University called Cavan McCarthy who did a performance which he called a poem but his poem was 'Music' and he had a little book that he'd printed as an artists' multiple thing which had some symbols on the cards and you were supposed to have some different physical response to these different symbols— clap if it was a circle—and he held them up and the people in the audience responded as they were supposed to and it made a sound, non-verbal sound… it epitomised the hybrid crossover thing that was going on then, just by its nature, it was a poetry conference and he called it a poem, but it was called Music and it was called that because it produced non-verbal sounds.[21]

Post-event correspondence between the Trent Book Shop and participants reveals that the event was deemed to be a success, with many
poets appreciating the opportunity to meet their counterparts. This is
evident in a letter sent by McCarthy to Martin Parnell:

> I still haven't recovered sufficiently from the reading and
> accompanying rush to be able to give a coherent opinion.
> It was a happening, really, I was at first terribly excited and
> nervous, then I drank some lunch… So: it was an incredible,
> fantastic day, exhilarating, I think the main use will be that it
> enabled people to meet on a personal level. I'm not terribly
> worried about people hearing poetry, I can't absorb more than
> very little, say ten, poems per day anyway, although this acts as
> a good excuse.

Despite this, Poetry '66 went largely unnoticed in the national press
and has certainly never been written about in any substantial way. A
letter from George Macbeth (who participated in the conference and
was also acting as Producer in the BBC Talks Department) commented,
"It's nice to see that the exhibition [Concrete/Spatial Poetry] got some
publicity, but I agree with you that it would have been helpful if the
conference had been noticed." The only additional publicity Poetry '66
received was a 45-minute programme based on recordings made at the
event transmitted on the Third Programme on 24th April 1966.

After Poetry '66, the Trent Book Shop expanded from its Trentside
location. The gathering momentum around poetry in the provinces
was a likely motivator for this expansion; it certainly wasn't down to
financial gain. Poetry '66 proved to be a costly financial venture for
Mills and Parnell. But in order to focus more on the sale of paperbacks,
which in the mid-1960s still made up a relatively small proportion
of all books published and sold in the UK, a decision was made to
open another branch. Bux (pronounced "books", a play on Midlands
pronunciation) was first located on the medieval Drury Hill. Bux
existed between 1967 and 1969 and announced its presence via a
frontage decked with exposed wood, the name of the shop set in bold
stylized letters. Just as the Trent Book Shop intertwined its identity

with its Bauhaus-inspired interior, this theme was extended to the logo used for Bux. Although undoubtedly benefiting from being located on a street that functioned at a pedestrian scale, the three floors that the shop occupied gave it a quaint charm and slightly haphazard feel, whilst also making it a paradise for shoplifters. While the Trent Book Shop remained an enclave for small press publishing, an important source of stock for Bux was imported books from the United States, Holland and Japan. Additional stock included the complete Methuen, Faber and Penguin ranges, which were sold and displayed openly alongside more controversial titles from the Olympia Press in Paris. Parnell comments, "If it was available somewhere I wanted it and I would do whatever I could to get hold of it."

Bux on Drury Hill was relatively short-lived because this part of medieval Nottingham became subsumed within plans for large-scale modernisation, the result being the much-reviled Broadmarsh Centre. When it became apparent that a long-term lease was not an option, Bux moved to Lincoln Street, a short road off Clumber Street, one of the main shopping thoroughfares in Nottingham's city centre. The Lincoln Street incarnation of Bux is the most widely remembered, no doubt due to both the size and the location of the shop—it was larger, easier to access and open to passing trade. Being in a central location and in a newly built retail unit, the second incarnation of Bux had neither the hand-crafted modern interior of the Trent Book Shop, nor the slightly ramshackle charm of Drury Hill. It was nevertheless a vital outlet for publications that would otherwise prove impossible to obtain. For budding local journalist Richard Williams:

> Bux was fantastically important because… he stocked the *Village Voice,* the *East Village Other* (another New York underground newspaper). He stocked *IT* when it was still *International Times,* and *Oz* of course and the more obvious stuff. But to be able to get the *Voice* and the *East Village Other* in particular was just amazing because it was like a mainline to what was really happening… And why he stocked them? There can't have been more than three people in Nottingham that would have bought them I wouldn't have thought, but anyway he did thank goodness… It was the only place in Nottingham

that you could get any of these things. Terribly important. And poetry, little poetry presses, underground culture and literature in general. It was a real, real focal point for me and some others I'm sure.[22]

Whist the Trent Book Shop and Bux were outlets for unusual literary offerings, they were also the focus for Nottingham's own small press.

THE TARASQUE PRESS

Tarasque. An animal which lived on the banks of the Rhone, and ravaged the surrounding countryside until it was overcome.

The Tarasque Press, "a small literary offering from a Midlands city" operated from the Trent Bookshop on Pavilion Road between 1964 and 1972.[23] Via its activities of publishing poetry books, pamphlets, postcards and prints the Tarasque Press effectively worked as an outpost for avant-garde poetry in Nottingham from the mid-1960s until the early 1970s. Simon Cutts, who co-ran the Tarasque Press with Stuart Mills began a career in publishing in 1964 when he:

> ...wandered into the Trent Bookshop... which was being run by Stuart Mills and Martin Parnell, and immediately struck up a relationship with Stuart. He was already in touch with a whole bunch of poets from Gael Turnbull and Migrant Press people to Basil Bunting and people like Spike Hawkins... and the immediate sympathy between Stuart Mills and myself meant that we had to produce something almost at once, and we decided to run the magazine *Tarasque*... and the subsequent publications that ran alongside the magazine.[24]

Cutts became a Saturday employee at the bookshop and found in Mills a shared interest in publishing, especially relating to poetry and art. One of the first things Cutts and Mills did under the label "Tarasque Press" was begin publishing a magazine entitled *Tarasque,* which ran for eleven issues between 1965 and 1971. The magazine acted as a platform for their work (in the form of both poetry and criticism), and that of other select poets, including Roy Fisher, Pete Brown, Gael Turnbull, Robert Garioch, Ian Hamilton Finlay and Hugh Creighton Hill.

The first issue of *Tarasque* was published in 1965 and began with the following statement:

A city needs a voice; a tangible proof of its spirit.
At its worst a city can throw out the arts with the slops, at its best it can nurture them all (with no hopes of immediate gain) as a parent.
We wish that this magazine should grow as the city grows, that like a city it should attract the best rather than insulate itself.[25]

Tarasque Number One was framed as a local issue including work by local writers such as Mills, Cutts, and Parnell (all from the Trent Book Shop) and Ray Gosling (who had received acclaim following the publication of his first book *Sum Total* in 1963). In its initial form, *Tarasque* was to be the voice of Nottingham. But it was not to remain a local interest magazine for long. As Cutts explains, "it got more esoteric as it went on" and "became more and more involved with the contemporary poetry scene and less to do with local issues. It became involved in the general discussion of poetry and the world and Britain."[26] The magazine's focus evolved throughout its seven year span, taking on board criticism, of both poetry and the wider arts, and increasingly towards the end of the sixties, concrete poetry.

The Tarasque Press was operating at a time in the mid-1960s when there was a proliferation of little magazines, alternative publications and other underground press activities. Individuals using cheap printing equipment, churning out low cost, and sometimes low print quality, publications were to be found across Britain.[27] The most well known were the likes of the *International Times* and *Oz*: publications at the forefront of the counterculture and linked to the Underground Press Syndicate.[28] These firmly countercultural publications were the most garish and purposefully shocking tip of a very large iceberg of such publications in the 1960s. By contrast, *Tarasque* participated in a longer tradition of British little magazines, those primarily concerned with publishing poetry, prose and literary criticism. Rather than engaging head on with the politics of the era, Cutts and Mills viewed their work as more "classically modernist", seeing "precedents and ancestry" for what they were trying to do in Wyndham Lewis' *Blast* and poets like Ezra Pound and T.E. Hulme.[29] The lack of interest that Cutts and Mills showed in other publications is evident in *Tarasque Number Seven*, which included a spoof "magazines received" list at the back of the issue. The titles read as follows (with tongue firmly in cheek): "Nugget, Lilliput, Esquire, Family Doctor, Locospotter, Penthouse, Practical Motorist, 'Poetry' Chicago, Meccano Magazine, Exchange and Mart, Health and Efficiency." Mills and Cutts thought that many of the underground magazines of the time were produced by a "stampede of carpetbaggers" which resulted in "a general aimlessness".[30] *Tarasque*, by contrast, had an aesthetic focus and a polemical stance.

The 1960s was the period of the "British Poetry Revival". As Andrew Wilson comments, "The voice of The New British Poetry was resolutely not a London-based one", with magazines such as *Poetmeat* in Blackburn, *Dust* in Leeds, *Phoenix* and *Underdog* in Liverpool, *Migrant* in Worcester and *Move* in Preston.[31] Indeed, according to Robert Hewison, there was an overwhelmingly provincial geography associated with these operations:

> Few [magazines] were published in London or took much notice of it; their life was ephemeral and their readership sometimes little larger than the circle of contributors and their friends. But their very cheapness and simplicity gave their creators freedom to experiment and express their enthusiasms. Anyone who felt they had something to say in print could launch a magazine, and many people did.[32]

The provincial bias of small press publishing was due not only to the location of the participants, but also to the infrastructure associated with these practices. Because of the small scale of such operations, importance was not placed on "rents and rates; it was just doing something out of your room."[33] Or indeed your bookshop.[34]

The Tarasque Press set out to be a platform that would use "poetry as an essential constituent of the artistic process".[35] Contributors to the magazine were chosen carefully, with a distinct bias towards British poets working in a modernist mode. The early work of Tarasque keenly promoted a particular type of written poem—the small poem—with *Tarasque Number Six* being an anthology devoted to short poetry featuring work by J.M. Synge, Ezra Pound and Georg Trakl. Contemporary writers of small poems included Jonathan Williams, Hugh Creighton Hill, Spike Hawkins, Pete Brown and Robert Creeley. Stuart Mills set out the parameters in his typically humorous fashion:

> The proper subjects for poetry are;
> the Seasons, the Affections, Fishing Boats,
> Inland Waterways, Non-Alcoholic Beverages,
> Certain Flowers, Certain Trees.
>
> Improper subjects are;
> Sex, Drugs, War and Self.
>
> Adjectives should be used sparsely, if at
> all, and not ever in proportion of more
> than one to every 9 nouns.[36]

By positioning itself in opposition to poetry about "sex, drugs, war and self", Tarasque critiqued the beat and pop poetry being promoted elsewhere in the UK by the Liverpool poets and New Departures. In the above poem we see a respect for a longer literary tradition, an older type of "popular culture" that privileges outdoor pursuits, seasonality and nature. This is almost a variety of pre-war vernacular through which objectivity is used to draw attention to the page, which works as a material and typographic artefact. This is modern rather than pop poetry.

Central to the development of the Tarasque Press's poetic and artistic affectations was Ian Hamilton Finlay, whose Wild Hawthorn Press played an important formative role in the work of Mills and Cutts. Finlay began a working relationship with Tarasque after Stuart Mills began corresponding with him. This led to a visit by Mills to

Finlay's Stonypath garden in the Pentland Hills of southern Scotland. When Finlay became involved with the Tarasque Press in the mid-1960s he was still developing his concrete poetry. His were the first concrete poetry works published by the Tarasque Press. Simon Cutts recalls:

> We were producing the first two [Finlay] prints, Star Steer and Acrobats or vice versa and we were doing Ocean Stripe Five, taking those texts of [Kurt] Schwitters and collaging them with photographs of fishing boats sailing under duress, from Fishing News.[37]

For Cutts, the transition from short poems to concrete poetry was a move "through the ever-encompassing, seemingly orthodox poem with its arrangement of line and stanza to a narrative and a syntactical concrete poem."[38] However, the Tarasque Press's involvement with concrete poetry came at a time when Cutts and Mills were "nestled on the edge of concrete poetry… we were outside the movement, we weren't ever at the centre of it. I think we were all working in an errant plastic poetry, heading to plastic things, rather than the mainstream graphical poetry."[39]

Simon Cutts has commented that Tarasque was primarily interested in "the written poem and the poem on the page and less the performance piece."[40] In the cards and pamphlets they produced it is evident that attention to detail and materials played an integral part in their poetry and aesthetic. Cutts and Mills were producing texts rarely more than twenty pages long, never larger than A5 in size, always with limited print runs. Knowingly working within a cohort of small press publishers in the 1960s, the relative obscurity of the Tarasque Press was largely self-imposed—they enjoyed working at what they termed the "derrière-garde"[41] of concrete poetry—and this enabled them to forge their own aesthetic, which was "witty, sly, understated, seemingly casual, and operating on a miniature scale".[42] For Mills this would "encompass the small image, the artifact, and (in those days) the so-called Concrete Poem… Simon Cutts would often be seen coaxing a small fretsaw through the intricacies of a piece of work no larger than a florin, and as the poems shrunk in size so did the format of the booklets. Some people responded. Mostly we were ignored."[43]

NOTES

1 Gosling, R. (1980). *Personal Copy: A Memoir of the Sixties*. London, Faber and Faber. p. 121
2 http://jargonbooks.com/stuart_mills.html
3 Ibid
4 Cutts, S. (2006 [2000]). An interview with Wolfgang Görtschacher. *Some Forms of Availability*. S. Cutts. New York, Granary Books: 14-43. (p. 15)
5 Author's interview with Simon Cutts.
6 'The Urban District of West Bridgford' *Nottingham Topic*, 1965, February, p. 41
7 Author's interview with Martin Parnell
8 Author's interview with Simon Cutts
9 Mills, S. (1972). "Read the Small Print." *Laurels* 1(3): 32-34.
10 Author's interview with Simon Cutts
11 Author's interview with Martin Parnell
12 Author's interview with Simon Cutts
13 Author's interview with Martin Parnell
14 Mills, S. & Parnell, M. 'First Circular,' (1965), MS487 (East Midlands Collection, University of Nottingham)
15 Author's interview with Martin Parnell
16 Poetry 66—Final Plans, (1966), MS487 (East Midlands Collection, University of Nottingham)
17 Cutts, S. (2006 [2000]) pp. 23-24
18 Programme for Poetry '66 (Nottingham Local Studies Library, L70.2). Williams was a poet and the founder of The Jargon Society, which published poetry, fiction and photography.
19 http://jargonbooks.com/stuart_mills.html
20 Adrian Mitchell, Robert Garioch, Alan Brownjohn, Hugh MacDiarmid, Edward Lucie-Smith, Bob Cobbing, Dom Sylvester Houedard, Tom Pickard, George Macbeth, Edwin Morgan, Jon Silkin, Roy Fisher, Anselm Hollo, Ed Dorn, Michael Shayer, Ron Johnson, Gael Turnbull, Jonathan Williams, Jeff Nuttall, John Furnival, Cavan McCarthy, John James, Nick Wayte, Peter Armstrong, Andrew Crozier, Tom Clark, Pete Brown, Tom McGrath, Brian Patten, Adrian Henri, Michael Horovitz, Spike Hawkins, Nathanial Tarn, Vernon Scannell, G.S. Fraser, Jim Burns.
21 Author's interview with David Briers
22 Author's interview with Richard Williams
23 Cutts, S. (1972a) p. 19
24 Cutts, S. (2006 [2000]) p. 15
25 Tarasque One (1965). UCL Special Collections: Little Magazines.

26 Author's interview with Simon Cutts

27 For a feel of the range of these publications see, for example: Spiers, J. (1974). *The Underground and Alternative Press in Britain: A Bibliographical Guide with Historical Notes*. Hassocks, Harvester Press; Görtschacher, W. (1993). *Little Magazine Profiles: The Little Magazines in Great Britain, 1939–1993*. Salzburg, University of Salzburg; Miller, D. and R. Price, Eds. (2006). *British Poetry Magazines 1914–2000: A History and Bibliography of 'Little Magazines'*. London, British Library Publishing.

28 See, Bizot, J.-F. (2006). *200 Trips from the Counterculture: Graphics and Stories from the Underground Press Syndicate*. London, Thames and Hudson. *IT* and *Oz* weren't low quality publications, *Oz* in particular was famous for its adventurous use of colour, which on occasion would leave it virtually illegible.

29 Author's interview with Simon Cutts

30 Mills, S. (1971). "Editorial." *Tarasque* Eleven/Twelve.

31 Wilson, A. (2004). 'A Poetics of Dissent: Notes On a Developing Counter-culture in London in the Early Sixties'. *Art & the 60s: This Was Tomorrow*. C. Stephens and K. Stout. London, Tate Publishing: 92-111. (p. 96)

32 Hewison, R. (1986). Too Much: Art and Society in the Sixties 1960-1975. London, Methuen. p. 95

33 Author's interview with Simon Cutts

34 The printing press for the Tarasque Press was housed in an outhouse at the rear of the Trent Book Shop on Pavilion Road.

35 Cutts, S. (1971 [2006]). A Note on Tarasque and Concrete Poetry. *Some Forms of Availabilty*. S. Cutts. New York, Granary Books: 50. (p. 50)

36 Mills, S. (1967). "Editorial." *Tarasque* Six.

37 Cutts, S. (2006 [2000])

38 Cutts, S. (1972). 'Metaphor and Motif.' *Platform* 5(1): 19-21 (p. 19)

39 Author's interview with Simon Cutts

40 Author's interview with Simon Cutts

41 Cutts, S. (1972). "Metaphor and Motif." *Platform* 5(1): 19-21

42 Bevis, J. (2006). Swings and Roundabouts. *Certain trees: the constructed book, poem and object 1964–2006*. Saint-Yrieux-la-Perche, Centre des livres d'artistes: 13–24. (p. 16)

43 Mills, S. (1975). From Tarasque to Aggie Westons. *Certain trees: the constructed book, poem and object 1964–2006* Saint-Yrieux-la-Perche, Centre des livres d'artistes: 141. (p. 141)

The Carshalton Steam Laundry Vision

Chris Torrance

29/4/2011. Today I found, lying on the soil, a metal serpent, a once electroplated belt buckle, the plating now all worn off, a late 1940s/ early 1950s artefact that pulled me back to a boyhood consciousness of Westerns, of heroes in boots & belts with holsters & guns that I used to see in cinemas. I'd seen other boys sporting this belt buckle, the attached belt made of some kind of rubberised fabric, blue with a white stripe in the middle. I *had* to have one of those, & eventually mum bought me one, of which I was very proud: this inexpensive boy belt. Probably my first conscious fashion choice.

So in 2011, when I see this object, pick it up & handle it, clean away the dirt & lay it in the "museum", an old stile by the house, the deeper organic mind writhes a little, SERPENT, something that wiggles & slides & has the power to strike like lightning—this boy belt buckle, poised just above the developing pubis.

*

I was 11 years old, living with my parents & brother Denis at Tellisford, 108, Shirley Avenue, Shirley, Croydon, Surrey. The family had moved down from Edinburgh, Scotland, in the late 1940s. I got a pushbike & this was the first freedom I experienced, flying about the suburbs & rural fringes of outer London, away from parents, house, school. From Shirley to West Wickham, to the terrifyingly steep Gravelly Hill I whizzed down. Then South into the birch woods of Shirley Hills and down into Penge. I was well into solitary habits by then. I retreated into my own worlds. *Treasure Island*, the *Kon Tiki Expedition*, netting tadpoles in the forbidden grounds of the posh Shirley Hotel. I was already a "library cormorant" (S.T. Coleridge), scouring the shelves for anything & everything that was exciting & mysterious in the world of books.

My father, a chartered accountant, was a distant, authoritarian figure who never really allowed me into his life. The faith school I went to employed corporal punishment & I received many whalings.

I was the only person I knew who was into jazz, apart from a boy called Dobbin, who was in a class above me. Boys in different class streams never spoke to one another. If I wanted to talk to Dobbin, we had to meet in an obscure corner of the school to mutter about Louis Armstrong, Kid Ory, the Dukes & Counts.

At 14 or 15, I joined the Army Cadets in a miserable attempt to get a life. Map reading, & drilling, in a hut in Purley. Blowing the bugle at the Green Howards barracks/parade ground in Croydon on a Sunday morning. Uniform. Boots polished up to a brilliant shine. I was suckered into all that. & then washed out, just not caring much.

Sometime in 1956, mum took me & Denis to her friend Mrs Dark's house, where we had tea, & weak cider, while lissom daughter Angela played over & over again the record she had just bought, 'Heartbreak Hotel' by Elvis Presley. This was a key moment, a pivotal experience: sensuous, bluesy, echoey rock'n'roll, with a few bars of exquisite jangly piano that added to the shivers up my spine.

At St. Elphege's youth club I met Terry Page, another jazz fan, & political too, from a committed leftie family. I also got to know the family of Mervyn Peake, who lived in a big house nearby. I remember jamming on piano with Sebastian Peake on drums in the little music room. There was an old Anderson shelter in the back garden which we wanted to turn into a jazz club but nothing came of it. Sometimes we had tea with Maeve Gilmore. I did meet Mervyn Peake once or twice but he was never really very well.

*

It was a relief when I started earning my own money, as a clerk for a firm of solicitors at Fitzroy Square—Fitzrovia! Virginia Woolf!! Car dealers of Goodge Street on the walk down to Soho—spivs & touts & bookies. Suddenly I was a London sharpie, in the know or pretending to be in the know, walking those areas, timidly enough. I had arrived at a place, a stage, where I could, however cautiously, *be*.

During the years 1957–1962 I assiduously pursued my interests in jazz, in reading, & wrote copious letters & diaries. Kerouac's *On the Road* came out, which provided me with a model for the fusion of writing method with the improvisational spirit of jazz. I wanted to be a musician. I wanted to be a novelist. I didn't have the discipline to be a musician, but I was always writing. I continued to work my way slowly up the legal ladder until I could call myself a legal executive. I began to explore the emergent night activities of the youth in edgy coffee bars & leftish pubs with folk singers, trad bands, whiskery cider drinkers, the British beats of their time. But I was unable to truly connect, to find the hip soulmates I felt I desperately needed.

*

Carshalton. A nucleated village with a big flinty church & acres of woody graveyard. Freshwater springs along the foot of the North Downs chalk. Ann Boleyn's Well, opposite the Ponds. The River Wandle, famous of yore for its unique & distinct species of trout. Famous also for its cressbeds. Herb farms & snuffmills, echoes of an Elizabethan age of grand manors, of smallholdings supplying London. A country village until swept up in the urban outspill from London in the 20th century.

*

The most important day of my life : It was a quiet Sunday evening in the summer of 1961 when I walked into the Spanish Bar at the back of The Greyhound, Carshalton. I carried my pint of Young's Special through the large room to the back pew in the corner, & settled myself down. Hooked out of the duffle bag: books. Take your pick from:

William Golding   e e cummings   Norman Mailer

Within a few minutes the pew was invaded by a volatile, seething crowd of youth, who eloquently took over the entire table, with me shoved into a corner. Soon, the two I got to know first, Barry Taylor & Phil Dudley Gill, were interrogating me about my books. "Have you read Henry Miller?" they demanded. All these guys were seriously into books & ideas, also jazz & blues. Mingus was God. & *Wednesday Night Prayer Meeting* was their anthem. This crew turned out to be The Mob. & I joined them.

The Mob first manifested, in the late 1950s, in Elmwood School, in Surrey. The core Mobsters such as Roger Yates, Don Bodie, Mick Collins & Chris Lovell graduated from rock 'n' roll through the blues to arrive at modern jazz, of the hot & passionate variety, rather than the cool jazz that was in vogue. They began using The Greyhound—"The Dog"—as their headquarters.

For a while, The Mob were an all-male cell, a boygang. We listened to our type of jazz. & there was the *Jesus Jump*, done to Mingus's music: a dance which consisted of lurching around with pints of sauterne, or passing Mick's duplicate book from hand to hand, filling it with spontaneous poems, stories & songs. Poetry & performance straightaway then.

The Mob was expanding & soon swept up people from Wallington, Croydon, Sutton & other areas. The big night at The Dog was Friday night in the Spanish Bar all squeezed up, cadging drinks, bumming rollups, animatedly discussing & arguing every topic under the sun. One furiously disputatious evening resulted in the challenge: to start a magazine, instead of just foaming away in the back bar. We needed a name. I was aware of a US mag called *Origin* edited by Cid Corman. *Origins,* I suggested. *Diversions,* said someone else. *Origins Diversions.* John Wood was appointed treasurer & collected our dues until we had enough money to get the magazine rolling. We had weekly editorial meetings at Dick Dyke's place or where my brother Denis & I now had a flat. Dick was the main editor & handled the production side.

At that stage I was still tinkering with the idea of being a novelist. I had managed to sell a short story (about Green Shield stamps!) to *The Croydon Advertiser.* I was beginning to contribute small items to left-wing & anarchist publications & then got hooked up with a Young Socialist paper called *Young Guard* as their jazz correspondent. I had never seriously considered writing poetry.

Our magazine activities attracted a flood of communications & manuscripts from the then thriving world of little magazines & small independent publishers. I was aware of space opening up for me, in the company of other Mob poets—Roger Yates, Don Bodie, Bill Wyatt, later on Richard Downing, Dave James & Jeff Morsman. If I was to write for the mag, some of it would be poetry. I began to read Ginsberg, Burroughs, Corso, Levertov & Ferlinghetti, G. M. Hopkins & Marianne Moore. My earliest poems, published in Dave Cunliffe's *Poetmeat,* were pseudo-beat, science fiction-type things, scratchy & derivative.

Each issue of the mag was launched with a reading featuring many of the writers involved, with guest stars such as Dave Cunliffe & Tina Morris, & later on Peter Bland & Allen Barry. Dave said I should invite Lee Harwood down. I wrote to Lee & met him at Carshalton Station one afternoon in the summer of 1964; & thus began the most influential of my friendships & one that was most instrumental in getting me writing properly.

& sometime during the autumn of that year I picked up a 2nd hand copy of *The New American Poetry 1945–1960* edited by Don Allen because I was attracted by the Beat poets represented there. After meeting Lee, this was the next most powerful influence on what I was writing. I gutted the anthology & still have the pieces, Olson's 'Projective Verse' essay heavily scored & annotated in red biro. In April 1966 I threw out all my old beginner poems & started again from scratch.

Dick & I also went on hitching tours meeting other activists including Clive Allison in Oxford, Alan Turner & Alex Hand (*Iconolatre Magazine*) in West Hartlepool, Dave Cunliffe & Tina Morris in Blackburn, Jim Burns in Preston & Ian Vine in Bristol. & the *Origins Diversions* crowd got involved in some of the London readings; we had our own reading at Better Books, & some of us read at Lee's celebration of the birth of Dada in 1966.

*

Just to backtrack a little. After working for 3 London law firms, I was working for a firm in Sutton, with my own desk, room, access to a typist, & a steadily growing stack of legal files. But the experience with The Mob was driving me to reject the black suit & shiny shoes image. The Mobsters were garden labourers & window cleaners, as well as clerks or apprentices—& I felt increasingly pulled to the outside.

In March 1965, I gave in my notice. I had secured a post as a garden labourer for the Carshalton Parks Department. By April 1965 I was picking up litter with a stabber & sack in Carshalton Park. A few weeks later I was transferred to the St. Helier running track to undertake groundsman duties.

It was wonderful to be free of the office, the responsibilities, of tugging barristers gowns at court hearings, or holding the hands of nervous clients. My mind was free. I wrote furiously that year. My first paid gig, in 1965, was at Nottingham University with Lee Harwood, Mike Horovitz, Pete Brown & Spike Hawkins; the reading was organised by Michael Skaife D'Ingerthorpe. I never felt I was *in* the London scene, which to me was a joyous polarity between the Horovitz-Brown *New Departures* tribe & the activity generated by Lee's succession of oneshot mags such as *Nightscene* & *Tzarad*.

On another occasion I went with Lee Harwood to the Bath Festival fringe where we were on the bill with the Liverpool poets & some of the Migrant poets. Brian Patten read. As he finished & announced the next poet, me, he drew a joint from his top pocket, lit it, took a few drags, then gave it to me as we passed each other on the steps. I had not read stoned before, & the experience added to my perception of myself reading, & of the acoustics of the venue. Reading my work live terrified me but reading out loud became a vital adjunct to the compositional process. I went to the famous Albert Hall event *Wholly Communion* and picked up cadences, modes, & the pensive silences & dramatic commitments of Harry Fainlight.

By late 1965 Lee had put me in touch with Andrew Crozier, who was bringing out *The English Intelligencer,* which went out by mail, sometimes as frequently as once a fortnight. I began sending in pages that became the foundation for my first book, *Green Orange Purple Red.* I began delving into the geography & history of the River Wandle and the most hidden corners & byways of Carshalton. Most of that writing occurred between April & July of 1966 culminating in what I call The Carshalton Steam Laundry Vision. I was mowing the narrow verge outside the laundry hearing the hissing & clanking of the machines & the voices of the women operators coming through open windows when I had this absolutely sublime moment when I realised that I *was* a poet. *That* was what I was going to do with my life. *Be a poet.*

In the autumn of 1966 I signed on for an evening class in English Literature at Carshalton Technical College. Mr. Derek Clout was doing Eliot, & a large class soon became absorbed in his knowledgeable discourse on 'The Waste Land' & 'Four Quartets'. It was in this class that I met my future wife, Val.

*

Val & I took off in 1967 for a summer season working in Jersey, along with a dozen Mobsters & associates. On the full moon of May we had a Buddhist wedding officiated by Bill Wyatt. Later that year Val & I settled in Bristol. Val worked as a lab assistant & myself as a parks department labourer on the Bristol Downs. We had a flat in the Cotham area. I continued writing but in retrospect the work I did there (collected in *Aries Under Saturn*) did not move for me the way it had done when I was in Carshalton.

I was in regular touch with poets in London & Cambridge, & one weekend in the late '60s Jeremy Prynne picked us up & drove us down to John Hall's place in Devon. It was an opportunity for me to learn as much as possible from a great mind & I quizzed Jeremy all the way, discovering that he seemed to be aware of every book that had ever been published, as well as knowing how poets & poetry worked. Jeremy always responded positively to my work & this was obviously a boost to my confidence in those early, sometimes very uncertain years.

On 6 June 1970, Val & I moved to our new residence in Wales. Thus we settled into the first stage of our rural idyll with those early days and the sense of being free. By now I had 2 books out, *Green Orange Purple Red*, containing poems written mostly in Carshalton, & *Aries Under Saturn*, written in Bristol, both from Andrew Crozier's Ferry Press. I began to write the book that became *Acrospirical Meanderings in a Tongue of the Time*. This was published by Iain Sinclair's Albion Village Press, who also published the first 2 books of series.

In retrospect, *The Magic Door* really begins with that first book *Acrospirical...* I set the theme to be that of an exploration of the Transformation Process in nature & in humankind. Experiences under lysergic acid & the Jungian studies, the mandalas in Jung's *Psychology and Alchemy*, dreams, & the beauties & rigours of the rural scene with its weathers & seasons combined with speculative forays prompted by the discovery of a line that extended from 2 local standing stones right through our front door.

The geology of the area was complex & fascinating, with the Neath Valley Fault being one of the oldest in the British Isles. Its movements had created a palimpsest of superimposed landscapes & an industrial history that stretched from as far back as the Bronze Age. The finest anthracites in the world, fireclays, quartz-rich rocks & extensive limestone provided the basis of successive waves of industrial innovation & revolution & endless inspiration for writing.

Another potent factor was the isolation, which changed the nature of personal relationships, away from the distractions of urban living. No TV or telephone, no fridge, & the nearest pubs were miles away. We had to learn how to work for & entertain each other. A continuous teach-in about the hows & whys of life & art. This was a time of hope. Gurus, mystics, charlatans, acid doctors—it was a time of chaotic madness full of blazing creative endeavour, woodshedding, blissouts & comedowns. Naked summer dawns.

I have to talk about drugs a bit because they've been a part of my culture and influence all through my adult life. Cannabis, both calming & arousing of the senses was projective, stretching time, opening out dimensions. Socially bonding. When dope appeared I found myself using it to enhance the light trance state of the first writings of a poem, or as a diagnostic tool later. Playing Burroughs-Gysin games with it. Chance operations were a stage of the work as well as the seriousness of desiring a resolution of shape, form & intent.

I had drifted West, further & further away from the London & Cambridge poetry scenes. *The English Intelligencer* was tailing off, but the small mag network was still strong & I sent plenty of work around, & began to get a few readings, as well as making connections to the Welsh scene. I already knew Peter Finch for *second aeon* & the readings he ran in Cardiff, & I was soon to meet poet activists such as Nigel Jenkins & John Tripp.

*

Late in November 1974 Barry MacSweeney & I were reading in Lampeter, in West Wales. When I joined Barry on the train he had already consumed a bottle of white wine and had a second bottle open in front of him. A bellyful of political troubles was poured into my ear; industrial action he'd been engaged in as deputy father of the union of Kentish Times journalists; threat to grants for *Poetry Review*; Northern Ireland despondency adding to my own Northern Ireland despondency. & I was in as gloomy a mood as Barry by the time we got to Carmarthen.

We arrived at the reading to find 3 people in the audience, plus the 2 organisers. We both read twice, cancelling the interval & crashing straight on, terrified of losing our audience during the break.

In 1993 in London we launched a book of our work plus work by Thomas A. Clark called *Tempers of Hazard,* published by Harper Collins. This was about the time Rupert Murdoch took over the publishing firm. I became resigned to the fact that the book was imperilled & indeed the print run was curtailed & the book was never promoted. I put that behind me, but it hit Barry hard, & may have contributed to his ongoing problems with alcohol.

My last meeting with Barry was at a reading in a café bar in Brighton in the 90s, when he appeared to be sober, full of confidence & talk as usual, & read like an angel. At the height of our friendship we were each other's "blood brothers"… I more & more feel that he was the outstanding poet of our era. I especially loved his work from *Black Torch* to the astonishing *Book of Demons.* I was sorry when he died.

However, poetry was alive & kicking. Allen Fisher's *Place,* Gavin Selerie's *Azimuth* came out, one using Poundian rhythmic springboard, the other more embedded in the radical/commune/ liberationist states of that time. By the late '70s, however, the scene was changing. The revolutionaries at The Poetry Society were edged out & the old guard were back in control. I was now becoming more involved with the poetry scene in Wales. I had been in touch with poet/musician Barry Edgar Pilcher & in the mid '70s joined his Cardiff-based band *Dragons Blood.* This became the setting for my first tentative experiments reading my work live with musicians.

There were up to 7 or 8 people in *Dragons Blood* & the regular line up was Barry Edgar Pilcher, sax & flute & contributing poems; Eve Pilcher, cello; Ray Paul, guitar; Tim Davies, mandolin, percussion, songs & poems; Val Torrance, guitar, songs & poems; Phil Maillard, guitar, poems; myself poems & programming. It was hard to juggle the dance of egos in this large, talented group, & to avoid clashes, let alone get things finely balanced in rehearsal & onstage. *Dragons Blood* broke up in the later '70s.

By the beginning of 1976, my marriage to Val was unravelling, & she left in the early spring. I entertained thoughts of leaving. I couldn't, however, neglect the garden, & once some fine weather arrived, I began cultivation. I borrowed money from friends, who also supported me in many other ways. There was income from readings & occasionally from farm work, so I was getting by.

One of the most significant visitors to the farm as that season developed was Sue, a troubled person & a student, at Cardiff University, later a trainee probation officer in Bristol. She soon regarded my place as a sanctuary & over the course of the year or so she poured out her life to me, sometimes following self-harming episodes & suicide attempts. Heavily influenced at the time by the likes of not just William Burroughs but also Hunter S. Thompson &—wait for it—yes Len Deighton—I faithfully kept a diary of each & every one of her encounters, including a voluminous correspondence.

After 2 years of seemingly continual crisis, Sue pulled away from her difficulties, having established a supposedly safe relationship with an older man. As a result of a series of incidents Sue suddenly found herself cut off, discarded. It was all too much. She took her car out onto Brean Sands one day & killed herself by feeding car exhaust into her car. The book I wrote then was called *The Diary of Palugs Cat*, the most intimate of any of my books. It was a very difficult book to write.

Palug was published by Galloping Dog Press, run by a new arrival on the scene, Peter Hodgkiss, editor of *Poetry Information*. His presence in Swansea meant that it became a hub of alternative writing activity. I did a reading there with Jim Burns, & there were readings by many others including Lee Harwood, Bill Wyatt, & the sensational Anne Waldman, whose rhythms in her poem 'Pressure' I was able to convert into the driving force behind my later long rap poem, 'Frinite'.

*

In the meantime I'd begun tutoring *Adventures in Creative Writing* evening classes for the then Adult Education Department of Cardiff University—a part-time job that continued for 25 years. As I'd never taught before, I was on a steep learning curve from the start. I told the class members that the instant they entered the room I would treat them as writers. That it was their class. I stressed how important was the commitment to the act of writing, & to delivery of the work, as Olson said, all the way over to the reader, the recipient. I stressed the act of performance of the work almost as much as its creation. In retrospect, the whole class was "performance" from start to finish. This engagement was facilitated by the opening feature, *Burning Issues*, which was designed as an open forum focusing on hot topics of writing & creativity. Another gambit was writing on the spot. Awesome atmosphere of a roomful of people writing in near silence with just a steady undertow of pens moving across paper…

This was the preamble to regular events of this type, retitled Cabaret 246 after the room number of the Humanities Building in which the classes were held, & the title of a magazine which ran for many years under various editors & published by Chris Mill's Red Shark Press.

As *Adventures In Creative Writing* rolled through the years, so new people kept showing up, especially in the wake of the Cabaret 246 events & publications. One of those was poet & activist Ric Hool, who was just then initiating a series of readings in Abergavenny, & publishing books with John Jones & others under the name The Collective. As the series has developed over the years, I have become increasingly drawn into these readings occurring mainly at the Hen & Chicks pub in an upstairs room providing an ideal venue. In recent years Ric has hosted the annual *Beneath The Underground Jazz & Poetry Festival*, basically a reunion of the old Carshalton crowd—The Mob—plus the many others who have been drawn into the various activities since *Origins Diversions* was launched all those years ago.

Jeff Nuttall's Carnival of Discord

GILLIAN WHITELEY

Blood let/melt light/apple bleed/catch sun
Sun late, gurgling in its westerly mess,
They run out, shrieking geese across the darkening, the dead
    girls.
    —From 'Blood let', *Penguin Modern Poets No 12,* 1968.

Watching Jeff Nuttall read 'Blood let' on Pip Benveniste's 1969 film
9 Poets,[1] is a visceral experience which is undiminished by time or
technology. Teasingly, his animated body writhes as he spits out phrases
in a sensuous physical performance. Similarly, with their scribbles,
inkblotches and tumescent appendages, Nuttall's drawings, paintings
and junk assemblages celebrated a Rabelaisian corporeality which
reflected his interest in the erotic and the comic, running from the
pornographic writings of philosopher Georges Bataille to the end-of-
pier ribaldry of Northern working-class club stand-up.[2] No sign here
of the "new affectlessness"—or "the degradation of awareness" as he
later called it[3]—that he felt was "becoming commonplace at an unnerving rate" in the Sixties and beyond.[4] For Nuttall, a pernicious
consumerism was eroding the capacity to "feel", accompanied by the
relentless commodification not only of art but, potentially, of life itself.
Consequently, his appeal for the need to sharpen sensory experiences
and confront complacency and uniformity was not just a constant
refrain: it was his credo.

The same sophisticated, often outrageous, combination of
sensuality and vulgarity[5] was expressed throughout Nuttall's prolific
body of work which, besides poetry, encompassed the founding of a
host of small "underground" presses, the writing and drawing of novels,
biographies, literary criticism and countercultural polemic, music-
making, performance and visual art practices, theatrical and educational
innovation. Indeed, the extent and diversity of his cultural production
over fifty years, demonstrates the ease with which he slipped from one
art form to another. Paradoxically, despite playing a key role in the
"British Poetry Revival" (he was Chair of the Poetry Society, 1975–6)

his insistent interdisciplinarity probably explains his remaining on the periphery as, until recently, his various contributions have remained unacknowledged even in historical surveys. As he himself declared, when interviewed for the *International Times* (No 9) 1967, about his latest venture—the *People Show*—he was intent on breaking down artistic conventions:

> "I paint poems, sing sculptures, draw novels. So I don't want a name for this latest excursion but you can call it theatre if you want."

In many ways, Nuttall's entire cultural output was grounded in the experience of Sixties' protest with much of it a response to the perceived "failure" of 1968. Thinking back, rather than poetry or artworks, it was probably through his writings on counterculture that I first encountered Nuttall:

> …the anti-bomb movement had been ignored. The Vietnam war was permitted… Affect was nowhere to be found. I wanted to smash the impenetrable glass bulbs in which people housed their apathy.
>
> *Performance Memoirs,* London: Calder, 1979

As a working-class hippy art student, in my black and gold kaftan and shaggy white Afghan coat, I have hazy memories of browsing *Bomb Culture*, Nuttall's idiosyncratic semi-autobiographical account of the build up to 1968. Of course, I would have concurred with his blistering attack on hypocrisy, conformity and authoritarianism: to demand the impossible was an urgent necessity.

However, my subsequent pursuit of the kinds of countercultural practices which took art out of the gallery and into the streets, meant that Nuttall's anarchic happenings and installations in the 1960s and 70s provided a starting point for more extensive research. Whilst studying for a PhD at Leeds in the mid-1990s, the rediscovery of Adrian Henri's 1974 book *Environments and Happenings*—and its account of the macabre *sTigma* environment which Nuttall, Bruce Lacey, Islwyn Watkins and others built in the basement of Better Books—set me on a journey which included studying private and public archives, interviewing fellow poets and artists and talking to former students, friends and family.[6]

Apart from the intensity of *affect* (with distinct reference to Antonin Artaud, evidenced by Nuttall's personal annotated copy of the influential *The Theatre and Its Double*), and an *absurdist* approach (with due homage paid to Alfred Jarry), a key element in his writings came from the visual arts—as it was *collage* which provided a core methodology. Remembered phrases and snatches of "found" dialect were pasted together or "cut-up", echoing the work of his contemporaries, William Burroughs and Brion Gysin. Nuttall wrote of his aim for "simultaneity", persistently employing montage techniques to create a dense mélange of imagery and ideas.

> The rubble bled with a viscoid scum. Out of the strong came
> forth sweat said the snoring lion with his paws in syrup.
> *The Case of Isobel and the Bleeding Foetus,* Turret Press, 1967.

Despite a relatively genteel upbringing, Nuttall, who was born in Clitheroe, Lancashire, in 1933, had a distinct familiarity with the backyard banality of working-class life and this went alongside a divergent set of influences from Dada, surrealism and jazz to the American Beats. Certainly, Nuttall was a key figure on the British "underground" scene, exchanging ideas and writings with contemporaries such as Burroughs, Douglas Blazek, Carl Weissner, Alexander Trocchi, Dom Sylvester Houédard and Bob Cobbing, initiating small journals such as the cut-up inspired *My Own Mag*[7] or collaborating on various publishing projects. Perhaps more importantly, besides being a significant poet, artist, performer and polemicist in his own right, as Michael Horovitz commented, Nuttall was a cultural *catalyst* in that he facilitated others through his various projects.

In the 1980s, Nuttall returned to painting, initially finding his subject around the Pennines, "a landscape mangled like a mongrel's scabby back with degradation... beneath its superstructures of bawdy humour, music hall, smoky-arsed orientated folklore, the hardmouthed toughness of a terrible ancient violence."[8] His writings, like his paintings, revelled in the dark terraces, the soaring valleys and the "lumpen, plump, blunt onomatopoeia" of the place-names around the Calder and the Colne:

> …Nabby Nook, Mankinholes, Lumb Butts, Midgeley, Widdop, Hoo Hole, Lob Mill, Hoar Nib, Turley Holes, Upper Stubbing, Great Jumps, Pisser Clough, Bog Eggs, Slode, Twine, Owlers…'
>
> *The Pleasures of Necessity*, Colne: Arrowspire Press, 1988

In such a short piece, it is almost impossible to sum up the incongruous elements that made up Nuttall's artistic and poetic sensibilities. One of his own phrases—a carnival of discord—seems to capture it perfectly for me. Alongside the "mangled" industrial North, there was also a neo-romantic element which sprang from a heightened awareness of the exuberance and vitality of organic forms and processes. Indeed, Nuttall's "Dionysian landscapes", as he called them, hark back to the Orcop valley in the Herefordshire of his youth. His poem, *Return Trip*, with profound notes of Dylan Thomas and D.H. Lawrence, transfers us to a bucolic landscape which bubbles and vomits with frenzied blossom and turbulent hedges. His late works—both in words and imagery—combine the hyper-realism of the nineteenth-century painter Samuel Palmer with a Blakeian sense of astonishment at the natural world. Yet, characteristically, there is always an eye for the farcical and the burlesque that, with Nuttall, was forever rooted in the anarchic sensibility of the Sixties.

> Walked through the spittle, dead cats, shattered phone booths
> Winced at rain-soaked mattresses amongst the willowherb
> Turned into the Fenton, bought a packet of Park Drive and
> > fifteen pints
> Took a bus to Otley, shot his bloodcoil into endless recesses of
> > midnight summer rain.
>
> *'Love Landscapes'*, *Objects*, Trigram Press, 1976.

NOTES

1 In 1965, Pip Benveniste (1921–2010), with the poet Asa Benveniste, founded Trigram Press, a publishing house dedicated to experimental typography and poetry—see Nuttall's *Objects*,1976

2 In 1978, Routledge and Kegan published Nuttall's *King Twist*, a biography of Blackpool comedian, Frank Randle.

3 Jeff Nuttall, *Art and the Degradation of Awareness*, London, Calder, 2001— his last major publication before his death in 2004.

4 Jeff Nuttall, *Bomb Culture*, p. 27

5 Seaside postcards were just one of the subjects Nuttall explored in *Common Factors/Vulgar Factions*, a study of popular culture co-written with Rodick Carmichael, published 1977.

6 I carried out extensive research for the exhibition, *The Life and Works of Jeff Nuttall: 1933–2004*, MidPennine Arts Gallery, Burnley, 2006. Also, see 'Sewing the "subversive thread of imagination": Jeff Nuttall, Bomb Culture and the radical potential of affect' in *The Sixties: A Journal of History, Politics, and Culture*, Winter 2011, Volume 4, Issue 2

7 *My Own Mag* was a mimeographed magazine of cartoons, political commentary, poetry and letters. Between 1965 and 1967. It ran to seventeen issues, included writings by Burroughs, Ginsberg and Marowitz and was distributed across Europe, the United States and North Africa.

8 Jeff Nuttall, *The Patriarchs*, The Beau and Aloes Arc Association, London, 1978.

Basil Bunting and Me

Connie Pickard

Friday, 25th July 1969
BARRY SCAUM'S HOUSE IN BENSHAM, GATESHEAD.

Sitting in the garden facing the sun—someone appears at the gate—bronze face, hair flowing: Robert Bly, back from the Buddhist monastery? No, it's Basil, looking incredibly young and large. He is working on a new poem, about the Isabella pit in Throckley which his father helped to sink—a poem about the life that takes over when the pit is finished: the "goaf"-waste, by-product—the hole left after the seam has been cleared—the dark hole with ice-cold spray—the dense foliage growing around the outside. Only children visit the site, for swimming, leaping in the air, half a dozen at a time. A completely different country, and only a few miles from Newcastle. Never-Never Land. My daughter Cath, playing with water, letting it flow through her toes. She is becoming a big, fat, earthy lass; suddenly lays into Basil for some reason. Basil busy with Chalmers Burns on Matthew Arnold's *Scholar Gypsy* for a memorial concert for Peter Ure (late Professor of English at the University of Newcastle). Have got to get a copy of *Nature*, look out for Moon Dust coming to Wylam.

April 26th 1975
AVENUE ROAD, BENSHAM, GATESHEAD.

Basil arrived. We talked and talked about John Collier, Spence Watson, Fox and Quakerism; about the split in Quakerism between pantheism and puritanism—the Bensham Settlement has been an attempt to harmonize the two; Whittaker and the Bach Choir; the Veitches and the People's Theatre. Basil's father and old Runciman had helped set up the first Labour candidate. It all happened here in a house in Jessy Dene.

On to Haughton Castle; we sit by the river, watch dippers. Great Whittingham. Narrow lanes and Bewick motifs. Batch of hens with very red combs; Taoist trees. Basil's face very lined now—lines of age, lineage like an ancient king, rattish laugh. Then talks of Abiezer Coppe with the enthusiasm of a young man. Sweet Sips of Spiritual Wine... he wrote in a prose style quite unlike anyone else... all that has been lost.

*

Abiezer Coppe would have got into Basil's good books on the strength of his name alone. One of the things I had noticed early on was the musical attachment Basil had to names. I was always "Connie my dear" not because I was particularly nice at all but it had a better resonance and he would always give your name its full weight and measure... and I am not talking about the Domenico Scarlattis and Eric Bloodaxes, but about ordinary names. When he said my little daughter Catherine's name it was always with a full trill on the "r". It sounded like a small fountain. And all of the former Catherines were there too: the mystic, the great letter-writer, the king's wives. The length of the "a" when he said "Matthew" was pastoral. I could never say my son's name in the same way.

The notes from my diary are so sparse—they were not meant to be anything more than a jog to the memory. I had asked Basil about the Bensham Settlement because I wanted to know more about his relation to the North-East, though I was curious, too, about its history. I knew that Joseph Skipsey had visited the house, and we loved Basil's story how, as a baby, he had been dandled on the knee of the Pitman Poet. While attending Gaelic classes at Bensham Settlement I had found out that another North-East writer, Jack Common, had attended classes for the unemployed there in the Twenties. I wondered if Basil had ever met him, but he had not, neither in the North-East nor London, where Jack Common had worked on *The Adelphi*—although Basil had been a friend of A.R. Orage and some *Adelphi* contributors had also written for *The New English Weekly*, Orage's paper.

Both Basil and Tom Pickard had been born in Scotswood. In 1900 this part of West Newcastle was still quite rural, still a residential area for well-known Quaker families. At the nearby pit Basil's father was the miners' doctor. By the time Tom was born, forty-six years later, Scotswood had become a slum. About the time Tom's family were moving into their house on one of the new post-war estates on the outskirts of the town, Basil would have been returning to England after being expelled from Persia.

We all finally met in Wylam, further up the Tyne, in a beautiful and substantial house overlooking the river. We sat in the garden, in Sima's domain full of raspberries and other good things. Sima was Basil's second wife, whom he had met in Persia. On that day she had just been playing tennis, her long black hair was tied in a pink scarf and her eyes sparkled. The Bunting children were quite young: Tom very plump, and Maria an exquisite figure from a Persian miniature. In the background Basil's mother, then in her nineties, fussed over the poet, calling him "Son" in a broad Northumberland accent. There were one or two Persian students and lots of animals in that big household. Sima cooked us a great spaghetti dinner and afterwards Basil made Turkish coffee.

On that first evening in Wylam, Basil, read us some of his poems. We were amazed and delighted: "Let them remember Samangan", 'Mesh cast for mackerel', but the revelation was 'Chomei at Toyama'. In 1931, when it was written, the story of the devastation of a city must have seemed something remote:

> To appreciate present conditions
> collate them with those of antiquity.

*

Tom Pickard and I were a very odd couple. Tom was eighteen and had recently published a piece called 'Workless Teens' in *Anarchy*. I was older. I came from a pit village and had graduated from King's College (now the University of Newcastle-upon-Tyne) and then taught until I was expecting Matthew. I was living with Tom, but, as I was not yet divorced from my first husband, I was naturally asked to leave my job; in fact, it was suggested that I should go and live in another town— advice which people still tend to give me. Good advice, but impossible. When some superannuation money I had applied for miraculously turned up—a whole £180—we decided we would start a bookshop. Crazy. I managed to persuade the City Fathers to let me rent a medieval tower in a very insalubrious back lane in downtown Newcastle for ten bob a week. When publishers' reps used to call they suggested that a better idea would be to keep pigeons. Basil thought all this was a hoot, but he did not discourage us.

By chance Tom had met Pete Brown while hitch-hiking to London, and Pete had invited himself to read in the Tower when he was to pass through Newcastle in a few weeks' time. We asked Basil to come to Pete's reading and were amazed when he said he would.

*

A few years before, poetry and jazz had come to the town, announced when the immortal words "Bird Lives" (Charlie "Bird" Parker) started to appear on walls among the graffiti. Our friends Tony Jackson and Roy Robertson were reading Rexroth, Patchen and Snyder. At that time we had still read only one poem of Basil's, 'The Complaint of the Morpethshire Farmer', and had been expecting someone quite different, so that we were pleased to find Basil shared our enthusiasm for Snyder. He introduced us to William Carlos Williams and Zukofsky.

When Basil himself read in the Morden Tower he had a great appeal for young people. He could not understand this. But just imagine him as he was then, his face quite thin, almost wolfish, or cadaverous, reading 'Villon' with the intensity of his own experience (Bunting had been imprisoned in 1918 for being a conscientious object during World War 1); add the fact that many of the people who came to the Tower had faced arrest in peace demonstrations, and some were lads who themselves had seen the inside of prison because of trivial offences, one begins to understand that Basil's reading was an impressive experience.

But it was not always solemn. Basil had a strong sense of humour and sometimes reminded us of Groucho Marx. During Allen Ginsberg's first reading in Newcastle he had dedicated to Basil the poem 'To an Old Poet in Peru'. After the reading Basil retaliated by out-singing "The Howling King of the Beats" (as Allen had ludicrously been described in the local evening paper). For every mantra that Allen performed Basil would sing a sweet Purcell aria or a lovely song of Campion's— the strong voice getting stronger and stronger in tone, the centuries rolling away, till after some very stern Victorian ballads we all collapsed laughing, and Allen fell with his head on Basil's knee.

Some years later there was another good day with Allen when he wanted to visit Durham Cathedral. I remember them both discussing prayer very learnedly in the cloisters, discussing the way Buddhist or medieval Christian monks dealt with wool-gathering. Allen was obviously never guilty of wool-gathering, because he quoted the inscription on Bede's tomb even before we reached it: *Haec sunt in fossa Baedae venerabilis ossa*. After we had also paid our respects to Cuthbert's bones, Allen noticed the little fossil remains of the sea lilies in the Frosterly marble pillars. Allen had a broken leg and Basil's eyes were not too great, but in no time at all we were clambering into the jalopy, driving over hill and dale and walking through fields until we came to the old working of the quarries of Frosterly. It was a day of huge time-scales. Often it seemed that we had stepped into eternity.

There were other times like that—when, for instance, Basil was writing 'Briggflatts' sitting in St John's churchyard and reading out some lines that he was really pleased with:

> You who can calculate the course
> of a biased bowl,
> shall I come near the jack?
> What twist can counter the force
> that holds back
> woods I roll?

Until then I had thought that when Pound had addressed Bunting and Zukofsky as strugglers in the desert he was talking about the difficulties poets face in making a living or getting accepted. It was only then that I realised it was something quite different: it was about the seriousness of the work itself.

I love 'Briggflatts', not only because it is a great poem but also because we were privileged to be around Basil while he was writing it, and I can see that it is only fitting that his ashes were scattered over the meeting-house in 'Briggflatts'. However, it is 'Chomei' that keeps coming into my mind. It could almost have been written for 1985:

Fathers fed their children and died,
babies died sucking the dead.
The priest Hoshi went about marking their foreheads
A, Amida, their requiem…

Anyone wishing to know what Basil Bunting was like in the last few years need only read the last few verses of that poem:

The moonshadow merges with darkness
of the cliffpath,
a tricky turn near ahead.

Oh! There's nothing to complain about.
Buddha says: "None of the world is good."
I am fond of my hut…

I have renounced the world;
have a saintly
appearance.

I do not enjoy being poor,
I've a passionate nature.
My tongue
clacked a few prayers.

Accent, Bunting, Caddel…

Tony Baker

The Cheviot in Northumberland has to be one of the world's worst hills to walk on—an unrelenting slog through unrelenting moor-grass to a summit so drearily sodden amongst unrelenting peat slough that no one in their right mind would want to reach it. The one time I got near the top I stopped short, seeing how the bootprints of earlier walkers were bedded in the slutch. Two skylarks flitted round the triangulation point in sole possession.

Likening Ezra Pound's *Cantos* to the Alps, Basil Bunting suggested "you will have to go a long way round/ if you want to avoid them". The comparison wouldn't have worked with the hills round Cheviot. They're easily avoidable. You can take the coast road and scarcely remark that they're there, though Cheviot itself is oddly visible, swelling from the skyline like a bruise. Yet these were the hills of Bunting's heart: born in sight of them, he died amongst them. He wasn't a man of crags and precipices; he belonged to the enduring, overlookable, shepherded slopes.

For long years of course people took the coast road round Bunting's own writing. While he travelled a great deal he always returned to Northumberland, living, perhaps happily avoided, in different parts of the region for the majority of his life. Part of him never left. His voice on recordings has sometimes been described as affected, as if the churring "r"s and prolonged resonances were an attempt to force exaggerated northron tones on an audience that ought to know who Eric Bloodaxe was but seldom did. Yet it really *was* an elaboration of the voice he conversed with, a voice both edged with bright consonants and foggy with vowel-ballast. It seemed quite deliberately drawn up from the well of his throat, a rising sap squeezed past the hedge of his beard to reach the air as meticulously filtered articulation. Supple like the turfs round Cheviot, yet nothing you might think or say would seem likely to budge it. His speech, readily clipped to the verge of irony, made human history seem an ephemeral blip before what was immemorial in the hills. He would rubbish cant: "Beware Bull," as his relished acronym advised.

If the small celebrity that followed the publication of *Briggflatts* in 1966 amused, even perhaps pleased, him a little, it didn't fool him. His self-estimation remained "a minor poet, not conspicuously dishonest". As penniless as ever, he quietly occupied the skyline and waited for folks to come to him if they wished. And mostly they didn't.

*

I first came across Bunting's writing in a bookshop in Richmond, South London in, I suppose, 1972. The shop specialised in selling review copies of books that reviewers had preferred to sell rather than write about which meant of course that it was unusually well-supplied with modern poetry, including amongst many spineless items, books from now-mythic presses like Trigram, Ferry and Fulcrum. I was at school at the time, studying Hamlet and Yeats and Spender, barely aware that there might be lands to explore beyond the world according to Faber or Eliot's Great Tradition. I was uneasy about it: words *did* excite me, but right there where it seemed they should be most exciting, in "modern poetry", I was somehow unconvinced. I think I felt it was maybe my fault: I wasn't reading right.

Then, three steps up a ladder in a south London bookshop, hard up against the ceiling, a book fell open at "I am agog for foam..." I'd learnt that poems opened up their riches when prised apart by the oyster-knife of Leavisite criticism and here was a script that remained more or less clammed shut when read that way. Yet it contained word-chains that gleamed like mother-of-pearl. It wasn't a moment of sudden illumination; my reading in fact was thin to the point that it took years before I recognised what Bunting's ode was "about". But I do think I heard something which hinted at other possibilities, which was properly, if indecipherably, convincing. The dance of Bunting's syllables may have sounded strange as surf on a distant shore but the undertow of their music was ineluctable. His words seemed true beyond all struggle.

Now this was a time that saw, or had recently seen, the International Poetry Incarnation at the Albert Hall, the establishment of Morden Tower as a reading venue in Newcastle, the Great Poetry Society Wars, Henri Chopin, the opening of the Oriel Bookshop in Cardiff and the Unicorn and Public House bookshops in Brighton, the Liverpool

Poets, Sparty Lea and little Sparta, A.L.P., 36 editions of *The English Intelligencer*, Horovitz' *Children of Albion, Place*, Writers Forum... all the thousand and one symptoms of what has become known as the British Poetry Revival. I missed it all. Absolutely every bit. Of all that activity, Bunting's poems—themselves marginal enough—were the first hint I think I got. And I record it here only because my experience can't have been very unusual. Two decades before the internet in a pre-Google era the visible parts of the poetry iceberg loomed like the whole story. It wasn't a question of mainstream versus counter-currents; I simply didn't come across all the local turbulence.

*

Same story at university in Cambridge. I caught other hints: the revolving stand of journals in the Faculty library that carried copies of a curiously home-made publication called *Poetry Information*; the over-subscribed lectures of J.H. Prynne on contemporary poetry where students stood in the doorway to hear him reading Olson; an oddly evaporating encounter with Prynne himself at a reading by Bill Bennett where, had I known it, the public probably included various notable Revivalists in person; a student seminar on O'Hara's 'The Day Lady Died', a poem whose form seemed an outrageous un-achievement and whose truth really did make me nearly stop breathing; a puzzlingly, pleasingly, provokingly unadorned thing about a red wheelbarrow... But for the most part I followed the instructions on the box: I read John Wain and Larkin and Sylvia Plath (who seemed a special case), but mapped none of it into what seemed to make a very pertinent or coherent terrain.

On one occasion I found an orphan among the library stacks, a thin, stapled thing entitled *Old Bosham Birdwatch* by someone called Lee Harwood. It contained no great density of words on each of its few, cyclostyled, unnumbered pages. It might have issued from the same back-kitchen manufactory as *Poetry Information*. I'd learnt to think that form was something wrested from matter—the outward evidence of a struggle to subdue content to the rigours of a recognisable shape. I didn't recognise Harwood's shapes and bewilderingly it didn't seem that he'd especially struggled to make them. If the truth of "I am agog for foam" rang clear before I'd worked at the words, Bunting's graft in assembling them was nonetheless self-evident: the poet *had* written with a very deliberate chisel. Harwood's writing however seemed to transgress the rules; one simply didn't enjoy reading—or writing—poems (if these were such) with quite so little apparent effort. The pamphlet—it was hardly more than that—impressed me to the extent that I wrote down the name and address of the publisher: "Pig Press, Newcastle-upon-Tyne". And somehow failed to lose the note for another 2 years.

*

None of these details are of any particular consequence except that they do probably reflect a very common experience among curious young readers with no guttersnipe rebellion in them in the mid-'70s. If your instinct was essentially to trust the integrity of teachers and mentors, you tended not to see beyond them. The information revolution hadn't happened. So far as writing was concerned, the circle that closed around reviewers, publishers, libraries, funding bodies and educational institutions, looked complete. If that now seems simplistic, it would be hard to over-estimate how it didn't at the time. You looked for clues within that circle because that was their habitat. The tools to unearth evidence of other worlds didn't come my way. It took Bunting's Northumbrianism and Richard Caddel's Pig Press—born in the Newcastle where Ric himself got to know Bunting—to demonstrate that not only was that *not* the only habitat to search, but that no such habitat really ever exists. Ric showed me that the writing that mattered would always give things a local habitation and a name. There was no other place for it. Any soil is local. Writing comes from where you plant your feet. Which in the late '70s came to mean for me the north-east.

*

I eventually wrote to Ric at the Pig Press address shortly before arriving in Durham in 1978. By return I got a brief, warm reply in a nearly illegible handwriting of big, thin loops and quick angular corners. The idea of the person I invented from it—wild, hairy, brittle-tempered, hasty—turned out to be only just short of completely wrong. Ric, who worked in the University Science Library, cut a steady figure: breathy from the asthma that had troubled him since childhood, I don't think I ever saw him break out of a walk. Squat and shambling, he was disarmingly unassuming yet attentive to detail. His eyes weren't good but his ears knew as well as any man's how to listen. He would patiently discriminate sense in what you said and quick-wittedly add colour to the non-sense. He was astute and remarkably—carefully—good-humoured. I don't recall ever hearing him raise his voice: his angers he would sink in irony. He was as respectful of forms as he was ready to dump empty formulas.

And he knew the meanings of the word *local*. Mostly they reduced to The Vic on Thursday lunchtimes though the New Inn would do if he was short of time. Five years older, he introduced me to beers, writers and writings, which gave coherence to the various inklings I'd picked up. I'm not sure that reading alone could have done that. It needed the shape of his concerns, his *lived* experience.

*

I'm nearly sure it was Ric too who introduced me to Peter Hodgkiss, the remarkable editor of *Poetry Information* and eventually Galloping Dog Press, who moved to Newcastle in the late '70s and managed the possibly unique small press feat of engaging eagerly with innovative writing as a reader and publisher while not actually directly creating it himself.

Peter was an enthusiast and avid cataloguer whose work epitomised one feature in particular of the small press world at the time: his publications were hand-made, home-made and essentially transferable. Since their entire means of production would go into the back of a car, a kitchen anywhere could be a publishing house. They weren't identified with any particular cultural centre. They might, materially, have been as easily (and quickly) made in Cornwall as Tyneside. Peter's methods, no different to those of a hundred other small press publishers, suggested a profoundly egalitarian alternative to the writing that issued from commercial publishing houses: they belonged to the tradition of pamphleteers and bill-posters in which anybody's news could be the news. They enacted Williams' notion that "the local is the only true universal": elsewhere is never more than another local place. Ric I'm sure deeply believed in this motto too: "...there is no 'away'/ to sling things to". Sling things away and you only sling them to another locality, not to some invulnerable Beyond. The universal is only the sum of every diverse local. Similarly Bunting clung to his Northumbria because he felt the force of the south, slinging its cultural debris towards the edge of the kingdom, and saw how it clung to his native earth like the coalwaste on the Durham beaches, slung out to sea and returned by the tide to blacken and choke the local growth.

Peter's approaches also guaranteed another sort of authenticity for if almost none of his publications ever had a very extensive readership, the readers they did have were free to approach them on their own terms. His books lived or died with the force of their own resources. They gave you the raw material. You invented your own ways of encountering them. And the writer enjoyed parallel liberties. As Ric wrote, *I've developed so much of my "craft" in the garden shed without much reference to what people thought, so can hardly be surprised if, when the buggy's finally out on the road, it fails to meet their notional traffic regs. Still, the ride is, to me, exciting... and "cryptic" and "sentimental" and "pretty" are all ways people have, whose hearing is other than mine, of saying, what was that? I guess. So on with it, anyway.*[1]

*

There are two other introductions that Ric made that I'd want to mention, though they're so closely linked as perhaps only to be one.

Morden Tower had been established as a venue for readings in Newcastle since 1964; just south, in Durham, readings at the Colpitts hotel began in 1975. The programme, decided by a steering group each member of which had the opportunity to invite a reader for a given season, had at least the virtue of being eclectic. Durham town with its great mediaeval skyline and mining history, overshadowed the hotel almost literally for it was sunk near the foot of the arches of the railway viaduct with its monumental blocks of blackened stone. A room with a décor that belonged to a post-war Omo advert was hired off the main bar and a core of a dozen or more people would usually turn up. Occasionally drinkers would wander in and find a group of consenting adults in private, listening attentively to poems, and would hastily or apologetically retreat. It felt like the annexe to a working-men's club that had inadvertently conceded admission to women.[2] In such a place *any* poet tended to sound a stranger. You might listen to Kenneth Koch and Anne Waldman with their east States accents and urban intelligence, but what you'd hear would be a counterpoint between them and the background murmur of voices from Pity Me or Esh Winning.

One time Peter Riley gave a reading in which he chose to intone texts that Pig Press published as *Five New Poems*. They were, by the poet's own reckoning, gristly writings and he decided to give the audience a second chance by repeating them in their entirety. It was, I think, two nights after John Riley had been murdered—no relation of Peter's, but a poet who had recently read in the same room—and the evening had been dedicated to his memory. Peter, perhaps gaunt with the shock of John Riley's death on the eve of Halloween, gave a reading of stark austerity that measured its tone against the hotel and the dark outside as it surely could never have done in a more likely venue.

*

Given that it's very hard to grab much sense from a poem at a reading, why do readings ever happen? Because "sense" has many phases other than that of the dictionary; because poetry is a vocal music, that needs to be heard (Bunting's insistence, obviously); because a poet's tone of voice gets under the skin and reads itself into your own reading of his or her work; because performance—good or bad—is a unique event. It dramatises the present. It suggests how the silent reading of words always veers off towards abstraction while the noise of words in the mouth is rooted in the theatre of the immediate. Performance defines the local by creating it. This too, albeit indirectly, was an idea Ric put in my path.

*

Twenty years later we exchanged a good few mails on the subject. I was dragging Ric towards listening to Bill Evans, he was pushing me towards William Alwyn. We tossed around thoughts about how performance implants an event uniquely in a place and a time and at its best brings with it a sense of what Ric (hesitantly) called *"privileged reality"*. *It's that sense… one gets from an individual, another one of us humans (using the term loosely) hitting or blowing or in whatever way making noises like that, and not like that or that.* Recorded performance is never more than an archive, shorn of a directly complicit audience, a limitation Ric said he found in recordings of Albert Ayler's improvised music: *you can't "participate" in it, cos its past, done deal… You come across it as photos of last nite's dinner, which was certainly stunning at the time, but loses many of its flavours at this remove…* His thrust was always towards reading as live/lived performance. *Without even claiming unique qualities for "my" work, I cherish the fact that the words come out different each time.* The ambiguity of the page as musical score meant that vocalisation was always a challenge. Referring to a reading of 'Counter' that he was then preparing he remarked, *so much of it will have to just stay open until I get up to do it. In that sense not a million miles from other pieces of course (Block Quilt always drains me, since it goes in different directions at the same time) but in another sense, well, apprehension-making.* Performance makes explicit what the hard-and-fastness of the page tends to mask: that any version of a poem is provisional, a point on the poem's trajectory. *Increasingly the uk train tame thaibles are EXACTLY what I'd posit mah pomlets to be: —partial articulations of possibilities for further exploration.*

Ric of course had been a practicing musician and he'd learnt directly from Bunting who never ceased to insist that poetry is a musical art. Ric's own art always stemmed from a local hearing: bees, trains, birds, voices. These were not just imagistic details carefully discerned: they were things listened to and embedded in a local geography. *Lying awake nights, I've noticed that the 3.00am blackbird down the hill is a jazzy one—percussive, slipnotes, bubbles and short phrases, perhaps a Monk. By 5.00 there's a blues merchant in the front street—long, languorous slides and a torch-song sadness reverbing off the wet tarmac—the divine Billy, perhaps? By 7.00 (if I'm still awake) there's too much other stuff going on and they all tend to be imitating each other till evening. It's those isolated utterances which fascinate me. In Rome, of course, the local hotel blackbird was a tenor, full of injured melodrama…*

*

Isolated utterances—as Cheviot is to the skyline, as "I am agog for foam" proved to be. But utterances in permanent overlap with neighbouring utterances: they might be distinct, individual, unclassifiable, but they have their place. *Seen in Japan, where things are organised better: next to the bin for CANS and the bin for BOTTLES and the bin for PAPER there's one marked OTHERS.*

In you jump, boy.

*

Bunting belonged with the "others" from the start. At the age of 18 he chose conscientious objection and was condemned to a bin that eventually produced 'Villon': "to the right was darkness and to the left hardness". He must always have been made of resistant matter. By the end of the '70s he was enduring, because he had little choice, in a house "like a tomb in a very bad part of the *Inferno*" provided by Northern Arts on a recently built estate in Washington New Town. Ric said I should ring him and gave me his number. "He won't mind if you take him some Glenfiddich."

His house was hardly a "home". Largely empty, it was painted a sterile white throughout. Tiled floor, large window to let in the reluctant November light. No decoration, except for two framed pictures by Wyndham Lewis making solitary islands on the walls. Perfectly courteous, he was as patient through an afternoon shared as no doubt he would have been silent had I not been there. He related anecdotes about Tehran, about planes and being in dogfights during the second war, about sailing—things he no doubt had ready on the pile for whenever the occasion required he pulled them out. At one moment some kids going home from school banged on the window. He shuffled across the room and shouted after them that he was busy, that they weren't welcome. "They come in here", he said, "last week they stole my scarf". But you knew he was disappointed not to be able to invite them in. I was a student: they were the "unabashed boys and girls" he wrote for.

The most enduring echo I have of his voice resonates from an evening during the March 1979 Pound Conference, in Durham, to which he must have been invited as an honoured guest. He put up with being feted as the nearest living thing to real Pound but he was no man for lingering at such events.[3] It was late into the evening and I'd escaped for a breath of air. The sky was clean and bristling with stars. After a while I was aware of Bunting with his cane, a few yards away, similarly loitering on the threshold, gazing up. I don't recall that he looked my way.

—Fine night.

(Pause)

—Yes. Yes it is.

(Long Pause)

Isolated utterances. Said low as the hills, surrounded by silence. Inconsequential. But thoroughly, utterly complete.

Notes

[1] This italicised quote and those that follow are taken from emails from Ric that date from around the year 2000.

[2] A selection of pictures of readings taken by David James can be seen online at www.poetsinalens.blogspot.com.

[3] See 'All the cants they peddle' and his note to the poem for what he thought of "poets' conferences".

Work Conchy

Tom Pickard

Towards the end of 1965 the "success" of the Morden Tower was paralleled by pressure from the dole to get me into a proper job. It became increasingly intense and hard to handle. I started getting visits from National Assistance Board (NAB) officers every other day.

> *thi sen an inspector roon*
> *each day of the week*
> *to see if am lookin for work*
> *but av got me coat on and walking the toon*
> *forst tryin to borrow a short*
> from *High on the Walls,* Fulcrum Press, 1967

Up until then it had been a low-intensity war between the dole and myself. They offered whatever work was available for a working-class youth without even the most basic qualification and I refused it. They offered more work with vague threats and still I refused it—citing my vocation as a poet. There is no such category of worker in any modern state and any work-shy element, they argued, could claim to be a "poet". If I continued to decline the jobs on offer I would be penalised. My generation of school-leavers were the first post WW2 babies to hit an already depressed job market. The North East was going through another of its depressions and the dole queues were long, but they had to fit me up with a job because I yelped that I was a poet while the state's money was feeding three mouths and the National Assistance Board were putting pressure on them to get me off the books.

We'd brought a range of international poets to the tower and discovered a regular and new audience for them and had published a loose-leaf pop-art one-off magazine devoted to Bunting, *King Ida's Watch Chain*, and his long poem 'The Spoils'—both designed by Richard Hamilton. My mate Bunting was a great poet and he was showing me the ropes; I *had* to be a poet. The Morden Tower is situated in an unlit alley—backing onto small factories emitting sulphurous fumes—where prostitutes took clients for a quick turn. It provided a focus for some of the finest talents in the region. Bryan Ferry, then a student at the Arts School under Hamilton, was a regular visitor, and Alan Hull—the singer songwriter of the folk-rock band, Lindisfarne—was to give his first public performance there. Hamilton was working in his studio at that time on the reconstruction of the Duchamp great glass, *The Bride Stripped Bare By Her Bachelor Even*, when we took Creeley to see him, and it, in late 1964. The campaign to rescue Kurt Schwitters' "wall" from the barn in the Lake District, where it was deteriorating, and bring it to the Hatton Gallery in Newcastle was also being organised by Hamilton. After Robert Creeley's visit he would also attend occasional readings and became a guiding hand, lending his name to the Morden Tower "committee". Before the NEAA (latterly Northern Arts) or Newcastle city council's cultural activities committee would recognise us we had to form a "committee". The young badger-eyed Gordon Burn was a regular at readings and recalled in *The Independent Magazine* in 1992, (p46) that he felt enabled, as a working class school leaver, to come to the tower:

> "I was 16 in 1964. Pickard was only two years older, and from a virtually identical background (his father shovelled coal in the railway yards in Gateshead;[1] mine worked in a factory on the Tyne). But whereas I was a conventional product of the system, a roll-on roll-off grammar-school achiever, he was already married to a beautiful older woman, Connie (a name throbbing with Chatterley connotations at that time) and four years into what he referred to as 'my working life on the dole'............the series of readings and 'happenings'... were the first sign to me that writing could be something more than a set text to be slogged through with dutiful encircling and underlining and comments of 'v.imp' and 'signif' in the margins.."

The rationale for investing public money in the arts was that it would "attract industry." The recently formed North Eastern Association for the Arts was peddling the argument that it could attract industry by making the perceived culturally-barren region attractive to the managers of multinational companies by creating an environment where they could experience an artistic *frisson* whilst putting the bite on clients—and it would give their wives something to do in the evenings. The Morden Tower gave no comfort to that mind-set and neither was it physically comfortable. To accommodate the numbers who wanted to get into the readings required us to be chair free and sit them on the floor. Brian Swann exemplified the NEAA's on-going state of mind when he recounted a conversation with the director (in 1974) who gave him the organisation's official brochure that was "full of imported arts," indicating that Northumberland was still regarded as an "outpost of the empire." The director thought Bunting's attempts to acknowledge a Northumbrian culture "fatuous… he's got no followers and has had no effect. He is rather an eccentric… Northumberland is dead, and its so called folk-culture.."[2]

A year or so before local governments could be persuaded to set up this regional arts council the more visionary architects of the scheme brought the playwright, Arnold Wesker, and other Centre 42 representatives to Newcastle to give a talk about culture. It sounded patronizing and we got into a kerbside argument with Wesker about the relative merits of sending a string quartet down a coalmine as opposed to The Animals playing in the Downbeat, or pit ballads, and the Beatles, for fuck's sake. Youth was wriggling out of the cages and singing. What was art, anyway? We could do it for ourselves. Wesker probably argued that "rock and roll" was commercial and therefore worthless, mere commodity.

The NAB thought poetry worthless, an "excuse to idle", and took up the war from the dole. I gambled that they wouldn't stop paying us the £9.10s per week because there was an infant to feed. But, as an able bodied potential breadwinner, they told me, I had a duty to provide for my family, and refusing paid employment could certainly be seen as a failure to maintain them, which is illegal. My objection to work was as much pragmatic as principled: as a teenager without qualifications or skills I could earn most by labouring on building sites, as I had done up until the Ginsberg reading in May 1964, but the pay was only £10 per week. When the compulsory national insurance stamp was deducted along with bus fares to and from work there would be no improvement in our circumstances, we would still run up debts, go cold some days without coal and hungry others. Being on the dole gave me time to read and time to write, time to spend with my baby boy, and time to spend with Basil on his lunch breaks over a pint upstairs in the Crown next to the old music hall—the Empire Theatre. On those occasions he'd read me a few new lines of 'Briggflatts' from his notebook, cast a critical eye over what I'd been writing, give me a tutorial on Marie Lloyd, Zukofsky, William Carlos Williams, Lorine Niedecker, Charles Reznikoff, Mina Loy or Whitman.

He was always sympathetic and knocked the self-pity from my helpless rage at the dole authorities with a "What the hell! You keep at those poems and you'll have a good book in no time." Then he might break into a music-hall song because we were next to the Empire Theatre, or a bawdy one from the First World War, assuming for the latter frowning eyebrows, a chin firmly set on chest and ponderous bishop-like scowl from which he uttered the brilliant trench profanities that inspired him to a howl of appreciative laughter. On the days when I didn't have to visit the NAB office in the afternoon and tell them which factory or building site I had solicited for work that morning they would send an official to our home. He would step into the living room and unpack my file and sit uncomfortably in an upright chair while I sulked, sprawled in another. So much of what he said was true, and so much of my position was indefensible, that I only shrugged in agreement with him. "Where have you been today?" Spinning him lies and uncomfortable about the necessity of doing so, I just wanted to tell him to get out of our home and mind his own fucking business, but I didn't because the baby had to be fed and the rent paid, so pretended just enough for him not to suspend payment of the benefit. I would continue to argue about my right to be a poet at the same time as pursuing half-heartedly some underpaid drudgery and it worked for a while. But they were only momentarily convinced of the sincerity of my search for a job. They also argued, correctly, that it wasn't their responsibility to support arts organisations such as the Morden Tower by paying the organiser. There were other departments of government, local and national, to take care of that.

Surprisingly the Lord Mayor, Teresa Russell, became an ally. Her son, a sixth form pupil of the fee-paying Royal Grammar School, started coming to the tower regularly so she thought anything that kept him off the streets was fine. Danny appears as an embarrassed guest in the D.A. Pennebaker documentary, *Don't Look Back*, when Bob Dylan visits Newcastle and our Lord Mayor doorsteps the startled singer in his dressing room and introduces her son and his friend Harry. Recently elected, she wanted to help us and was pestering her colleagues to award us a running grant. Her proposal was that I should be employed as a Youth Worker and paid £750 a year to run the Morden Tower as my parish, or youth club. The machinery of local government ground into action and a proposal was put on the agenda for discussion at the next meeting. About this time I heard that Edward Dorn was in the country so I wrote to ask him if he'd come and read for us. He replied on the 12th of January saying he'd wanted to come "since Creeley told me of his visit there." [3] The stakes were getting high and this was to be an important date for us. The Lord Mayor and the chairman of the Cultural Activities Committee, Mrs Gladys Robson, magistrate, leader of the council, and later model for Bunting's satirical poke at municipal morons, 'What The Chairman Told Tom', were to attend the reading. Ed Dorn didn't really know what he was walking into. In a letter to Charles Olson he sets the scene:

> "They take things very seriously up there, have a thing called the North East Arts council which gives money pretty much all round, but not that freely because since it was discovered Tom lives on the dole while he is a POET 'at the same time' they took a closer look and thus the Lord Mayor, plus the Sheriff, of Newcastle came to my reading." [4]

Dorn was a tall, wiry, Midwesterner with a lived-in face and was sharp as a blade. We were instantly comfortable with him. Bunting prepared me for the meeting with the council officials by suggesting that I curb my usual truculent impatience and treat Mrs Gladys Robson with diplomacy. She was partially receptive to his ex-Wing-Commander's charm because, although a bit raggy-arsed, he was a cut above her. However she was clearly contemptuous of my poverty, aspirations and frame of mind. We had met before when the Lord Mayor invited me to a civic reception they were holding for a visiting dignitary, thinking it, I suppose, a reasonable opportunity for me to network with members of the Committee. But, alas, I had no social graces and was undiplomatically curious of the Lord Sheriff's official duties when he spoke wearing his ceremonial garb. Each link of the chain of office was stamped with the names of his predecessors, many of whom had exercised their right to be present at a scaffold. In a poem I preferred to see it otherwise;

"The Lord Sheriff's gold chain
sparkles with the names
of hanged men
whose lifeless limbs
dangle and decorate his chins…"
From *High on the Walls,* Fulcrum Press 1968

When he told me that he could lock me up if I caused a disturbance in the town, I asked him who could lock him up. The question was pertinent because policemen at the Pilgrim Street nick had recently beaten up a few of my old school friends. I had been gathering information and making notes about the most notorious, Muscles, who enjoyed thrashing any of the young roughnecks unlucky enough to be arrested on Saturday night brawls in the Bigg Market, or who had been caught thieving. Prisoners were often punched or kicked unconscious by Muscles and at least one other officer. There was a great deal of violence at weekends around that cluster of marvellous pubs in the Bigg Market and I would often turn sick at the sound of a bottle breaking or a table going over at the start of a barny. But that didn't justify the routine violence being metered out in the cells, where a number of men had been killed. About one thirty on the morning of March 18th 1964 Muscles visited the ground floor flat where Connie and I had a narrow single room with our four-month-old son, Matthew. When the policeman shone his torch into our window as we slept he woke Matthew first and then their laughter woke us, so I went out and confronted them, thinking it was the lads being stupid. The police had come looking for Franky, my old school friend from Blakelaw, who would occasionally doss on the floor. The cops stunk of alcohol and I refused to let them into the house without a warrant.

Barry Scaum, an art-student friend of ours, rented the flat, and each of the other three rooms was sub-let to students. We shared the bathroom, kitchen and outside bog with the students and a continuous flow of their friends and drifters. Situated in the otherwise respectable middle-class suburb of Jesmond, student flats were part of the landscape and their occupants' sometimes unruly behaviour was tolerated as part of the initiation into a professional life, or as the necessary sowing of wild oats. I came from Blakelaw and Cowgate where equally exuberant but working class youths were by definition delinquent. We had no business in that part of town unless we were housebreakers—and, it can't be denied, some of us were. The great Russian dystopian writer, Zamyatin, lodged in Jesmond in 1915/16 and was so impressed with its stultifying uniformity that he named and located the mythical country of his satire of the English bourgeois, Jesmond.[5] And Jesmond was where my mother had cleaned houses, both as a girl in 1916 and later in the '50s and '60s.

Mrs Gladys Robson attended the Dorn reading because the Lord Mayor insisted. She had already cancelled two previous visits in her capacity as chairman of the Cultural Activities Committee and that meant our case being dropped off the agenda. The delays were crippling for us as the NAB was either threatening prosecution or a complete denial of benefits. The civic dignitaries came to the reading, which was well attended, and Dorn read superbly. Everyone behaved politely towards the officials, and they left satisfied that we were a going concern. The next day's *Newcastle Journal*, reported the event with the headline:

> I SUPPORT BEAT POETS, says Lord Mayor.
> …After the meeting last night, Alderman Mrs Russell telephoned Councillor B. Abrahart, chairman of the Youth Committee. "I told him that I gave my wholehearted support to the group, and that I think it is something which Newcastle should be proud of."

We were hopeful when we read that, as Ed hurriedly got ready for the breakfast we'd been invited to at the Royal Station Hotel with the Lord Mayor. She sat with the majority leader in the National Assembly of Korea, Mr Kim Dong Hwan. Ed, conscious of his duty, made polite conversation over coffee.

"The Lord Mayor... invited me to see the town w/ her the next day which I did in her chauffeur driven Daimler limousine (cant have Rolls apparently because it wld bug the people who still remember Jarrow and might throw stones etc.) We drove thru Jarrow incidentally, scene of depression strikes and hunger marches where she pointed out to me (out the polished windows) what she called 'the more interesting poverty.' Dig that. I was, I assure you, speechless; I mean my eyes sort of fell out and rolled around on the deep, posh backseat. But I don't want to make her sound that flippy. Aside from those arch defenses, she's a good socialist, and ran on that ticket... and in her study in the mayoral mansion she had pictures of Lenin, one signed, to her father and pictures of Engels. Her father was a famous Talmudic scholar. His books where elegant, dry things lining the walls. She's a dark handsome woman in her late 40s I'd guess..." [6]

The Lord Mayor had a frigate-launching on the Tyne to attend and she invited Dorn to accompany her. The invitation didn't extend to me so I said I'd see him back home later.

Later that day we read an editorial that we had missed earlier in the morning paper:

POETRY AND PROSE

To turn the Morden tower into a poetry centre was a spirited venture full of the fire and imagination of youth. An out-of-work teenager from a secondary-modern D stream has played an important part in Newcastle's cultural renaissance.

In order to give the Morden Tower his full time attention, Tom Pickard relied on the £9-a-week National Assistance and dole money to support his wife and child. Now that has been withdrawn and Mr Pickard must either get a job or starve.

However he does not see the choice in such simple terms. He has asked the North Eastern Association for the Arts for a salary as the Morden Tower's professional organiser, and he has approached Newcastle Youth Committee in the hope of getting a Youth Leader's wage.

The Morden Tower may have to close down if neither of Tom Pickard's ships sail into harbour. This would be a great pity, but it does not improve his case for an added subsidy.

Tom Pickard should take heart from the poetic achievements of such men as W. H. Auden, an ex-school teacher, Basil Bunting a newspaper sub-editor, and Wilfred Owen, a soldier in the trenches. It may be very prosaic for a poet to do a job of work but it helps to pay the gas bill.[7]

Dorn stayed on for a couple of days and we took him for a lunchtime drink with Basil.

"Basil Bunting is a fine old man, very funny the way he'll stare at you with this silly grin on his face, up close, and you think he hasn't got it until suddenly he makes his answer. A real, seedy old gent, but very straight, I liked him immensely, he hasn't any of that put-off porcelainity I thot Zukofsky had…"[8]

He gave me a signed copy of his autobiographical novel, *Rites of Passage*[9], with a hand-drawn map to locate the geography for us. It is tenderly inscribed: "all about a place not so long ago and not all that different from Newcastle, but far." It has a chapter about an unemployment office, where a stuttering man frustrated with the bureaucracy, ends up shouting: "WHAT KIND OF A MISERABLE GODDAM JAJOB IS IT ANYWAY—POPOKING PEAS UP A AA RATS ASS?…"[10] It was a gift I appreciated and he greatly helped maintain my resolve to plough on. We talked continuously. I railed, naively, about getting money for poets, and setting up a poet's union or some sort of organisation with muscle that could ensure proper payment for readings. Dorn was doubtful but we chewed over the issues in the bars of Newcastle and shivering in the flat. The City council rejected the Youth Leader idea and the financial situation for us worsened when the Committee took up the bugle call from the newspapers and ran with it.

"Councillor Abrahart said he understood Mr. Pickard was receiving national assistance after his unemployment benefit was stopped. 'Now the NAB have threatened to stop payment because he is not seeking employment. He is arguing that he cannot do anything but this and would be unable to do it and work. I cannot understand why he cannot do a job of work as well as this'...".[11]

However they coughed up £150, half of what we owed.

*

I was shown where no claimant goes, unless escorted in transit—as I was—through the inner office of the building, past rows of desks where clerks typed reports or studied a file of someone like me, to the foot of a narrow and steep staircase. It was wide enough for one person only, and the clerk ushered me to climb. My resolve weakened as I remembered a dream of just such forbidding stairs. This grubby makeshift building built to service makeshift people; this warehouse peopled with need. I mounted the first step conscious of being boxed-in on either side with my retreat shut off by my escort following closely behind. We entered a small room with a low roof. The desks were laid out along three walls, leaving space for a chair in the middle. The desks were occupied by representatives of the disciplinary committee of the NAB. The manager continued to remind me of the legal obligation to feed, clothe and house my family, and the consequences of failing to do so. They spoke quickly like bingo-callers chiselling bids at an auction of repossessed houses. I said I would like to be a poet and if I couldn't then I'd be a lighthouse keeper. And they went on to say we want to give you another chance before we cut off your money, we want to send you to a Rehabilitation Centre where you'll get back into the habit of working. I refused and they offered the alternative of a Re-establishment Centre, which I again refused. Finally, they formally cautioned me that unless I accepted their offer of a place at a Re-establishment Centre they would prosecute me for failing to maintain my family, and the current mandatory sentence for a first offence was six months in jail. It was clear that I had to get the NAB off my back. There was no way that I wanted a labour-camp experience, to be taught the meaning of real work, or to be bludgeoned into a healthy work habit. The editorial in the local paper that suggested I find gainful employment spurred a response from Jonathan Williams who sent this letter to *The Journal* (March 2nd) with the support of a sympathetic Herbert Read:

I have read your editorial of February 8th *Poetry & Prose*, with interest. As an American poet who recently read his work at the Morden Tower, as a publisher of poets, and as a critic of poetry, may I add a few remarks to the discussion of the Tower and Mr Tom Pickard.

One gathers that poetry is not one of the refinements of life offered to youths in secondary-modern school's D stream curriculum. Putting it plainly, it seems to me that there is a considerable amount of resentment in Newcastle that Tom Pickard concerns himself with the writing of poems and the running of the Morden Tower Book Room instead of being a day labourer i.e. what he was "educated" to be and what his "class" is supposed to limit him to being in the first place. A reporter for the *Evening Chronicle* expressed astonishment that I should walk into his office in my Burberry clothing ("a world famous poet—an American at that") accompanied by a "long haired unkempt teenager", namely Tom Pickard. Being poor, twenty, and used to insolence, are three reasons for being unkempt. What is <u>not</u> unkempt is his poetic style. Mr Bewick's miniatures are no more refined. Northumberland should consider itself lucky to find another wild flower in its nettle patch.

Few people nowadays like what they are doing: few care about anything much but their paycheck. This is particularly true of journalists, often incipient writers, so I am not surprised to read an editorial condemning Tom Pickard because he does not want to join the other pigs routing at the economic trough. I am much more surprised that members of the NEAA take the same attitude to the profession of poetry i.e. <u>that it is not work</u>. Very correct, it isn't! It is a form of ancient play—like religion and ballet & football. Playing with words in poems enhances life, even makes it possible for many. And it holds the world together in the mind. We assume that monks have enough to do, that they have a "vocation". They are asked to make no profit. We do not ask Nureyev to dig ditches in his white leather raincoat. The ACGB pours huge sums into the performing arts in order to entertain the "cultivated" and keep social life whirling. The "uncultivated" pour huge sums into football in order to be entertained by the likes of Greaves, Osgood, and Charlton. And let them be ready for Saturday afternoon and not worn out from labouring. It is a question of <u>what</u> you value. Poems have little currency. Paul Potts says some very accurate things in his autobiography *Dante Called You Beatrice*. "The work I did was not sufficiently valued by my contemporaries for them to arrange things for me, as they did for others. No real artist can make a living out of his writing, but often can make one because of it, I've never had a pound in my life that had more than seventeen shillings in it. When I was a little boy I used to take things out of the house to give to the poor. I once took a whole joint of roast beef and gave it to a family of vegetarians. If all the people I owe half a crown to suddenly turn up at the Albert Hall on the same evening there would not be enough room for a dwarf to get in."

Orpheus, the first poet, was the gent who sang instead of spoke, played instead of worked, still he developed quite a following. As his man in Newcastle may, if given half a chance. There is plenty of work connected with Morden Tower and with poetry for Tom Pickard to do—if the community will recognise it as such. I disagree completely with the preachment of the last paragraph of the Journal editorial, all about the enlivening effect of drudgery all blessed by John Knox. I cannot see that the fact one is able to survive Belsen is any justification for being put there in the first place. What virtue is there if a man of Basil Bunting's formidable qualifications came back to his native country from Persia at the age of fifty and could do no better than a hack job on a Newcastle newspaper, forced to this by the need to feed and house a number of dependants? The local community (not to mention London, that Mecca of Establishment poeticules) made nothing of his genius for poetry. It now begins to having been shown by a few Americans and young outsiders like Tom Pickard and Stuart Montgomery of the Fulcrum Press.

Another question: why should Tom Pickard take heart that Wilfred Owen was forced into the trenches? Like many other people he died there, and we are left with a handful of poems and a nice legend. It is true, finally, that a test of being a poet is remaining one and writing poems. The surrounding community would do well to lend its support as best it can, and not fret over the shiftless ways of poets. Edward Dahlberg gives us some good advice in his recent volume of aphorisms, Reasons of the Heart: "trust any devil but one who does not steal, cog, lie, pimp, or whore. Hard of heart is he who has nothing to show for his life but his virtues. I have no confidence in a man whose faults you cannot see."

Yours sincerely,
Jonathan Williams

Notes

1   He was a goods-porter in British Rail's Forth Goods Yard in Newcastle.
2   'Basil Bunting of Northumberland'. *St. Andrews Review*, spring/Summer 1977, pp.33–41. Also quoted in *Basil Bunting Man and Poet*. Ed C.F. Terrell. Orono, ME: National Poetry Center., 1981 pp 410–411
3   Morden Tower papers Literary & Philosophic Society collection
4   Charles Olson Papers, Archives & Special Collections, Thomas J Dodd research Centre, University of Connecticut Libraries. Used with permission.
5   *Islanders*. Yevgeny Zamyatin. (Russia, 1918).
6   Edward Dorn's letter to Charles Olson 23/2/66. Charles Olson Papers, Archives & Special Collections, Thomas J Dodd research Centre, University of Connecticut Libraries. Used with permission.
7   Editorial in *Newcastle Journal*: 8/2/1966
8   Charles Olson Papers, Archives & Special Collections, Thomas J Dodd research Centre, University of Connecticut Libraries. Used with permission
9   When reprinted in 1971 by Frontier Press re-titled *By The Sound*
10 *The Rites of Passage*. Buffalo, NY: Frontier Press, 1965. p54
11 *Newcastle Journal* 11/2/1966 p 3

Here & There

Kris Hemensley

1

The Book of Beginnings is labyrinthine, its expanse infinite. One's only ever quoting from it, always awaiting the time when its definitive writing can start. Not the rude and huge chronology, despite obvious merit, but Midrashic: continually and expansively present in its references and epiphanies. Writing at this end of things, of one's beginnings in poetry and inevitably, on the scene, one's only too well aware of the personal and poetical changes which have transpired in the forty-odd years one's been there—changes of a degree which don't disturb the inventory but do affect the mood. And mood is probably very much to the point, thus the "temper of the times".

For instance, when F.T. Prince (Frank Prince), in 1970, aged 58, then Professor of English at the University of Southampton, during one of our many *tête-à-têtes* (which continued to the mid '90s, whenever I visited England), invited me, aged 24, to agree with him that the young poets were defined by "protest", I flustered and blustered a denial which would never have occurred to me to make in the early to mid-Sixties! For though my political fire and motivation was undiminished, poet and poetry now related to matters of style and poetics (the double edge of literary seriousness), which an education gloriously on the run, since dropping out from Southampton Tech College in '64, had provided. Prince's comment smacked of 50s/60s Angry Young Men and Ban the Bomb more than the New Left/ Hippy/Yippy Counter Culture with which I'd run in Melbourne.

My earlier persona, spawned by cumulative immersion in Lawrence, Whitman, Ginsberg and Yevtushenko, *was* Protest writ big—indignant, passionate and prophetic! And yet my younger brother, Bernard Hemensley, and I—jointly embarking upon what we imagined as the quest for the truth vested in jazz, folk and rock music, in poetry and literature, in "gotta-get-outa-this-place" travel—were also discovering William Carlos Williams (chanced upon in an issue of the post-war American magazine, *Perspectives*, given me by our Uncle Dennis on the Isle of Wight in '65). I found the names, ever practical Bernard bought the books.

96

William Carlos Williams was hardly a firebrand, but so different to traditional British poetry, suggestively like some of the Eastern things we were looking at; light, almost fleeting, "natural", exact, direct, uncluttered. The Eastern resonance was a direct legacy of our father's similarly untutored esoteric reading, especially Indian and Chinese classics. Another of his books was at the very least an important subliminal influence throughout our young teens—Derek Stanford's *The Freedom of Poetry* (Falcon Press, London, 1947). I seriously read it in the couple of years before I emigrated to Australia, identifying with its paraphrase of Erich Fromm and its absorption of Romantic humanism. For example, from Stanford's introduction (p. 17), "Poetry makes its decision, then, in freedom; approaching a given attitude not with analysis but imagination. It will not be dictated to, for poetry like love cannot rise from an endeavour of the conscious will alone." Yay! exclaims the teenager, the young twenty—yeah, yeah, yeah!

One could say now that this was also a model of "protest", ironically of the same era in which F. T. Prince was making his mark, following a similar middle way, perhaps, between MacSpaunday and the New Romantics. Looking at Stanford's book I note the absence of Dylan Thomas. Probably regarded as established by the '40s, he would yet have sat well with Gascoyne, Keyes, Raine, Moore, Comfort, Durrell and others in the book. Prince described to me his meeting poets of the day in a Soho pub, Dylan Thomas at the bar in the middle of the scrum. Prince stayed on the periphery, as innocent of the big city ways as a character in a Thomas story, noting the high jinks and alcohol, the dearth of poetry. An incidental image I know but "on the periphery" is the true sub-text of this entire excursus, every last bit of it…

What would I have said to F. T. Prince in my defence? Anti-war *was* part of it—"peace and love"—but so too the rationales of the new poetry, the new novel, the new theatre, the new cinema, the new music— participatory, experimental, democratic: the new world indeed. I would probably have stammered to Prince about the new materials obliging poet and poem some place other than traditional lyric. He doubted the efficacy of my propositions, and wouldn't let go his bite of the "protest" slipper. "Being happy and holding hands surely isn't the point, what?", he said, in his signature Oxfordese. He meant politically and poetically.

"I support the young, the new", he said. True, which was why he kept faith with Eric Mottram's editorship of *Poetry Review*, remaining on the Poetry Society's committee during that vexed period, and always responded to my solicitation for subs to Tim Longville and John Riley's *Grosseteste Review*.

I hadn't heard of F. T. Prince until Lee Harwood mentioned him to me at a lunch arranged by Amanda Wade, a Fine Arts lecturer in Southampton, whom I'd met via one of her students, Dave Rogers, a painter. Serendipitously, not long after my return from Australia in late '69, Dave attended the same astonishing sound-poetry reading given by Bob Cobbing in Southampton. With our respective partners, Loretta and Ricky, we became friends and colleagues in that season's quest for "alternatives". We took along my brother Bernard (who began his Stingy Artist press in '78, dedicated to such English poets as John Riley, Paul Buck, David Miller, Owen Davis and Americans like Larry Eigner and Ted Enslin) to meet Lee. Regarding my ignorance of Prince, Lee said, "Very few people in England know him at all, but the Americans (Ashbery and co) love him: you're living in the same town, you should look him up." By the time I contacted Prince, Stuart Montgomery had sent me a bunch of Fulcrum Press titles, including Prince's *Memoirs in Oxford*, which I subsequently reviewed in my magazine *Earth Ship*. Rereading the review I'm startled by the forthrightness of my comment that its "very contemporary longings—*reach out and touch / a naked man and free*—offset the old stumpy rhymes." I was vindicated, to an extent, when Prince told me he was pleased I appreciated him as a poet of true feeling, and also that he probably wouldn't write in such a way again. In a letter to me, commenting on my criticism, which I published as an addendum to the review, he stated that such feelings "had to be expressed in a more 'distanced' way because my whole background and education were 'English' in the sense that scepticism, empiricism, dissent, were the accepted principles—the 'liberal' mind."

Prince said I was an untypical Englishman, full of "colonial energy", like Pound! Once upon a time he was similarly motivated, he told me. Like me he'd come to England from overseas, South Africa in his case, because England was the centre, where Eliot was. Of course, unlike him, I was English to begin with. My "colonial energy" was the complexion I'd picked up in Melbourne. Over the next couple of years he'd often ask me about the new English poets I'd encountered on my travels and via correspondence. I related the fascination and puzzlement J.H. Prynne, as a man and poet, generated (affecting some of his students and non-Cambridge readers alike). I describe my admiration for the *Grosseteste Review* poets, especially John Riley and John Hall and because of Prince's appreciation of French symbolist poetry, I pointed out Paul Buck's burgeoning contemporary translation project.

Influenced by the intensely localized activity I'd enjoyed in Melbourne, I felt hamstrung by the regional diffusion I now experienced; in many ways it was "London or the bush" (as ever it was, Prince concurred). Thank heavens then for an oasis like Nick Kimberley's self-contained poetry department at Compendium Bookshop. Even so, Nick often castigated us out-of-towners for failing to coordinate our meetings—for example, fancy John Riley, down from Leeds, and I, up from Southampton, missing Jim Burns, in from Preston, by half an hour (no matter that we hooked up with Lee Harwood, Dick Miller and Andrew Crozier later on)! In my case, London often came to the bush: Allen and Elaine Fisher, Opal and Ellen Nations, John Robinson, and from around the country such poets as George Dowden, Colin and Frances Symes, Hall, Longville and Riley, David Tipton, Jeremy Hilton. On my Southampton bedsit's doorstep was Jacqueline (now Vale) Benson from Edinburgh (who'd known Ian Hamilton-Finlay as well as the Incredible String Band), and a new Anvil Press poet, Philip Holmes (who later became acquainted with F.T. Prince). Tim Longville was the indefatigable go-between, putting me in touch with Hall, Chaloner, Gael Turnbull, Martin Wright, John Freeman, Tipton and many others. He felt the "hippy" Hemensley and the "beatnik" Tipton (still grieving after an awful family tragedy in Peru, where he'd been chasing Vallejo's missing manuscripts) might hit it off, as we did famously in Southampton. We met again in Sheffield over a weekend hosted by John and Genevieve Freeman, who mimeographed the latest issue of *Earth Ship* at the university for me. Ever personable, John had been lauded as one of the younger poet-critics to watch. From David's point of view he was irredeemably "Oxbridge", but for me he was yet another example of what had yet to occur Down Under: a younger academia's participation with new Ango-American poetry and poetics.

Prince asked me to arrange a meeting, sometime in '72, with some of the younger poets of my advocacy. John Hall was studying in town and John Riley visiting from Leeds for the weekend. You bring the poets, I'll get the beer! Prince said. It was generally amiable but flecked with irritation: while Riley and our host enjoyed discussing their enthusiasm for Orthodox icons, both he and Hall sensed an unwillingness from Prince to connect on poetry and poetics. It was nothing like the engagement Andrew Crozier had hoped for when he encouraged me to go ahead with such a meeting. Andrew said it was "important" that Prince meet "our" poets, evidently imbued with a similar sense of continuum. It was a matter, perhaps, of tickling destiny into the realm of our own potential and not accepting the *fait accomplait* of historically separated generations.

I'm not suggesting that F.T. Prince was a pivotal figure, on a par with W.S. Graham, David Jones and others advanced in Iain Sinclair's *Conductors of Chaos* anthology (Picador, 1996), but, for me, he came to be as important as the poets and poetics I met through Longville and Riley at *Grosseteste*. His ideas of "shape" and "resistance", his sense of form as antidote to sloppy thinking and expression and as facilitator of a larger kind of poem, finally took hold of me in the '90s, by which time my credit from the experimental '60s and '70s was spent. I ultimately understood Prince's "resistance" psychologically if not also politically, similar to Ortega's thought about the crucial contention of generational energies within a dynamic model of individual creativity and social formation. Accounting for who and where I was, and telling my story *vis-à-vis* history, my restored imperative. "Tuning into the music", in terms of subject and sound, whether counting syllables or just "running on", my salvation and knowing it all as the experimental impulse with which I first flew.

2

In the late '60s and through the '70s, the urgency and intoxication of one's own emergence together with other poets of the generation, and the feeling that poetics was palpable, literally being developed poem by poem, explicated in voluminous correspondence around the country and, indeed, the world, undoubtedly fuelled that sense of mission which necessitated clear distinction from the mainstream. It also led to the silliest ideological extrapolations, the pettiest political behaviour. Undoubtedly though, it was momentous to be a poet and small mag editor in England, 1970–72, as it had been in Melbourne, '67-69. Fantastic to contribute, via *Earth Ship*, to the new British poetry with poet-editors like Tim Longville and John Riley / *Grosseteste Review*, Allen Fisher /Aloes, Andrew Crozier / *The Park*, Peter Riley / *Collection*, Stuart and Deirdre Montgomery / Fulcrum, Opal Nations / *Strange Faeces*, Nick Kimberley / *Camel*, David Chaloner / *One*, Paul Buck and Glenda George / *Curtains,* Richard Downing and Andi Wachtel / *Sesheta*, Eric Mottram / *Poetry Review*, Tony Ward / Arc, Peter Finch / *second aeon*, John Robinson / *Joe di Maggio* and numerous individuals.

Relevant to say that this was a new British poetry largely uncomfortable with Michael Horovitz's *Children of Albion: Poetry of the Underground in Britain* anthology (Penguin, 1969). Such a tag obviously misrepresented many contributors, just as the revolutionary, if not apocalyptic banner unfurled was probably harder to take than the anthology *per se*. For all the charm, in retrospect, of Horovitz's social and poetical inclusivity, the attempt at amelioration is fudged, "Others retain detachment", Horovitz declared: "Crozier, Evans, Finlay, Fisher, Guest, Torrance and Turnbull employ cooler aesthetic approaches", in contradistinction to the song and dance of his exuberant Ginsbergean rationale. I had, of course, been cut from similar cloth then. Imagine me in Melbourne, wowed by a picture of an hirsute Charles Olson, enquiring in a letter to Nathaniel Tarn whether, like the rest of us, he had long hair?—"No", he replied, "but my spirit is hairy!" Ecstatic or not, I was now consciously seeking a change of clothes and scenery.

By the time I returned to Southampton, I was more than ready for a second English education. After three years in Melbourne on something like the Sixties' front line (the anti-war movement, new theatre and new poetry) I was a counter-culture vet. What I desired now was time for reflection after the Australian freneticism. Through 1968, the late Melbourne poet Michael Dugan's invaluable collection of British mags and small-press books allowed me to update the Liverpool Scene and Horovitz "Wholly Communion" models with which I'd emigrated. We enthused about Barry MacSweeney's *The boy from the Green Cabaret tells his mother*, pored over Dave Cunliffe and Tina Morris's *Poetmeat*, Jim Burns' *Move*, Simon Cutts' *Tarasque*, James' *Resuscitator*, the Longville/ Gordon Jackson *Grosseteste Review*. I provided counter-culture papers like *International Times*, proclaiming the importance of Nathaniel Tarn's article, *World Wide Open*.

3

When I announced my little mag, John Hall strenuously advised I should replace the intended title and concept, namely *Earth Ship Survival Manual* with the simpler *Earth Ship*; a telling example of the difference between my Melbourne mind-set and the English I was keen to learn from. I'd invited my erstwhile Southampton student friend, Colin Symes, to co-edit the mag because of two common projects: the 'James Joyce Letters' I intended writing him from Dublin around New Year, '69, and his magnificent 'Poet Tree' flow-chart of Anglo-American modernism we wanted to publish. Different people remarked that its timing was propitious, in fact I published David Chaloner's article which ruminated upon the parlous state of the "new poetry" small press in England. It seemed that *Earth Ship* would fill the temporary hiatus! My purpose was both prospective and advocatorial: to catch the pulse of the surrounding British poetry and to carry with me into England some of the Melbourne poetry—an example of which had arrived before me in the person of Garrie Hutchinson and his *Yam* magazine, through which I first read Ulli McCarthy, Jeff Nuttall and others. (It's long occurred to me that there's a rich and intriguing unwritten chapter here on Australian/British connections, or better said, a chapter on the unwritten relationships. The Peter Porter, Clive James, Randolph Stowe stories are well known; not so that of David Miller, Jas H Duke, Ted Kavanagh, Joanne Burns to John Forbes, John Kinsella, Tracy Ryan and Laurie Duggan. And more in the other direction...). The Australian imperative to overcome the "tyranny of distance" easily transferred to the English situation and then across the Atlantic, informing the style of the magazine.

I often and fondly recall a letter Wendy Mulford wrote me in 1970, a couple of paragraphs of which I printed in *Earth Ship* #2, where she objected to my "global village" sentiment and repudiated my opinion that contemporary English poets were "afraid to speak". Our exchange perfectly encapsulated the difference between my English ear, transported (no pun intended) by the American poetry (its fulsome embrace of the outward and material world, especially of sex and politics, even as it forayed the mystical dimensions of religion and language) that I was turning on to in Melbourne, and her own which could not help but *passionately* keep faith with the English tradition though no less aware of the American models. She wrote, "I want the energy you speak of alright, but for me it thrills as well through Blake, or Cowper, Browning or Clare or Byron or Christina Rossetti or or or for example." She used the phrase "syntax of survival" which, to the internationalist my experience had made of me, sounded defensive. Yet the term is probably as fair an encapsulation as any of the perspective described by the seminal little mag, *The English Intelligencer*. As the decades wound by, it was obvious that what she called the "shooting stars of Europe & America" were only truly visible when one unembarrassedly acknowledged one's birthright, thus her "small island off the west coast of Europe. Ah Greenwich Mean Time!" Or, those features initially articulated as "birthright" developing their own dimension, territorially unbounded yet acutely embodied.

4

At several junctures of the perennial retrospective, I was glad not to be living in the UK as a poet, especially in the decade from the late '70s through the '80s. During that time, when I was a member of the Association of Little Presses, corresponding with Paul Buck, John Robinson, Peter Hodgkiss (Not Poetry), Yann Lovelock, David Miller, Paul Green (Spectacular Diseases), Allen Fisher, Bill Griffiths, Alan Halsey, Ken Edwards and others, one often couldn't escape the impression of isolation and embattlement from parts of the scene. Perhaps if one had been there, on the ground, what appeared to be a desperate turning-in would have been crucially qualified. From a distance, though, some *avant-garde's* mutual exclusivities seemed wrong-headed. The choice was between *avant-garde* bloody-mindedness and confident amelioration. Not that Australia didn't have its own version of "the poetry wars" but it was probably a kinder society and culture which accommodated us than English accounts suggested of there. The lesson one ultimately learned in Melbourne, and I mean by the '90s, shared I think with the Americans, was the impossibility of not mixing it with an ever *broader* poetry community. With equanimity one had now to interject one's dissenting moves as though into a commonwealth.

Such a change in England, it seems to me, is marked by Carcanet's recognition of the '60s and '70s new poets, including the publication of the Crozier/Longville anthology, *A Various Art,* in 1987. It was as though Michael Schmidt had taken a prospectus, akin to William Cookson's *Agenda,* out of the heritage manor and into the contemporary estate. Unlike Oxford University Press's sterling service to the classics, Carcanet's simultaneous fielding of ancient and modern revealed a far deeper appreciation of the "tradition" than when Schmidt's project began in opposition to the "slavish Americanism" the "conservatives" feared. Who then would have forecast John Ashbery as a Carcanet mainstay? Carcanet's exposition of tradition is dynamic: from John Clare to Michael Haslam… it's a history defined by continuum and not chronology, where contemporaneity of and for its subjects is the prerequisite. Similarly, Neil Astley's Bloodaxe, publisher of Basil Bunting, J.H. Prynne and Jackie Kay, having begun as a regional counterweight to perceived metropolitan publishing bias, now waves a flag for the poetry of every part of Britain and Ireland, the wider English-language world, and poetry in translation, especially that basted by surrealism, from every continent. Astley determinedly overrules the distinction between popular and esoteric, nowhere better represented than in the numerous Bloodaxe anthologies.

Yet even today I'm not sure, despite what appears to the Antipodean follower as the pluralist publishing of the two major poetry presses, variously augmented and extended by etruscan, Chris Emery's Salt, Tony Frazer's Shearsman, Tony Ward's Arc, Ken Edwards' Reality Street, Alan Halsey's West House and others, that the folly has been overcome—that is, the myopic, aggressive and often extramural partisanship that reduces and clutters our attempt at critical discussion and understanding. Those presses deserve whole chapters in their favour, though surely not as the *avant-garde's* last stand. This concerns a wonderfully heady amelioration;

not political compromise but what I'd call humility before the fact.

An abiding English exception to poetical and political parochialism and a possible legatee of Wendy Mulford's challenge, has been Nicholas Johnson's *etruscan books*, with its books and *Readers*. Etruscan seems to me the best survivor of the type of small press in which I'd come of age, publishing experimental and traditional British poetry in its musical and textual modes, cheek by jowl with a particular strain of Americans. Writing an article, intended for John Kinsella's *Salt* magazine in the mid-'90s, I suggested Johnson's fricassée best defined the British post-modernist prospect. I also considered Alice Oswald, who'd just published her first book with Oxford University Press, as bright a hope as Johnson in her hybridism; younger exemplars of an undogmatic, post-modern practice. Martin Corless-Smith's poetry, first sent me by Alan Halsey, excites in a similar way. Quite simply, the poetry scene is not a command economy equipped with a PC template of quotas and forms. The moral: far better the graces of pluralism than the heroics of zealotry, *avant-garde* or otherwise.

Charge of the Light Brigade

Peter Finch

Poetry barely featured in the way that I grew up. Sitting next to his huge brown steam radio my grandfather once read me 'The Charge of the Light Brigade'. I'd been given a toy sword for Christmas and it prompted this celebration of great military events through the medium of verse. The sword was made of steel. "No one can break that—strongest metal known," advised my Grandfather. For declaiming this truth I got beaten up by yobs in the rec, the golden sword taken from me, bent in two, and thrown in the brook. Poetry and violence. Such common bedfellows.

I was born in 1947 in Cardiff. Cardiff was big and Cardiff was safe. You could cross it with ease on your bike. Up to Lisvane, the Garth, through the Penarth Dock tunnel, to Lavernock and the beach of sewage, to Llanederyn, along the coast road to Newport. Westville Road, Ty Draw Place, Queensbury Road, Waterloo Gardens, Bangor Street, Lakeside Drive, Stalcourt Avenue, Waterloo Gardens, Mafeking Road, Kimberley Road, Kingsland Road, Shirley Road.

Nobody in the family wrote and hardly anyone read. There were book club editions of popular fiction on a shelf in the hall. A couple of paperbacks, now and again. The newspapers we took were the *Sunday Pictorial*, the *South Wales Echo*, the *Daily Express*, the *Daily Mirror* and the *Daily Sketch*. My grandfather read the *Telegraph*. He was a law unto himself. I read to fill up space. These were the long yellow-lit days before television. Knitting. Games of marbles. Cards. Plays on radio. Dance band music. Forces favourites. Ted Heath. Billy Cotton. Vera Lynn. I went through every science-fiction book on the shelves at the Roath Park Branch library. When I got to the end I started again at the beginning.

An early girlfriend gave me Jack Kerouac's *Dharma Bums*. Jack in his check shirt on the cover. Handsome. Beat. Iconic. When I think back on it this has to be the seminal moment. Read this, you'll like it. How did she know? Kerouac consumed me. And his fellow travellers. Ginsberg, Corso, Burroughs. My copy of *Protest*[1], the British anthology of Beat writing published in paperback by Panther, sanitised Ginsberg's earth-shattering and totally amazing *Howl*. Nonetheless I'd never read anything like it. I went hunting for the real version. Found it unaccountably in the Society for the Promotion of Christian Knowledge Bookshop in The Friary, Cardiff. Ferlinghetti's City Lights Books edition, San Francisco. I was now reading poetry. The stuff was so different from anything I'd imagined. It was free. You could do anything within it. So it seemed. Ginsberg wrote long stanzas which finished only when his breath ran out. Corso took benzedrine and stayed up all night writing as fast as he could. Kerouac put in the sounds of the sea and the sounds of the streets, rhymeless rhythms of speech. They all quoted Carlos Williams as their master. *Paterson*. And then Pound spun me in circles, nowhere to set myself down.

I wrote songs. Blues songs. I listened to Dylan. I got a guitar and got bleeding finger tips managing the chords. I bought an harmonic harness. Put bottle-caps on my shoes. I was a one-man band like Jesse Fuller. I bought *Snaker's Here*, Dave Ray, a white American blues singer playing a 12-string. Listened to Tom Rush. Wore cord jeans. Liked railroads and wide-open spaces. Looked for trails that went somewhere. From the heart to the spirit. The Kerouac scenario. But this was Wales where the roads went up valleys and got lost among pits and sheep and trees.

I had no voice, it turned out. Not for singing. Being a poet was the only way I could contain, sustain, enrol, and envelop these things. But I had no real idea what being a poet actually was. Ginsberg and his vision of Walt Whitman in a supermarket in California might be the way on. It took a long time to learn. I'd heard about Tom Pickard putting "poet" down as his occupation on his passport. I just loved that idea.

Late 1966 I began my magazine *second aeon*. I was a devotee of the Bauhaus and their typographical theories. Punctuation unnecessary, everything in lower case, in sans serif type, simple lines and pure circles. The weight of the face would always be enough. That was me. Early *second aeons* dropped commas, started sentences in lower case, never used exclamation marks. Tried to be Twentieth Century. Hard anywhere, but especially in ancient Wales. Here it was seen as affectation. Reviews of the magazine claimed my work was like monkeys jumping on typewriters. "Finch may have more energy than anyone else around but you don't win prizes for that." "*Second aeon* is a mere comic, our other literary magazines are the real stuff."

For most of its life—its twenty-one hard-fought issues—the magazine was mistreated and misunderstood in its own heartland. It might have begun, a hundred-copy-circulation foolscap six-pager, as a vehicle for its editor's own poetry but it soon outgrew such myopic concerns. I wanted at first to show just what was going on in contemporary British poetry. I wanted to show it all. Great changes were afoot out there, buzzing, misrepresented and misunderstood. The old guard were falling foul of the avant-garde. The line that came from Thomas Hardy was being bent and battered. The new pop poets were making verse for lit-illiterates. Adrian Henri, Roger McGough, and Brian Patten were mixing music with poetry and letting it loose on a pop culture obsessed world. There were visual experimentations and foreign influences rolling across our landscapes like fog. There were other languages in the universe than English. Listen and you could hear them shouting. The battleground was waiting. Unlike others I had no history or reputation to get mashed. I could do what I liked.

I went out and found translators. Found visual poets. People who worked with smears and splatters. Poets whose reputations were built on American or East European accents, or on dope or booze. Outsiders. Centre screeners. Cutting edgers. Old stagers with the guts to keep on changing. I wrote to them, phoned them, made a nuisance of myself at their publishers. Sent them stamped addressed envelopes. Told them how important I thought their work was. Kept at it. Got them to contribute. And so they did.

The magazine began to get coverage in most of the underground press—in *Oz*, in *International Times*, on John Peel's radio show. Pop stars were subscribers, the University of California set up a *second aeon* archive, Argentina exhibited the magazine's visual pages, in France Henri Chopin celebrated *second aeon*'s cause.

Yet despite the TV-producer and OUP poet, John Ormond, championing my poem machines[2] on 405-line BBC Wales and Herbert Williams interviewing me for the *South Wales Echo* and for the *Western Mail*, most of Wales remained highly suspicious. Herbie was brilliant. Long associated with left-leaning literature he recognised spark when he saw it. He was a poet too and interested in non-conformity. For his formative-years support I owe a lot. John Ormond taught me how to take poems apart and put them back together again. We sat in the front bar at the Conway. He showed me his poem about salmon. Told me how he'd made it and explained how my stuff might work much better if I took the ending and put it at the start. Work on things, he advised. Pick them up, put them down, pick them up again, never stop.

This was around forty years ago. Writing in Welsh, the senior literature, culturally took pole position. Subsidised volumes of verse brought out by the Welsh presses like Gomer or Christopher Davies sold as few as 150 copies a time. No wonder I failed to make many inroads. Even as late as the mid-1980s many established Anglo-Welsh poets—or Welsh writers in English as they had become clumsily renamed—still failed to understand the job that *second aeon* had done. Wales had no tradition of avant-gardism. Still hasn't. Wales liked poetry to be poetry. How it always had been.

The Pineapple pub was up the road from where I lived on Maplewood Avenue. It exerted a magnetic pull. John Tripp and I would go in there to work. He was reviews editor. We'd sit over a few beers in the dark interior and talk. *second aeon* had a section towards the end of each issued called *The Small Press Scene* where I tried to list everything that was going on. This section of the magazine had proved so successful that it had got completely out of hand. Cavan McCarthy, the concrete poet, once told me that what was missing from the present day (i.e.1960s) poetry scene was information. "No one had a clue what's being published. No one is collecting these things. Most people don't know that they come out."

I wanted to change this and had gone about it by offering exchange subscriptions (I send you mine, you send me yours and we both mention each other's work) to anyone who wanted to join in. The hundreds of small press (and increasingly big press) publications that were starting to arrive at Maplewood Court turned into thousands. Getting them into the flat was the first problem. Opening them, stacking them, tracking them, listing them, thinking of something to say about them was the next. Some of these publications were far too important to just list with a price and an address. I kept them in boxes and then laid them out across the floor in alphabetical order by country of origin. Most of the stuff came from the UK and the USA but increasing piles slid in from Europe. South Africa, Australia and Asia. John Tripp had offered to help.

He would scuff through the stacked mags and torrents of pamphlet paper and haul away things like *Balzac* by V. S. Pritchett, *Behind Hesslington Hall* by Cal Clothier, Walter Benjamin on Charles Baudelaire, Dannie Abse's *Corgi Modern Poets In Focus*, Dave Calder's *Cube*, Philip Roth's *The Great American Novel*, David Rhodes' *The Last Fair Deal Going Down*, Charles Bukowski's *Mockingbird Wish Me Luck*. "These are longshot poems for broke players who run with the hunted & the cold dogs in the courtyard... yarns & anecdotes... this articulate Buffalo renegade who tries to live up to the hilt."

I edited in the evenings. The days I spent doing paid office work. I came back late through the south Wales drizzle to distant Llandaff North, Llandaff Yard, where the Canal had once flowed, where my father had been brought up. I read manuscripts on the bus. The volume of unpublished and unpublishable manuscripts received was incredible. But in reality the unsolicited slush pile, the life blood of many little poetry mags, actually gave up very little. 10% or less in the magazine's whole lifetime. In the end the bulk wore me down. Sacks of the stuff arriving everyday by every post. Brown envelopes like kippers. I cut back to reading the first poem in the stack only going further if something sparked. It rarely did. Submitting authors tried to catch me out. They sellotaped poems together. Inserted hairs. Put pages in upside down and then when I sent them back this way wrote to me long accusing letters about how I was undermining their creativity and doing a disservice to the whole world of verse. I filed their letters in the bin. I put the phone down when they called and call they did. All hours. On answering to some irate voice asking to speak to Peter Finch I'd say hang on I'll get him, put the phone on the floor, and carry on with what I'd been doing before. After fifteen minutes or so I'd quietly put the handset back on the hook.

Change was the spirit of the age. The concrete poetry movement, born in the '50s, really came on as a force in the sixties. It did so on the back of Marshall McLuhan's *Medium is the Message* philosophy. That idea, that what is significant is not what is said but how it is said, was very important to me. Olson had worked the territory too with his form vs. content arguments. And when I opened the box and looked inside I found that the surrealists and before them the futurists and most importantly the dadaists had all worked the field as well.

These discoveries set me on fire. F.T. Marinetti, Russolo, Duchamp, Kandinsky, Hans Arp, Khlebnikov, Carlo Belloli, Raoul Hausmann, Hugo Ball, Man Ray, Kurt Schwitters, Tristan Tzara. In America were e e cummings, Dick Higgins, Jerome Rothenberg, Jonathan Williams. In Europe Ernst Jandl, Henri Chopin, Diter Rot, Frans Mon, François Dufrène. The Anglo-Welsh Poetry anthology of the period was titled *Dragons and Daffodils*. Where else could I go but the avant-garde?

If I had to nominate a point when I changed direction it would be when I first met the great late sound poet, Bob Cobbing. I'd already realised that if *second aeon* was going to be any force in the world then I had best stop thinking that the mailbox was the answer. I wrote instead to those who, it seemed to me, were making a difference and asked them to contribute. Roland Matthias, who'd published my diatribe against parochialism *A Welsh Wordscape* in his *Anglo-Welsh Review* and given me an early boost suggested that I ask the poet Bob Cobbing. To this day I don't know if Roland understood Cobbing for what he was, an innovator and ground-breaker, or had merely come across the name. I'd never heard of Cobbing but I tracked him down. London, Randolph Avenue in Maida Vale, tan tandinanan tankrina tanan tanare tantarane tan tan… You know the rest.

Bob taught me how to pick something up and make a poem from it. He'd pulled a label off a jar. Make the sounds, he said. Take the letters apart. There are sounds inside them. Henri Chopin calls these language's microparticles. We sang the instructions for making Nescafé. Once you've recorded something onto tape, Bob told me, you can then process it, slow it down, speed it up, cut it, slice it, reverse it. Hear your old voice made completely new. And, having heard that processed voice, you can then imitate it. Take it further. Remake it again. There was little difference between sound and visual either. The trick was to turn one into the other. I did. That older stuff I'd worked on—the faux Beat Generation in the South Wales drizzle, my R. S. Thomas dribbles, my Shelley fantasies, my blues song ramblings—I put them in a drawer in an old cabinet. Locked it. Lost it. Just as well.

This experimental work—material that goes under the banner of innovative poetry today—was a much harder act than emotion recollected in tranquillity. So many things needed to be put in a straight line before the work could flow. Not anything would do. Concrete poetry and the grappling to understand what it was all about was a huge factor in my beginning writing career. I won an early bursary award from the Welsh Arts Council to pay for materials to make concrete poems. I bought large point dry transfer lettering, inks, brushes, card, paper. The poems I made were never much good but the process of making them and the fact that I was making them then was vital.

Peter Mayer was sticking things to the exhibition panels with a staple gun. Dom Sylvester Houédard typestracts. John Furnival lettertowers and skyscrapers. Cobbing duplicator blurs. Purity from the Brazilians. Colour from the French. Henri Chopin typewriter shouting. A couple of mine were there. *The Boom Poem. The Sun Poem.* This was the Museum Place Gallery, ground floor of the Welsh Arts Council. At the opening reception Norman Schwenk explained to me that in addition to intellectual wonder there was also free wine.

The librarian at California exchanged his overstocks with me for copies of *second aeon* and associated publications. I got boxes done up with American sellotape and protected with American brown paper. Inside were the great concrete books. The biggest prize was Mary Ellen Solt's great *Concrete Poetry: A World View* (Indiana University Press, 1968)—the whole deal. Re-reading it now it's easy to see that at the time it was published the academic backdrop to the movement was desperate to find legitimisation. Today we'd simply take that for granted. Back then critics struggled to pin down this surging and all-embracing beast. That was concrete poetry. Hard to believe today.

second aeon ran a terrific course and took me with it. Its circulation rose to three thousand and it became a marker for where British poetry was. It closed in the mid-seventies when I took on the job as bookseller for the Welsh Arts Council's new venture, Oriel. The Council was a major *second aeon* funder and if I worked for them then subvention would need to cease. The magazine's internationalism, its outward looking willingness to embrace the whole poetic scene coupled with its desire to plug the information gap had brought me into contact with a poetry world that was considerably larger than I'd imagined it could be.

Readings became now increasingly important. I invited the world to Cardiff. Gavin Ewart, Eugène Ionesco, Jackson MacLow, D.M. Thomas (who famously demolished a sculpture with an arm gesture while adding extra meaning to one his poems), Edwin Morgan, Adrian

Mitchell, Brian Patten, Roger McGough, Adrian Henri, Iain Sinclair, Bob Cobbing, Margaret Atwood, Jeni Couzyn, Michelene Wandor, Fiona Pitt-Kethley, Fred D'Aguiar, Jeremy Reed, James Simmons, Friedrich Dürrenmatt, the actor John Laurie performing William McGonagall, Thomas A Clark, George Dowden, Clayton Eshleman, Tom Pickard, Bill Bissett, Lee Harwood, Bill Griffiths, Allen Fisher, John James, and Barry MacSweeney all came.

As time moved so did the scene. The poet Chris Torrance, a famous outsider living now in the Brecon Beacons, found work running a weekly evening class, *Adventures in Creative Writing*, at the University in Cardiff. Torrance was a man of habit and his weekly big-city trips ran to an absolute pattern. Market, park, friends, coffee, pub. He'd visit me at the Oriel Bookshop mid-afternoon. We'd talk about poetry, the latest books, the weather, crops, who'd written what and when and where it all might be going. He invited me to talk and read to his class. A fellow traveller. We worked the same furrows. I took along tapes and tubes and a speaker system and showed his group how sound poetry worked. Cobbing impersonations, Schwitters shouting, futurist mumbling, Finch process and permutation. The session went down well. These were *Adventures* after all. Chris's class met in room 246 of the Humanities Building at the top of Park Place—on the site of the old Taff Vale Railway wagon works and engine sheds. That number turned out to be significant.

To get his writers out and into the real world Chris organised what he called "a sort of cabaret" in the upstairs room of the Roath Park pub on City Road. I went as a guest and the class put on a show. What really distinguished this from a regular reading was the spirit of engagement with their audience that was often missing from elsewhere. People stood and read and actually projected their verse. No paper shuffling. Little rambling. It looked and sounded as if thought had gone into things and that people might have rehearsed things earlier. Pints, applause, laughter. We all enjoyed ourselves. Some of the poets—Dorcas Eatch, Ifor Thomas, Tôpher Mills, John Harrison and others wanted to do the show again. So we did. Called it Cabaret 246, that Humanities number, and began to meet weekly, on our own, outside and away from Torrance's class. We'd try out ideas. Criticise each other. Work out in public just how we wanted our poems to sound. Experiment. Get it wrong then get it right. With mutual support.

I'd been doing this kind of thing for some years on the London scene, working with Bob Cobbing and a whole range of other innovators—Andrew Lloyd, Clive Fencott, Lawrence Upton, David Toop, cris cheek, Sean O Huigin, Bill Griffiths, Adrian Clarke, Eric Mottram—mostly edging at the avant-garde or more likely *being* the avant-garde. Performances were long and exciting. Roaring, edgy, innovative, ground breaking, new blood, new age, new speed, new words, new strength and style. Audiences were desirable, yes—but not essential.

By contrast Cabaret 246 went for the audience by the throat. The scene was transformed. Poetry moved into the entertainment business. People who'd never read poetry before found that there was something here to enjoy. Cab 246 lasted for about five years putting on public performances monthly at Chapter and at other venues, travelling to London, Swansea and Liverpool, working with musicians and performers and loonies in costume and blokes with strange haircuts and women who shouted. Cab 246 had its own eponymous magazine and spawned Red Sharks Press. The movement eventually ran out of steam and transformed itself into the poetry slam. Elsewhere stand-up comedy had taken off in a big way and alternative entertainment nights were springing up everywhere. Poetry had come out of the closet. Some would say, of course, that this performance stuff wasn't really an art and to a large extent they'd be right. But it did open doors and it did change the way people wrote. It gave me a new edge, that's for sure.

Oriel Bookshop, which I'd turned into a sort of centre for poetry, "largest selection available anywhere outside London" was my claim, closed in the nineties. From then until recently I've run The Academi, the Literature Promotion Agency for Wales (recently reborn as Literature Wales) which has given me a new handle and new budgets to carry on what I began years ago. It's considerably easier today to make headway with poetry. The stuff is now everywhere. Audiences are less readily shocked and are open to things that in the seventies they were certainly not. People no long say "T.S. Eliot would spin in his grave if he heard this…" Which means that either poets are no longer pushing at boundaries like they once were or that audiences now comprehensively understand how poetry works. I know which one of those I think it is.

Being an outsider, an underdog, is a very Welsh condition. All my life I've been an organiser, an administrator and have picked up experience from a number of fields outside the arts. That's all served me well. Being an avant-gardist or an innovator doesn't mean that you can't tie your shoelaces. As Marshall McLuhan and other 1970s media philosophers predicted, the written word today seems to be actually increasing its penetration. Dada wasn't for nothing. The future is bright. The signs are good.

Notes

1. Feldman, Gene and Max Gartenberg (eds), *Protest* (London: Panther 1960).

2. The best of these was an eight foot diameter revolving construct of rods and globes covered in text. The poem permutated before your eyes.

We Must Talk Now

JOHN FREEMAN

My father recited the 'Immortality Ode' and my mother seemed to mint language, though of course she got it from somewhere. A child shivering with cold was shrammed and a crying one was winnicking, a nail sticking up out of a floorboard was proud, and we must all dree our own weird. We had an anthology of poetry printed in larger-than-usual type, which was the only sign it was intended for children. In it were 'The Tyger' and the poem that gave its title to *The Ecchoing Green,* and by the age of eight at the latest I was rhyming. I went on doing this into my lonely teens, but in between neat stanzas I wrote anguished prose and free verse in a jagged scrawl which, looking back after a few weeks, I could see was more alive than my clever quatrains.

The bus that passed our house went to Trafalgar Square where I alighted and walked up Charing Cross Road. There was a shop called Better Books with a novelty, a coffee machine, and seats. I don't recall using either, but I felt free to stand and browse, and was transfixed by a conversational love poem spread across the page by a poet I had not heard of. Neither had most people outside America then, since his work had only just found a British publisher. "Of asphodel, that greeny flower,/ like a buttercup/ upon its branching stem – / save that it's green and wooden – /I come, my sweet, /to sing to you." I had to have this book by William Carlos Williams*, Pictures From Brueghel and Other Poems,* and the current flowed through the previously broken circuit between the terminals of poetry and speech, my father's quotations and my mother's larger-than-life discourse. And that transcendent element, which my humanist father had regretfully banished, renouncing the church of persecutions while nostalgically singing the hymns of his East End childhood, guyed or straight, the mysticism I had sneaked back in through *Endymion* and *Hyperion* in my pocket Keats, was here again in chastened form. "What power has love but forgiveness?/ In other words/ by its intervention/ what has been done / can be undone. / What good is it otherwise?" "Don't think/ that because I say this/ in a poem/ it can be treated lightly/ or that the facts will not uphold it." "Inseparable from the fire/ its light/ takes precedence over it... In an eternity/ the heat will not overtake the light./ That's sure./ That gelds the bomb,/ permitting/ that the mind contain it." "Only the imagination is real!/ I have declared it/ time without end./ If a man die/ it is because death/ has first/ possessed his imagination." One of the Black Mountain school, I think Fielding Dawson, ended a tribute to Charles Olson by quoting something the master had written and commenting, "I knew I had found the guy." So with me and Williams. I was for a while intimidated by a T. S. Eliot essay sneering at "spilt religion" in poetry; for him religion was the Fire Sermon or the Anglican Church, and poetry was something else. But Blake, Wordsworth and Shelley were prophets of a new testament, supplementing or opposing orthodoxy, and so was Williams, and so were other poets I was later to recognise.

At John Newton's instigation I read Robert Creeley's *The Gold Diggers* and the stories led to the poems, with their electric tension and solemnity about love and sex. "My lady/ fair with/ soft/ arms, what// can I say to/ you – words, words,/ as if all/ worlds were there." "For love – I would/ split open your head and put/ a candle in/ behind the eyes…" There were poems which resisted comprehension, such as 'The Innocence': "Looking to the sea, it is a line/ of unbroken mountains.// It is the sky./ It is the ground. There/ we live, on it…" Somehow I came to trust the poet enough to stare with religious intensity at these poems until I knew them by heart, waiting for some kind of illumination to strike. Occasionally, it did.

I sent poems to two magazines I found copies of in a shop. One was *The Wivenhoe Park Review*, edited by Andrew Crozier, and renamed *The Park* by the time of the double issue (4/5) I appeared in, when Crozier had moved from Essex to Keele. My other choice was *The Grosseteste Review*, whose editor, Tim Longville, began to educate my taste with funny and illuminating letters and issues of the magazine. Soon I was discovering John Riley, George Oppen, and Jim Burns.

Burns, from Preston, was a breath of fresh air. He clearly knew his way round modern poetry, but his poems in verse and prose were grounded in spoken language with telling quotations from working-class people, and centred on emotions generated by tough real-life situations. Burns wrote simply and movingly about a stranger knocking on the door when his father had died, saying, "I've come to say goodbye to my friend," and sitting with the body for a while before replacing his cap and leaving, without explanation. Another piece described reproaching a man who has admitted having attended Fascist meetings in the thirties because, as he goes on to explain, they gave out black shirts, and in those days a black shirt was better than none.

Oppen and Riley both used the transparent language I felt drawn to, but challenged the reader to see how one statement connected, across the white space between lines or around single words, with another. You had to slow down and take in the implications of each statement to tune in to the implied current of thought. The American Oppen had a concern for working and unemployed people, like Burns, and an air of profundity that made him seem like a puritan version of Wallace Stevens, as his gaunt face and spare physique, when I saw pictures of both poets, contrasted with Stevens' plumpness, as if the author of *Harmonium* had been redrawn by Giacometti. There was an urgency, a sense of human crisis and the need to respond:

> We must talk now. I am no longer sure of the words,
> The clockwork of the world. What is inexplicable
>
> Is the "preponderance of objects." The sky lightens
> Daily with that predominance
>
> And we have become the present.
>
> We must talk now. Fear
> Is fear. But we abandon one another.

I spent a year in York beginning a doctorate, which took me eleven years to finish. I was reading Shelley's letters and corresponding with poets. Magazine publication had been an entry into a community. I took a train to Bicester and visited John Riley. I remember pulling into the country platform and seeing a short man with long lank hair and a long beard standing very straight, smoking a pipe and pulling a pocket watch from his corduroy jacket. John's Russian studies in the R.A.F. had led him to the Orthodox Church. I could not share his faith but felt nourished by the poetry he made of it:

It takes a prophet
To understand a prophet : and it's not just the word
But a man's whole life, that edifies.
                                                Thus
Overflowing with joy and gratitude and
Fear, let him beg for the light he lacks.

I was drawn just as much to an intensity, a kind of mysticism, in
Oppen, though he was a resolutely materialist Marxist: "The small
nouns/ Crying faith/ In this in which the wild deer/ Startle, and stare
out."A sceptical reason in tension with a drive for spiritual affirmation
is a state I see as bearing fruit in Oppen and William Bronk as well as
in Shelley.

In 1970 I married a Frenchwoman, Geneviève Rauch, moved from
York to Sheffield, and became a father. Longville put me in touch with
David Tipton, who had just come back from several years in South
America and had fetched up in the same city. David was an admirer of
Byron and in many ways Byronic. We were chalk and cheese, but fellow
poets with common reference points, and with nobody else around of
whom that was true. He wanted us jointly to launch a magazine to be
called *Julian and Maddalo*, after the poem in which Shelley immortalises
his friendship with Byron under those pseudonyms. It did not happen,
but we heard the chimes at midnight, and the swift thought, winging
itself with laughter, lingered not, but flew from brain to brain. David,
originally from the midlands, settled down at first in Sheffield and then
in Bradford, and went on to publish many books under the imprints
of Rivelin, Rivelin Grapheme and Redbeck Presses, including, I am
glad to say, three of mine. Those early Rivelin pamphlets, appearing
in batches, were especially important in defining and giving a public
presence to a swathe of mostly northern or northern-based writers.

My first meeting with David was early in 1971, by which time I had
had a visit from Kris Hemensley, back in his home city of Southampton
from Australia. Kris had brought out the first issue of a magazine he
called *Earthship* and I had offered, with the cooperation of a secretary,
to run off the second issue on the Gestetner duplicators at Sheffield
Poly where I was teaching part-time. The ground-floor flat in the house
where we had the first floor was briefly empty, and we spread out the

foolscap pages of *Earthship* 2 on a long table in a cold room and moved round it, Kris and the heavily pregnant Gen and I, picking up the pages in order, ready to be stapled.

John Riley moved back to his native Leeds where I occasionally went to see him. With a friend who had a car, I visited Riley and Longville in January 1972 when they had rented a house in Fowey. We had a strenuous walk on Exmoor and I quoted from *The Return of the Native* the observation that the heath darkens before the sky, and John wrote a poem ("Rough Tor, Cornwall, this landscape what song") saying that it doesn't. It was my first meeting with Tim, which felt odd as we had exchanged so many letters. A bit of a shock to discover the otherness of the other, especially when he has an inescapable physical presence, being a very tall and large figure: not fat, just *big*. Perhaps this is the place to say that he is an underrated poet, not least by himself, which may be partly why he gave up poetry to become an expert on landscape gardening. What I learned from his poems more than anyone's was the structuring effect of well-handled syntax, long but clear sentences woven entertainingly over several lines like a baroque melody. I think I first saw Tim with John, unless I dreamt this, as we drew near the house in Fowey, heads nodding over music stands, playing something elegant on large recorders, very expertly.

John remained a lodestar for me when I moved to Cardiff in the autumn of 1972. In those days before email, writing a note to John would often be a way of getting me into my day, rousing enough motivation to do the next thing. I was in Wales to teach English Literature, more than ten years before we managed to get creative writing onto the syllabus. I soon met Chris Torrance, Phil Maillard, Peter Finch, Pete Hodgkiss and others. Finch was famous as the editor *of second aeon* and ran an outstanding poetry bookshop, Oriel. Chris' habitat, already beautifully presented in photographs and poems in his early collections, was and still is the remote farmhouse at Glynmercher Isaf, the Vale of Mercury. This became a legendary site and I am glad to have tasted its magic and the brisk walk to the Lamb and Flag. An Italian colleague at the university, Spartaco (Gino) Gamberini, invited me to edit an English-language poetry section for his Italian magazine, privately distributed and not for sale, *Lettera*. This collaboration lasted for several issues and I printed work by famous and unknown American and British poets, reprinting a special issue of *Lettera* as *Poetry in English Now,* under my own imprint, Blackweir Press. I also published pamphlets by Roy Fisher, David Tipton and Phil Maillard. Eric Mottram invited Finch, J.P. Ward and me to read together, at one of the Poetry Conferences he presided over in the Polytechnic of Central London. Tom Pickard and Barry MacSweeney were there, representing the North-East. I introduced myself to Jim Burns and told him I was writing an article about him and began one of my most sustained and sustaining friendships with poets.

There was a busy connectedness about the poetry scene in those years of the mid and late nineteen seventies. Finch and others organised poetry readings in Wales—I organised a few myself—and Mottram's large-scale conferences flourished for several years, with poets from America and all over Britain. I remember a camp-fire on Great Malvern one midsummer night where poets including Gael Turnbull and Jeremy Hilton, who was then living nearby in Pershore, read and performed music under the stars. There were other readings in Malvern at more conventional venues, and I guess that they lay behind the eventual appearance of the magazine *Fire*, edited by Hilton, which was a significant outlet for a remarkable diversity and range of poetry in English for two decades. Other new magazines, crackling with life, appeared and lasted one issue or many issues. Who remembers *Spindrift, Saturday Morning, One*? They shone, they nourished. Hodgkiss edited *Poetry Information,* which did, invaluably, what the title says, as well as adding analysis to fact. There was an association of little presses and there was as there still is tireless reviewing of new work by Burns in *Ambit* and elsewhere. I published an article called 'New Poetry and Where to Find It' and a couple of follow-ups at intervals. At Finch's instigation I fronted the Welsh Association of Small Presses.

And then? Peter Hodgkiss phoned me at 7 one morning. "John Riley's been *murdered!*" He had been attacked and killed while out walking near his Leeds home. He was forty-one. To quote Lee Harwood: "years pass". We go on writing, we stop writing, we start writing again. Publishers do and don't and do again want to take us on. There are new movements and revivals. Poetry never quite expires. Poets rarely agree, and different tendencies coexist, ignoring or attacking each other like revolutionary splinter groups. The baton passes. But several generations of poets are writing at the same time, never more so than in this period of increased longevity. Sometimes the spotlight is on the long-established, sometimes on the young. So it goes. Some of us live long enough to come in for a certain archaeological curiosity, but are still re-inventing the poem each day from first principles, and looking around for inspiration from fresh sources, experiential and literary.

In the Second World War serious reading increased, partly from boredom, partly because they were dark days that made people look for something to confront them with. John Riley: "It would be foolish to suppose that everybody is not searching." (Try saying that when looking for your keys: it will stick.) Dark days have not gone away. What sustaining poetry will searchers find in years to come?

A lot of the poetry that most satisfies me lies outside the mainstream of publishing, the metropolitan élite, and popular taste; but there is enough polarisation in our fragmented culture without refusing to see anything good in what is popular, or written in ways that do not look "innovative". I regret having for a period been blinded by partisanship to anything good in Ted Hughes, and I deplore the viciousness with which some attacked him just because he had so many readers. Similarly, the popularity of the Bloodaxe anthologies *Staying Alive* and *Being Alive* is not proof that they are some kind of collective disaster. I, at least, have discovered Irish and American poets in them by whom I have gone on to buy collections, and whose work has been like lifeblood to me: Kerry Hardie, Jane Kenyon, Jack Gilbert, and Alden Nowlan, among others, not to mention translated poets such as Tomas Tranströmer.

The relationship of poetry to speech is where I began, and it has a political element, a democratic vista. It has been a perennial theme in English poetry. Many lines by Shakespeare and Donne still sound like someone speaking spontaneously, now; Wordsworth wanted to get back to the real language of men, and Hopkins and Robert Browning in contrasting ways both sought that authentic note of speech under the pressure of passion. But how are we to reconcile it with intensity and form, especially now that we understand so thoroughly that every style is chosen, not given? Edward Thomas, Robert Frost, Eliot, Pound, Williams, Ginsberg, Burns, Oppen, John Riley, Lee Harwood, and, I would add, Jane Kenyon and Kerry Hardie, are among those who have contributed in this respect to "that great poem, which," as Shelley wrote in *A Defence of Poetry*, "all poets, like the co-operating thoughts of one great mind, have built up since the beginning of the world." It matters. Humankind, as Mahler reminded us in German, and with a solemnly beautiful musical cadence, lies in greatest need. And as Friedrich Hölderlin had affirmed in the same language, after asking urgently what use poets are in a time of dearth: what remains, though, the poets create.

It's All in the Garage: Possibly Reliable Memoirs of a Small Press Publisher

Peter Hodgkiss

I'm looking at a tatty cardboard box measuring 37cm x 29cm x 17cm. On one long side in red felt tip pen the letters GDP are faintly depicted surrounded by a circle. The box contains 62 books + 2 falling-apart account books and represents the Galloping Dog Press archive, accompanied by a collection of cardboard files housing correspondence and a large box full of "miscellanea". It has moved from landing to attic to garage 1 to garage 2 in two houses in Newcastle to its present residence in Whitley Bay. What strikes me now twenty years on is the fact that the books vary considerably in appearance from the early A4 mimeograph jobs to the later much more sophisticated litho printed bookshop-friendly books and pamphlets.

In the autumn of 1974, having worked as a librarian in London for 5 years, I moved to Swansea to study English at the university as a mature student (I was 29). For much of my time in London I had edited the reviewing and listing magazine *Poetry Information* which had gradually expanded over the years. Part of the reason for moving was to use whatever spare time I had to develop the magazine. Since I was not a model student this proved to be entirely feasible and I managed to produce two substantial issues a year for most of my stay in South Wales. Despite this I still had time on my hands and decided to join the brigade of little presses listed in the magazine. I can't remember the exact motive for this—probably it had something to do with the desire to get amongst the poets rather than just dealing with them at arm's length as I did as editor of the magazine. I should add that I was one of the few small-press operators who did not also write poetry.

Having made the fateful decision, what was I to call myself…? I must have been reading Joyce's *Ulysses* because that's where the lean and hungry dog came from. Page 52 of the Penguin edition describes a dog on the beach loping off "at a calf's gallop". At the time I was living about 100 yards from Swansea beach and the description fitted most aptly (apart from the calf bit, of course). So it had to be Galloping

Dog Press. The press motif, which appeared on some of the duplicated books, came from a Gustave Doré illustration of *Don Quixote*.

The first two publications were small, stapled pamphlets done on the trusty Adler electric typewriter I used for *Poetry Information*. *Playing It Cool* was by *Poetry Information* stalwart & Beat specialist Jim Burns & consists of short, laconic observations on life, the best of which had a witty edge to them. *A Graph of Love* was by David Tipton who had contributed a piece on Peruvïan poetry for the *PI* Latin American issue. Overtly autobiographical, looser in form and more highly charged in tone than the Burns. Both were widely published in magazines and a good pair to start off the press I thought. They were both printed by Tony Ward, who was attached to the Arvon Foundation at Lumb Bank in Todmorden, & did a good neat job.

The next book was much more problematical. After I had published his book David Tipton mentioned that he had been hoping to publish a travel journal by the American poet Clayton Eshleman whom he knew while teaching in Peru. Since he couldn't afford to do it would I like to take it on? I had been impressed with Eshleman's recent Black Sparrow collection *The Gull Wall,* which contained some intensely-wrought tributes to poets & musicians he admired. He was also a "big name" in the American poetry area that interested me. So I said OK. The book *On Mules Sent From Chavin* was to be printed by Tony Ward. The problems lay mainly in Clayton's expectations—he wanted a paperback book with a spine, a special signed collector's edition etc etc. All quite reasonable in many ways since the guy was used to dealing with experienced American publishers, not a naïve Englishman publishing his third book. Costs escalated, the book took ages to come out &, by the time it did, I was fed up with the whole business. In the event it looked fine, but despite American distribution did not sell particularly well. I also felt no particular rapport with the poet. Fortunately, as I did not receive any grant aid, I was assisted by friends Neil & Sue Carne, who also helped with a couple of other later projects.

While waiting for the book to emerge I made a decision that the point of my publishing was to get stuff out quickly & cheaply even if that meant sacrificing a little quality. So I went back to the duplicator (I had used a Roneo for several of the London issues of *PI*). I did a couple of pamphlets to see how it panned out. I managed to borrow a Gestetner tabletop model from Geoff Towns, tolerant proprietor of Dylan's second-hand bookshop where I worked on and off during the vacations, toasting myself in front of his one-bar electric fire, eating his biscuits and "liberating" tasty books to add to my burgeoning collection (he used to make periodic visits to liberate them back again). I should also add that by now I actually possessed a table top since I had moved in with Annie Wood, even more tolerant (and we're still together after all these years—aren't I lucky?), so I was able to bash out the books to my heart's content.

I am proud to say I was an integral part of the "mimeograph revolution" which burgeoned in the '60s and '70s & which *PI* helped to document. It seems like the dark ages in our brave new world of the internet but it had an energy & immediacy which I found attractive (and still do). It was, however, very time consuming and could be messy (depending on how good a typist you were). The basic component of the duplicator was an ink-filled drum around which was wrapped a stencil, or "skin". The stencil was typed on and ink was forced out through the cut letters etc. on the stencil. The main problems happened when mistakes were made, which in my case were fairly frequently. Vivid pink correcting fluid had to be painted over the error, allowed to dry and then the correction overtyped. Easy peasy, eh? Not always the case... What sometimes happened was that the fluid was not allowed to dry completely and the overprinted letters merged in with the originals resulting in a messy splodge when printed. Look at any mimeographed book or magazine and I can almost guarantee you can spot the corrections. That was one mess; the other happened less frequently and involved ink spillages. Duplicating ink was thick and viscous and if the drum was overfilled could get all over the place. The least said the better really, suffice it to say that I sometimes walked around looking like a Black and White Minstrel. Apart from these setbacks I enjoyed most of it.

Back to the plot... The honour of providing the first mimeographed Galloping Dog fell to Phil Maillard for *Grazing the Octave*, a loosely linked set of poems in 22 sections. Hot on its heels came *Parflèche* by Colin Simms. Both provided a pointer to the basic preoccupations of many future books, in that they are driven by a strong sense of place and the poet's interaction with his/her surroundings. The Simms book presented particular challenges in that he uses very long lines. This meant I had to present the book in landscape format. I managed to obtain an old IBM long carriage typewriter with a golfball head (theoretically this meant that I had the option of several typefaces but I never worked out how to use it properly so I was stuck with only one). The other problem was that Colin's manuscript was handwritten in his tiny spidery writing. Despite, or maybe because of, these problems it remains one of my favourites and one I can still happily rediscover. Four other Swansea books followed including a collection by the absurdist, Opal Nations: *a pen some paper many dreams & other eye movements*, which leads me to talk about live performances…

When I moved to Swansea the only contact I had was Glyn Pursglove who lectured in the English Department at the university and who became a valued contributor to *PI*, as well as gently guiding me through my academic studies which ended in the attainment of a magnificent 2:2 degree. On arriving I made contact with several local poets including Spanish expert Malcolm Parr (who also became a contributor to the magazine) and Alan Perry who supplied the cover design for *PI 12/13*. (I produced 7 issues of *Poetry Information* in Swansea all of which were printed at the University print shop). There were already several presses and magazines based in South Wales so I figured my role would be to use my contacts to provide some variety. This included putting on readings in the city centre. The first reader was Jim Burns who launched *Playing It Cool* at the No Sign Bar in Wind Street. There followed two highly entertaining events at the Buffalo Social Club (the Royal Antediluvian Order of Buffalos is a working-class version of the Masons). I hired the downstairs room for readings by Opal Nations and Lee Harwood. The former featured an electrifying rendition by Opal (real name Martin Humm; he used to sing with the R&B group The Hummingbirds) of a song by William Blake; a stand-out feature of Lee's reading was the coincidental appearance of a herd of lady and junior buffaloes returning from a junior boxing session. Other readings took place at Old Nick's, a converted chapel on the seafront, which provided a more congenial venue. Performers included the fast talking Anne Waldman, Chris Torrance who lives high above Swansea on the edge of the Brecon Beacons, Sorley MacLean who encouraged by the audience gave a wonderful reading in Gaelic, Barry McSweeney and Tom Pickard, Thomas A. Clark, Bob Cobbing with musicians David Toop and Paul Burwell (water was heavily involved I seem to remember), jgjgjg (Lawrence Upton, Clive Fencott & cris cheek crawled around the floor with some effect). It was a varied and cosmopolitan bunch. Audiences were in the main large and appreciative.

Having left university in the summer of 1977 I managed to get a temporary job with West Glamorgan Council Planning Department (job creation, as it used to be called). This involved "compiling a register of mineral deposits" in the county (i.e. counting coal mines) and when they got fed up with me hanging around the office reading Joseph Conrad they provided me with a Datsun van and a camera & sent me off photographing coal tips and playing pool with my mate Alan (they didn't know about the last bit). I then applied to be a postman but was rejected for being too clever (I got all the "spot the difference" diagrams right but I think "motivation" may have been the main problem). Then fate sent me to the other end of the country and I then got a "proper" job in the cold North East as manager of the Arts Council-subsidised Ceolfrith Bookshop in Sunderland. This was part of Sunderland Arts Centre and as such operated at the whim of the director, who decided that the newly-elected Margaret Thatcher was a jolly good thing and made me redundant after only six months (he had no alternative apparently…). Fortunately Annie had landed a good job as a film editor with Tyne Tees TV and we stayed on and have been living in Newcastle (now Whitley Bay) ever since. The air and the company seem to suit us…

We started off renting a large ground floor flat in Jesmond which crucially had a wide corridor suitable for installing 1) a Roneo duplicator purchased from a defunct solicitor's office in Durham, 2) a large manual guillotine heroically transported on a flat bed truck from Swansea by Phil Maillard, 3) a clamp. These plus a large sweet jar containing binding glue meant that I had the means of production as well as, crucially, time. I was unemployed for about 18 months in which time I managed to produce roughly a book every two months as well as the final 180-page issue of *Poetry Information*. I'd like to say this was a labour of love but, looking back, it smacks of obsession and a determination to prove I was worth something despite being on the dole. However, I can't say I was desperately seeking employment (I remember having an interview as a petrol-pump attendant but not much else) and eventually I ended up doing another job creation stint, this time working for Newcastle City Libraries reorganising school libraries and reading stories to the kids.

The duplicated books produced in Otterburn Terrace varied in format. Chris Torrance's *The Diary of Palug's Cat,* is A4 in size with a lettered spine. This became the favoured style of most of the books, hence the binding glue & clamp mentioned previously. I have to admit it wasn't an original idea but one copied from Allen Fisher's New London Pride editions. It worked well and it was possible to produce quite lengthy books. I quite enjoyed the repetitive work of printing, guillotining, gluing and binding as it meant I could explore my large collection of jazz on vinyl and not feel too guilty about "wasting my time listening to music"—do I detect a hint of the Protestant work ethic? Oh, I think so…

Since there was already a thriving literary scene in the North East it meant that the performance side of things was already catered for and I could go along to readings at the Morden Tower in Newcastle and Colpitts in Durham purely as a member of the audience. One important contact I already had was Ric Caddel who operated Pig Press from his house in Heaton, later Durham. I had already published an article by him in *PI* and we became good friends over the years. I published several books by him, from the minimalism of the elegant *Baby Days & Moon Diaries* (with matching cover by our friend Tony Flowers) to the more expansive (if that's the right word for Ric's poetry) *Uncertain Times.* Our tastes in writing coincided to a great extent and there was a certain overlap in the writers we both published (Mottram, Griffiths, Harwood, Kelvin Corcoran, Maurice Scully etc). I think Ric had the idea that I was a secret scribbler but my role was always one of appreciation rather than practice (slippery things, words…).

Another friend I made (and published) was Tony Jackson who, like Ric, died too soon. When I got to know Tony his multiple sclerosis had started to tighten its grip and he progressed pretty quickly from walking with a stick to terrorising pedestrians in his motorised wheel chair. He had a fearsome reputation going back to his early performance poetry days (fake blood in Leazes Park has been mentioned) but I always found him a good and generous companion. He had developed a surprising passion for cricket and I drove him several times to see Durham play. He was a big man and getting in and out of the car could be a tricky operation; I remember once dropping him on the pavement outside his flat to the accompaniment of anguished howls. Fortunately a hefty Geordie gent picked him up with one hand, unceremoniously dumped him into his wheelchair, and strolled off without a word. Towards the end of his life Tony became increasingly immobile and was confined to his flat—"I measure my life in inches, Pete…"

One of the first books I published when I moved to Newcastle was *Ghostie Men* by Tom Leonard, a slim quarto pamphlet graced with a fine cover by Robin Campbell, a Swansea friend (a Scot who reputedly had been a champion cycle racer under "another name"—make of that what you will). Incredibly it was so popular that it ran to two editions of 300 copies each—the first yellow and red, the second a pleasing shade of light blue. I had first met Tom in the bar of the White House Hotel next door to the Poetry Society which provided a licensed before-and-after-reading sanctuary for poets & audience and was struck by the direct and uncluttered way he talked about writing—this man means business I thought to myself… (He also made me laugh—very important). This meeting led to his ground-breaking article on poetics through the work of William Carlos Williams which appeared in *PI 16*—I would urge anyone interested in language in its widest sense to read this piece (it was reprinted in *Intimate Voices*). Tom's description of himself as a "language activist" hits the mark. After *Ghostie Men* I published the book that really kept the press going financially for some time to come. *Intimate Voices* first came out in 1984 in grey, then in 1985 in caramel, finally in 1988 in lime green (I like to distinguish my reprints; there haven't been many of them…). All were printed by the Tyneside Free Press Workshop in Newcastle. Total print run 3,000, all sold. Joint winner of the Scottish Book of the Year Award for 1984. The fact that the book was published by an English press meant that sales outside Scotland received a considerable boost. It is crucial that, although some of his work is written in Glasgow dialect, it isn't confined to a Scottish readership—it's what's going on underneath that matters—and I'm proud to have helped in that. Random House under its Vintage imprint published a rather scuzzy version of the book in

1995 (a reduced-size reprint on inferior paper) and Nicholas Johnson's etruscan books did a handsome edition in 2003. So, the book still lives, as indeed it should do. I would add that I received grant aid from the Scottish Arts Council for all three editions which obviously helped considerably—in fact, it turned out that they were indirectly helping to subsidise many books by English and Irish poets along the line. I published two other pamphlets from Tom: *Situations Theoretical and Contemporary* in 1986 and *Nora's Place* in 1990. Both sold out quickly and are reprinted in *Outside the Narrative* (etruscan books/Word Power Books 2009). Tom Leonard is an important voice and it's good that he has been well served by his non-establishment publishers. Of all the poets I have dealt with he has been the most demanding in his insistence on textual and spatial accuracy (in amusing contrast Ralph Hawkins wanted his misspelling of snowy owl in one of his poems to stay—it appears as "snowly").

At the end of 1981 we moved across Jesmond from our ground-floor flat with its slugs and drafts to a three storey terraced house near Jesmond Vale which is where the dog remained until its demise in 1991. My son Joe was born at the end of 1983 and I was told in no uncertain terms that the guillotine had to go—apparently babies and sharp instruments do not go together, surely even I could understand that! A nice man from the Tyne & Wear Archives came to take it away and it's probably in their basement to this day. I can't say I was that sad to get rid of it since I was allowed to use the power guillotine at the Free Press. I managed to produce several duplicated books before I got rid of it—Eric Mottram's *Elegies,* another Colin Simms, books by Bill Butler, Maggie O'Sullivan, Geraldine Monk, Ken Edwards, Alan Halsey, Maurice Scully's *5 Freedoms of Movement* and several others. The Swansea connection was maintained with the fourth part of Chris Torrance's *Magic Door* epic *The Book of Brychan* (using Robin Campbell's illustrations) and for some reason a different Galloping Dog logo which looks more like a wild boar than a dog, Nigel Jenkins' *Practical Dreams,* and a tricksy production of Peter Finch's *Blues and Heartbreakers* got up to look like piece of 45" vinyl. I really enjoyed the business of suiting the production to the work rather than the other way round which is often the way with poetry publishers who are keen to present a unified front, a "house style" to the world. Just to keep my hand in with the duplicator I conceived a series of short pamphlets which I named *Quick Jobs*—spur of the moment, work-in-progress sort of things. Particular favourites are Ian Breakwell's sardonic *Rural Tales* and *Counting Coups* by the Canadian poet Guy Birchard, whom I met in Dublin and who told me he never read his poems in public (probably still hasn't, even though he's a terrific poet).

Oh, not to forget the prose magazine *Not Poetry* which I started in the flat. I've always been interested in work that doesn't quite fit conventional categories and decided to give it a platform. The result was six issues, which appeared from 1980 to 1985—later I published prose books by John Muckle and Phil Maillard. I had always wanted to publish some work by Douglas Woolf, one of my favourite writers and his *Being Normal* appeared in the final issue. I particularly treasure his long format postcards depicting American motels—he seemed to be constantly on the move. There were plans to do a book, which unfortunately never materialised. I also published some drawings by Glen Baxter, another favourite who also contributed the cover to issue 4 (well, they *were* "not poetry"). Looking through the issues they are a very mixed bag with such "big names" as Kathy Acker, James Kelman, David Almond, Paul Metcalfe and people I'd never heard of before contributing pieces about natural childbirth, heroin addiction etc.

The last few years of the press were taken up with publishing conventional typeset books, most of which look great and I enjoyed doing—nicely designed with striking covers, carefully chosen typefaces and all that. The sort of books that mainstream bookshops were willing to stock (by this time I was working as a rep for Yale University Press which helped to find homes for them), but I think my heart was really in the muck and sweat of the clunky and irritating business of feeding that bloody duplicator & swirling that bloody guillotine handle and gluing those bloody pages together until hey presto a really rather nice book appeared (not that many fell apart, either...).

So, there we have it. Over 20 years of small press activity, publishing the poets of my choice. I'm glad I did it, but I'm glad I stopped and came to realize that there was a life out there away from the printed word. The only contact I now have with the small press world is chewing the fat over cribbage with my friend the poet Peter Baker (he did some prose pieces for *Not Poetry* and edited *Skylight* magazine), and the occasional meeting with Tom Leonard. I'll end on one of Eric Mottram's more portentous pronouncements: "You'll be a footnote in the history of English Literature, young Peter". (I made up the young Peter bit—poetic license you know…). If that's the case it suits me fine.

In Conversation

ALAN HALSEY & DAVID ANNWN

AH: I was thinking the other day about the eighteen years I spent running The Poetry Bookshop and it struck me that I became friends with a lot of poets through that rather than through my own writing. I was thinking particularly of the poets I later collaborated with and whose books were among the earliest titles I published under the West House imprint. Gavin Selerie, Kelvin Corcoran, Martin Corless-Smith … and, need I say, you—although I can't now remember when and how we met. You've sometimes referred to a group reading we took part in at Oriel—I suppose that would have been in '82 or '83?— my memory's fuzzy, I did several of those—Oriel under Peter Finch's stewardship was such a vital place. But perhaps we'd met in Hay before then—you would have been in Aberystwyth at the time?

DA: I was finishing a Ph.D. at Aber when Jeremy Hooker gave me a lift to Hay, primarily to browse Anne Stevenson's Poetry Bookshop and there, with a welcome encounter with Sally Purcell and, later, a bartender-dog, we had a fine old time. Later, after you took over the shop and after my '81 move to Wakefield and having ordered several of your books, I wrote and asked you whether you welcomed discussion of your poetry. Hence it was your work hand in hand with my wish to revisit the bookshop which finally led to our encounter of circa '82. You were kind enough to give B&B to the vagabond poet. Then I revisited a year or two later with Adele Kaye and then again to visit Capel-y-ffin. The Oriel reading was '86 or '7, after North and South got going.

AH: I'm interested in how readers become aware of the less visible poetries. I tried to make available as wide a selection of "other" poetry in my shop as I could but of course people tend to find only what they're looking for—although everyone has lucky moments and perhaps that's what it all depends on. Was it at Aber that you found out about the broader spectrum?

DA: Your Broad Street shop opened out myriad poetic alternatives but I was lucky at University College Wales. Care of Clive Meachen I met Ed Dorn and Robert Duncan and was muddling my head with reading R.S. Thomas alongside Tom Raworth and Eugène Guillevic. I came to Lorine Niedecker's work through Ronald Johnson's *Eyes and Objects* but it was you who sent me *From this Condensery* and Loy's *The Last Lunar Baedeker.*

AH: To some extent what drove me at The Poetry Bookshop was the memory of my own isolation in the mid-'70s, when I had no idea what a rich vein of poetry had been opened up in the UK. Not a hint of it in *Agenda,* for example—just a peculiar mismatch of homage to the modernist masters and some outstandingly dull new verse. Then, around 1976, I read an article by Jeff Nuttall in one of the Sundays, a short piece on Allen Fisher, Eric Mottram and Bill Griffiths. His remarks about Griffiths particularly grabbed me and I ordered a copy of *Cycles* at once. Those opening lines

> Ictus!
> as I ain't like ever to be still but
> kaleidoscope,
> lock and knock my sleeping

—what a revelation! And through Bill I made a lot more small-press discoveries. Ric Caddel suggested I send my *Yearspace* MS to Pete Hodgkiss at Galloping Dog. I learnt a great deal from Pete and his *Poetry Information.* That's another Oriel connection—Pete Hodgkiss launched *Yearspace* at an ALP (Association of Little Presses) bookfair there. Glenn Storhaug bought a copy and knocked on my door a week later—and so began my long association with Five Seasons Press. Glenn introduced me to Gael Turnbull and I did my first reading at one of Gael's midsummer festivals in Malvern. That's where I first heard Roy Fisher, Chris Torrance and quite a few others. Why is Gael so undervalued?—not only as poet but enabler, one of those people around whom things just seem to happen—and not forgetting that *Migrant,* both press and magazine, was the precursor of much later publishing. I saw him a few weeks before he died, with a fistful of copyshop pamphlets of old and new poems, looking forward to taking his latest Poetry Machine out on the streets of Edinburgh. Tremendous energy. In a healthier climate he'd be a deservedly popular poet.

DA: Yes, Gael: it seems to me that he was one of the most polyphonous and delightfully open artists in the sense of having many voices and skills and trying various routes with so little prejudice shown. He wrote to me about how generous Robert Duncan was to him when he started out and Roy Fisher writes about how crucial Gael was for his development. Bill's 'Ictus!' is terrific. Ronald Johnson's *The Book of the Green Man* and Roy Fisher's work hit me like that. We need more people like Gael kicking over the traces and not settling for what are fundamentally boring party lines.

AH: The conservatism of the avant-garde is as stifling as any other. But tell me how North and South got going.

DA: Around 1986 Peterjon and Yasmin Skelt were visiting me in Yorkshire and said they'd come up with the idea of a poetry press and wondered if I wanted to be involved. A little later Frances Presley joined us.

AH: So your *King Saturn's Book* was one of its first publications? I remember being impressed at the time by the production quality of North and South books, some unusual designs and formats alongside paperbacks, which would sit pretty on any high-street bookshop's shelves. It was an interesting period with longer-established presses like Pig and Galloping Dog switching from mimeo to commercial offset. Yasmin seemed very energetic in repping the books around London and I wonder how successful that was. I guess it was just at the end of the era of independent booksellers, before the corporate chains got a stranglehold. The press was active for, what, seven years or so?—your selected, *The Spirit / That Kiss*, was one of its last books?

DA: Yes, and in between: Lee Harwood's *Rope Boy to the Rescue*, Frances Presley's *The Sex of Art*, Kelvin Corcoran's *The Next Wave*, Ric Caddel's *Against Numerology*, the Louis Zukofsky anthology and works by Elaine

Randell, Eric Mottram, Geraldine Monk, Catherine Walsh, George Mackay Brown, Jonathan Williams, Bobbie Louise Hawkins, and the Sinologist Lisa Raphals, a real range. How successful was any repping? Who to compare with? We never had a grant of any nature. Yasmin was also interested in making films, hence a couple of North and South videos. There was a series of readings, at the Victoria Miro gallery to start with. We worked pretty hard getting the designs of the books right. Peterjon did all of the setting. The Skelts also established another press, Solaris, to feature the work of Eric Mottram more extensively. I think *Prospect into Breath* (1991), a book of interviews with North and South writers, is a real map of the times. It starts with Peterjon's dedication to Paul Evans and ends "Alan Halsey's Poetry Bookshop in Hay-on-Wye remains a principal source for obtaining poetry publications in the British Isles." Were you aware of your shop as a place for roving poets to meet up, a kind of floating community? You were in touch with most of the small presses and the folk who ran them so you must have held/still hold a pretty good overview of poetics in Britain.

AH: Less so now. The shop did bring in poets of very different persuasions and allegiance. And I guess it had a certain reputation which made some stay away—I remember Christopher Logue popping in for a chat while his pal Craig Raine kicked his heels outside. But for the most part a shop is a relatively neutral meeting-place, simultaneously public and private. There's an element of performance involved, and not just by the proprietor—also the fun of never knowing who might turn up and maybe stay for supper or come down to the pub after a hard day's browsing. I tried to stay out of the crossfire of sudden spats and ancient quarrels but got caught a few times—'Table Talk' is an oblique account of one particularly gossipy and backbiting summer. I often think of that line of Pound's, "Their asperities diverted me in my green time." A wonderfully ambiguous word, "diverted".

DA: Indeed. This business of allegiance is a strange one. Someone once told me that Bob Cobbing came from Plymouth Brethren stock and hence his zeal. The lines form wherever you stand. Robert Duncan said that as soon as people began to draw a line, they could put him on the other side of it, but his rows with Denise Levertov show how difficult this is to maintain. We talked recently about whether one does or doesn't take all poems to be primarily about and involving language is something of a boundary-marker in Britpoetics…

AH: Years ago I had a conversation with Jerry Hooker. He was enthusing about the "Objectivists" and I remarked that it seems to me that the common "objects" in their poems are words, words treated *as* objects, rather than common objects signified. I regard this as a point in their favour but Jerry seemed to find my remark quite offensive. It sticks in my mind because I'm sympathetic to Jerry's writing—at the time he was just about the only contributor to *Anglo-Welsh Review* whom I found at all interesting. But it seems that he shares a widespread suspicion that in the "wrong" hands poetry becomes mere playing with words—rather than seeing wordplay as an opening, a way into, content and meaning. To me poetry *begins* with words, in certain or uncertain displacement—a poem is a thing made of words and to a greater or lesser degree creates its own meaning—as your own work, which I'm sure Jerry knows very well, shows with great exuberance.

DA: I suppose some people see the notion that "a poem is a thing made of words" as a statement of limitation, a mundane condition, not an opening on vast energies. Of course one doesn't want a restrictive homogeneity in thoughts about the nature of language but there's this insistent and recurrent view of language as shoddy and imprecise but also, potentially and simultaneously, transcendent. It seems as though many "mainstream" authors buy this line uncritically. Though the work of authors as various as Allen Fisher, Randolph Healy, Robert Sheppard, Geraldine Monk and Thomas A. Clark which embody totally different senses of language should surely give these folk pause.

AH: Let's step back a bit. Two of your earliest books were published by Bran's Head, a press I know hardly anything about except that it was run out of a bookshop in Frome by Grahaeme Barrasford Young. Tell me about your involvement there. One of those books was a study of Seamus Heaney, Geoffrey Hill and George Mackay Brown, which suggests your interests shifted a good deal in the following decade or so.

DA: Grahaeme kindly wrote to me and asked if he could publish *Foster the Ghost*, my first volume of poetry, as well as the critical book *Inhabited Voices* which was related to the subject of my Ph.D. My involvement with Bran's Head press was minimal—Grahaeme took the projects on himself and I remain very grateful to him. Because my work concerned myth and history in and as poetry, Hill's *Mercian Hymns* seemed very vivid and innovative at the time. You've said how much you admired it too but he never took up the promise of that volume. Heaney's work seems Neo-Georgian now: closed-off and pedestrian. It's as though he's trapped linguistically but one must remember how exquisite and open-ended some of those explorations of place-names in *Wintering Out* looked at the time. Heaney was also very generous and warm to me as a research student and spoke with me about how much he admired Gary Snyder's work. What I'm trying to say is that, quite naïvely at the time, I had no knowledge of the divisions: the Faber power-brokers, the North-Atlantic turbine, the London poetry wars making Eric Mottram's life a misery; I assumed poetry was an open arena where differences enriched the scene. It heartens me to remember how much Jeff Nuttall, with all his affiliations, continued to admire George Mackay Brown's poetry and give his books favourable reviews.

AH: I don't know Mackay Brown's work at all well. You're right that Hill's *Mercian Hymns* engaged me at one time, particularly after my move to Hay, 1977/8—among other things I was intrigued by his treatment of a geographical-historical patch new to me. But the shine wore off quite quickly. The comic anachronisms don't bear many re-readings and are nothing like as entertaining as Griffiths' in *Gesta Alfredi*. At times the poems seem like a sequence of aerial photographs—certainly the work of a man who doesn't like to get his hands dirty. What I wanted was a view from the ground and I had a yen to write about my experience of the Marches and more particularly about living and making a living in Hay. I'd twigged that Hay was a kind of micro-economy and that this hadn't just to do with the bizarre trading practices of secondhand booksellers—the book trade was plugging into a local ethos which had always been eccentric, at least from a metropolitan point of view—or rather it offered a kind of warped reflection of the macro-economy.

I had a lot of trouble even beginning to write about that but then I hit on the verse letter. That seemed to do the trick and those letters 'On Change & Exchange' grew into a long series, from 1979 to the mid-nineties. They allowed a useful licence to turn insides out, to range from ephemeral events to overviews and back again within a few lines. I used some of the same material in my last Hay writing, *The Art of Memory in Hay-on-Wye*, a memoir of sorts. By then I'd foolishly got involved in local politics and confrontations with the neighbourhood moneymen. There's a line in that text, "Me I'll be an incomer all of my life", which pretty much expresses how I've felt wherever I've lived. I suppose it goes back to growing up in an area of South London with still visible war-damage and suffering further destruction by the brutalist civic developments of the late fifties—alienating enough to make me feel that I came from nowhere in particular and will never really belong anywhere else. But maybe that's a very personal thing. Chris Torrance who comes from a similar background has been able to write about Wales as if it were his homeland. I could never do that. The experience of Wales must be very different for you although I'm sure you're pretty uneasy about a category such as "Anglo-Welsh poetry".

DA: I feel a considerable association with the Welsh borders, perhaps because my mother's family came from Knighton in Powys. Yet if I lived there I'd feel probably as much if not more an outsider than I do in West Yorkshire. What do these places expect from us anyway?

Am I uneasy about a category such as "Anglo-Welsh poetry"? To be honest I get rather bored with the popular point-scoring board-game called 'O Duw What's My Identity!?' which used to waste so much print in *The Anglo-Welsh Review* and *Poetry Wales* in the '70s and '80s. For better or worse I've a very diverse sense of what Welsh and Anglo-Welsh poets have been and *can be*, and we've only skimmed the surface of that as yet. For some, both inside and outside the Welsh diaspora, such an issue might seem fraught with dire complications. I find such fretting about titles both counter-productive and pointless. I come from a line of Welsh poets yet I see myself as made up of very different realities: Englishness, Welshness and of a presence that writes poetry as well as many other realities intimately related with these. These are givens; I can't see them as problematic.

AH: A curious twist, isn't it, that you and I for quite different reasons moved from Wales to Yorkshire? You implied just now that you feel like an outsider here. Do you see 'The Lighters of Wakefield' reflecting that? It's quite a bleak sequence—moments of love and intimacy shine up now and then but within a violently degraded cityscape.

DA: 'The Lighters' is a sequence of 43 sections and many of these are positive and humorous celebrations of a shared home. The anecdote recounted in XXXIII still cracks me up. And XXXVII is a real lift, or supposed to be.

I fancied forms which let graffiti, street-slang, bus-stop names, Disco, even limericks leech into all the sliding verbal/lexical play, some of which is admittedly quite gnomic:

> Somewhere between Bounty and deserto Rosso
> There was a young miller called Harris
> Made a film in a town called Embarrass

Which is all about Richard Harris's appearance in Lindsay Anderson's film *This Sporting Life*, shot almost exclusively in Wakefield. Yet parts of that sequence, say 'We had the slagheaps…' and 'state of the art security system', are more documentary in feel, just the people of this northern city speaking for themselves (with little mediation from myself in some cases) in the middle of all this urban conflict, light industry and rumbustious play.

John Goodby asked me about these and the 'placing a funnel' poems in *Bela Fawr's Cabaret*. Part of my reply was:

> I want to get into subsonics and sub-atomics, into languages, into the places implied in language, behind the f açade, behind the frontage at big Dance Clubs and shops and council buildings. The designs people have on us through creating surfaces, the underlying structures of environments and interiors for work and leisure are highly important for me. They help shape and channel our lives and so are beguilingly suspect.

When all the Fat Controllers put up signs reading "KEEP OUT" it's like a red rag to my bullish muse. Hey, wake up, what about the evolution of *Memory Screen* and the byways of Sheffield?

AH: Well I didn't mean to overlook the humour in 'The Lighters' or suggest that your treatment of the bleaker side is wholly negative. In fact I think that the balance between seriousness (serious rage, perhaps) and humour is one of the resonances between your work and mine. I guess my *Memory Screen* and *Dante's Barber Shop*, insofar as they're "about" Sheffield, log the familiarity we gradually form with a new environment and the shifts in self-perception this triggers. I felt able to do that only in text-graphic form and it was the first time I used mostly camera-based visuals. I took most of the photos late 1999, early 2000. When I was finishing *Dante's Barber Shop* in 2001 I revisited some of the sites and they'd practically all been demolished—an astonishing instance of urban mutability—giving an entirely unplanned local-historical twist to those pieces. How swiftly evidence of around 200 years of industrial life can be swept away. In Sheffield that life must have been sheer hell for its victims and no one can regret its passing—but it does show how vulnerable the historical/cultural record, or for that matter human memory, can be. The "screen" in *Memory Screen* is both the focus of projection and the screen that hides.

DA: What a good idea to place a CD of *Memory Screen* within the back covers of *Marginalien*. The sequence springs into life now on a PC monitor as freshly as at your Sheffield show which I saw in 2010. A seeming alien, but also palpably inner-urban human, graffito ushers us in. One of the things which impresses is the fact that we flex between inner and outer data of reception. Intimate collages, typewritten sheets segued with newscuttings, emblemata, lakeside gargoyles and abandoned walls with beautiful traces of decay feature among fragments of Dichotomedes, Quarles and Beddoes. You seem to trespass into previously human territories now demolished and/or made off-limits and overlap them with the alchemy of your lexical and graphic discoveries made in the creative space of your own home. In 'For "Gutenberg: the Movie"' as well as *Memory Screen* you also seem to be exploring the gaps and analogies between the lexical/graphic page-space and film screens.

AH: And the backlit screen which is quite different from the projected film image. The variety of new media has opened up a perplexity of grounds for my kind of visual work. Because in making *Memory Screen* I used various media more or less simultaneously you could argue that none of the "versions" is the work itself. In the traditional sense it consists of "originals" which are photo-based collages and electronically treated images spliced with typewritten text. But is that sense of "original" enhanced or undermined by its several transformations? It becomes a many-headed monster but also, I hope, a mixed-media version of the old "memory theatres" which I feel also underlie *Bela Fawr's Cabaret*— appearing in that work of yours as an arena for the performance of a panorama of historical events re-enacted through the quickfire repartee of the music hall.

When we started this conversation I was wondering if there was any factor which might associate the ragged band of West House poets and maybe there's something here. Gavin Selerie's use of stage drama and film, yours of the music hall, Geraldine Monk's of lost or disregarded urban spaces as locus for imaginary conversations, Kelvin Corcoran's of the travelogue, Martin Corless-Smith's of doubtful manuscripts… these are artifices aiming to penetrate what, as you say, lies "behind the façade"… am I pushing this too far?

DA: No, not at all. This raggedy band certainly probes lived spaces around us for realities which are left out of the official record and effaced. That's also one big difference between the modernist approach of David Jones, Pound et al and the tangent taken by Roy Fisher amongst others. Jones was on the look-out for touchstones for anamnesis, in Eliotic terms, fragments to shore against ruin. Fisher, along with the West Housers you mention, looks for what is out of bounds, as in this from *A Furnace*:

> Iron walls
> tarred black, and discoloured,
> towering in the sunlight
> of a Sunday morning on
> Saltley Viaduct.

Arcanum. Forbidden
open space [...]

In your words on *Memory Screen* I like the sense of flux between media that you convey, the "original" proving as elusive as the origins of different memories. After all, I'm interested in the ways your materials interact in each instant rather than an initiating text or image. Although I'm interested in the first text or image too, if truth be known.

AH: I noticed you called that image a "seeming alien" while my text describes it as androgynous and "monkey-like". In fact it was one of two graffiti spraycanned on adjacent garage doors beneath Castle Market and the other was a crude angel-like figure which did have the caption "Alien". I never managed to use that, perhaps because (despite the tempting question about aliens and angels) I felt it didn't hold a particular mystery—whereas "Memory Screen"—why write that on a door, what has it to do with the figure? Perhaps it proved so fertile for me precisely because it's anything but a "touchstone for anamnesis". What you said on that score is dead right although it only appears in a particular line of Anglo-American modernism.

DA: And modernism seems to have been an urban revolution of taste. The poetic hegemony of the urban south has always been a problem in this country. Michael Horovitz's anthology *Children of Albion* was deeply problematic for the right-wing poetry establishment. Iain Sinclair in *Conductors of Chaos* put the success of *Children* down to the zeitgeist of "frivolous times" but despite its obvious failings, lack of women writers in particular, it also contained the work of David Chaloner, Paul Evans, Ian Hamilton Finlay, Andrew Crozier, Roy Fisher, Harry Guest, Lee Harwood, Tom Raworth, Stuart Mills and Anselm Hollo. There's a good variety there, but it's as much a London-based publication as many subsequent anthologies.

AH: I'd like to go into reverse gear and look back much further than we've done so far, back to first enthusiasms. Did poetry play any part in your childhood? It didn't in mine. My mum and dad weren't at all bookish—my dad had one small bookcase with three neat rows of Travel Book Club publications. African explorers and so on—I think he read them going to and from work, on the train between Thornton Heath and London Bridge, blotting out the dreary terraces of South London with imaginings of the savannah. As I remember I didn't read very much before adolescence although I had a passion for Robin Hood books, which I picked up at jumble sales—I guess I was blotting out the same sad terraces with an imaginary Sherwood Forest. It was a friend I had at grammar school, Kevin Holmwood, who got me hooked on reading, when we were twelve or thirteen. American fiction initially— Chandler and Hemingway were particular favourites—Hemingway's short stories and those stunning vignettes from *In Our Time*. Then Kevin hit on e.e. cummings and oh what an excitement—the grasshopper poem with its letters leaping every which way—so that's what poetry can do?' Until then the only poetry I knew was Barham's 'The Jackdaw of Rheims', which I'd recited for a primary school play, and some dull narrative verse from a classroom anthology, of which I only remember Macaulay's 'Horatio at the Bridge'. It wasn't long before Kevin and I were churning out our own typographical extravaganzas, mine on a veteran heavyweight Underwood typewriter which was a fingertip's worst enemy. I started drawing at about the same time, I don't know why but the verbal and visual have always come together for me. I suppose that was what eventually led me to Dada and painter-poets such as Schwitters, and Klee whose paintings so often seem texts you can nearly but never quite decipher.

But that was three or four years later. I can't remember what came after cummings although we soon got going on the Beats. I had a great liking for Gregory Corso

> Should I get married? Should I be good?
> Astound the girl next door
> with my velvet suit and faustus hood?
> Don't take her to movies but to cemeteries

which I still associate with the cemetery near West Norwood Library where I found all the Beat literature, a remarkable gathering not just of City Lights and Grove Press books but many more out-of-the-way publications. I was talking to Allen Fisher about this recently—we didn't know each other then but it was one of his haunts too and we were pondering how it came to have this collection. An individual librarian's choice? I owe him or her a big thank you if so and I'd love to know who s/he was.

So then I was lounging around in Croydon cafes pretending they were bars in San Francisco. No mean feat but certainly not the way to write good poetry. I should say, though, that Croydon was quite buzzy at the time, particularly the revivalist blues clubs—but that in itself shows how we looked to America for, what shall I say, the "real" thing? What swung it round for me was—I vividly remember *Penguin Modern Poets 10* coming out—Henri, McGough and Patten. I saw it, bought it, remember starting to read it at the bus-stop going home—Henri in particular, 'The Entry of Christ into Liverpool'—the sudden realisation that there *was* a way of using the Americans' techniques to make authentically English poems. Maybe I'd had a sense of that before then, reading Adrian Mitchell's blues-inflected work, but the contemporary British verse I'd mostly encountered was in Alvarez' *The New Poetry*, a somewhat misleading title. So my writing found a fresh impetus and I had some apprentice poems published in a few magazines which, apart from *second aeon*, are happily forgotten.

And then for a while I lost interest in poetry altogether. I was expelled from school just before A-levels—apparently I was a "rebellious influence" or some damn thing—and I drifted around for a while. Then I signed up for a philosophy BA course at Northwestern Polytechnic, which at that time meant you were an external student at the University of London. For those three years I read nothing but philosophy, particularly Wittgenstein—which perhaps tells its own tale in that Wittgenstein's texts have a peculiarly poetic quality. After that I was drifting around again and started re-reading Pound. I'd read him in a half-cocked way years before, I remember opening *Section: Rock-Drill* in a Croydon library and falling in love with the look of the page although I hadn't a clue what it was "about".

The "ideogrammic" method was what I was looking for in 1972 or '3 and it started me thinking about writing poetry again. But I also moved down to Dartmoor, lived with my first wife Bridget in a caravan for four years, had no idea what was going on elsewhere—no sense of anything like a poetic "community" or how important that might be for what I was trying to write. But that's something else again—I've rambled on since I asked you what you may have found in your family bookcase.

DA: That reveals some fascinating crossovers with my own reading past. My mother read us poetry from an early age. As a young woman she'd given recitals and comic readings and I think this rubbed off on us; I particularly remember a rhyme about "Three little bearsisses…" My father would quote bits of Shakespeare sometimes and was especially fond of Belloc's 'Tarantella' and Gray's 'Elegy', both of which he'd had to learn by rote during his own schooldays. He was also a talented potter and scribed some phrases on his ceramics. We still have tapes of myself (shockingly revealed to be the verbal equivalent of a 5-year-old miniature George Formby) reading Rupert Brooke's 'The Little Dog's Day' (stumbling over "Jam incipiebo…") and my sister reading William Allingham's 'The Fairies'

> Green jacket, red cap
> And a white owl's feather!

the imagery of which gave me the shivers.

It was revealing to talk to Geraldine Monk about the wonder for her in childhood of certain words in the Latin Mass. We attended the "New" Queen's Street Methodist Chapel in Congleton, which John Wesley had visited. Wesley wrote: "(March 25th, 1768,) I turned aside a little to Burslem and preached in the new house. That at Congleton is about the same size, but better contrived, and better finished." Coming from a Methodist background, in amongst my developing sense of prosody and words were hymns: William Gardiner's setting of 'The Lord's My Shepherd' (1812) which I sang repeatedly and hymns like 'The Saviour has come in His Mighty Power' and 'And can it be…' ('Amazing Grace'), with words by Charles Wesley (1738) set to music by Thomas Campbell in 1825. At the Sunday School at Queens' Street I had my first ever awareness of phonic high jinks, hearing "Pity my simplicity" in the prayer 'Gentle Jesus…' as "Pity mice implicitly". We had a small collection of books: tomes on Bewick, pottery, wood-engravings and amongst them a crimson-bound *Poems from the Nineteenth Century* including Arnold's 'The Forsaken Merman' which I loved for its billowing, submarine effects.

I was fourteen when I came across *Love, love, love, The New Love Poetry* (1967) which included work by the Liverpool poets, Anselm Hollo, Frances Horovitz, Tony Jackson, Paul Evans and a poem by one Tom Pickard titled 'Connie'. (I had long forgotten that poem by the time I sat in Connie Pickard's kitchen chatting over tea before I read at the Morden Tower.) The reason those poems (as well as some from another Corgi book, *It's Love that Makes the World Go Round, Modern Poetry selected from BREAKTHRU International poetry magazine*, 1968) hit me was that here were words about chipshops, tramps, buses, the life all around me and, suddenly, poetry wasn't another world; it was ours and it dealt with the daily events in our lives. A lot of those poems were about sex and sleeping with girls. That was, of course, exciting and I started to write pages of stuff that was part-verse/part-lyric. I was living in the grounds of Red Bank Assessment Unit in Newton-le-Willows and going to school near Liverpool and, all of a sudden, we saw hippies in the streets and felt this Beatles-inspired energy, part of which was obviously ('I am a Walrus') to do with words and imagery. My first draft of a novel, *The Right Side of Wednesday*, was punctuated with Donleavy-esque lexical doodlings. I'd read Hunter Thompson's *Hells Angels* and dropped snippets of American slang into the speech of Scouser characters because it felt hip. Even Gerald Durrell's prose was ransacked. Talk about quaint confusion. At Wigan Tech doing A-levels I discovered William Blake, Chaucer, *Hamlet* and *Dr Faustus*. Blake seemed a friend, the visionary next door. My brother Gwyn was in a rock band and I grew obsessive about trying to make mixtures of lyrics and poetry. I expect half the youth of the country were doing the same.

AH: Yes I was one of those and very bad at it. I guess the point here is that it wasn't the poets but, initially at least, Lennon and McCartney who opened up a way of writing distinctly English songs in what had been a predominantly American idiom. Of course Bob Dylan had shown us how to draw conclusions on the wall but, again, he was as remotely American as any Beat poet. It was fifty years before I got a ride on Highway 61 but even South London had its Penny Lanes where I was already sitting and wondering why.

I'm glad you brought up hymns, which I should have mentioned as a little oasis in my poetry-starved childhood. I loved singing them at primary school morning assemblies, without the faintest idea they might be the words of a master-poet. One of my favourite verses was

> A man that looks on glass,
> On it may stay his eye,
> Or if he pleaseth, through it pass,
> And then the heav'n espy

so maybe it was George Herbert who first taught me the uses of skewed syntax and irregular lines with odd syllable counts. It's easy to forget that for many people and for many generations hymns would have been just about the only poetry in their lives, along with the King James Version. And nonsense rhymes and folk songs and murder ballads. Not quite such a minuscule audience...

DA: Yes, and rhyming cant of course!

A Life in Poetry

Fred Beake

Early Childhood

I used to get worried about the "baby on the tree top". And there was: "I'm the Little Red Engine and I am pulling the King". I used to be sung to by my mother and grandfather: mostly old songs from the *National Song Book*—'The British Grenadiers' or 'Men of Oak' or 'Molly Malone' and an obscure ballad about a frigate called the 'Arethusa'. I was read 'How Horatius Kept the Bridge' because my mother had loved it as a child, despite becoming more or less a pacifist later. And I was read 'Drake's Drum' because I liked an account of the Armada in a child's annual. And because I liked 'Drake's Drum' I was read J.R. Green's account of the Armada in its sonorous Victorian English. My mother read it with severe correctness; my grandfather chanted it like a poem. I used to think of my grandfather reading years later when I heard the great Sorley Mclean.

And on the Radio there was *Take it from Here* (and *The Glums*) and *Journey into Space* and *Hancock's Half Hour*. And there was frequently jazz and light music, which I bounced about to, not to mention the odd classical concert on my father's lap. And there was *Children's Hour* and a poem about dragons of various colours, which overlaps in my mind with *East of the Sun* and *West of the Moon* with its fine pictures by Kay Nielsen and a good book of retellings from the classics.

When I was four I demanded to have *Robinson Crusoe* read to me, because I liked the pictures and my Mother obliged, editing a lot. *Robinson Crusoe* was the book of my childhood. But between four and eight I was also read *Swiss Family Robinson*, *Treasure Island* and *Coral Island*, not to mention Alice and *The Wind in the Willows* and Pooh. I first saw a television at the Coronation. The whole family crowded in front of this little grey box in my Aunt and Uncle's darkened front room at Leek. We did not have our own television till the early Sixties.

LATER CHILDHOOD

When I was five my father's work took us to Wharfedale. We had a lovely house, with views over the river valley. I loved Jack Frost's brilliant abstracts on the windows in winter. I had a tree house from which I climbed up and gazed at the glorious northern sky with its crystalline blues and weird cloud patterns. I often wandered through open fields to the river. I was lucky in my school at East Keswick. There was not even a school gate and while there were walls round the playground they were not forbidding. I remember walking into the main (Junior) class room on my first day and seeing great bursts of September light coming through the window. A very large proportion of the children from this tiny school passed the Eleven Plus without cramming. We just worked hard and were well taught. There was some superb art teaching. We were taught to think of pictures as colour and pattern and not something laboriously drawn and then painted. Music too was of a very high standard. We sang well in two parts. And we worked our way through 'The Wraggle Taggle Gypsies' and 'The Mermaid' and a great variety of other old songs in our singing lessons. Our headmistress from time to time let us have 78s of Grieg and Tchaikovsky on during lunch, provided we listened and did not talk. Pop Music was notable by its absence, though films like *Davy Crockett* or *The Battle of the River Plate* or *Reach for the Sky* were very important.

All this led, however indirectly to my later to my later obsession with English 20th Century music and the interplay between Vaughan Williams, Havergal Brian and my own poetry from the Seventies right through to the present. Folksong and film lurks frequently at the back of that music. In poetry I remember Eliot's 'Skimbleshanks' and a Robin Hood ballad and Marryat's highly satirical 'The Captain stood on the Carronade' (his novel *Midshipman Easy* was also a great favourite) as well as Tennyson's more patriotic 'The Revenge'. Curiously I did very badly with the metrical rhymed exercises, but thought one day I would write poetry. This is very hard to account for. That it might be possible I discovered when I found an extract from Whitman's 'Out of the Cradle Endlessly Rocking' and discovered free verse when I was only eight or nine. The idea was still there waiting to be used when I was sixteen.

There was a fine children's History encyclopaedia with lots of Victorian history paintings. I read a lot about the Elizabethan seamen too. However, I also read a lot of ordinary children's books, not least Arthur Ransome, though I unfashionably preferred *Missee Lee* to *Swallows and Amazons*. But most important (other than *Robinson Crusoe*) was Charles Vivian's retellings of the Robin Hood legends with its fine pictures by Harry Theaker. This (like *Robinson Crusoe*) was essentially an oral text. Whenever my grandparents came to stay I got them to read it for hours at a time.

The leap from East Keswick Primary School to Tadcaster Grammar in 1959 was immense. I went from a school of around 50 children to one of 1350. Overlapping the two schools was a private obsession with the History Books of the Old Testament and later the Books of the Maccabees in the Apocrypha. Essentially a historical rather than a religious interest. Later on in the Sixth Form I did A level Scripture and got interested in Hebrew Poetry, not least its use of parallelism.

However, there was a lot else going on in my head at Tadcaster: Eliot's cat poems, Lawrence's 'Snake', Eliot's 'Journey of the Magi', Tennyson's 'Morte d'Arthur', 'The Rime of the Ancient Mariner', Browning's 'My Last Duchess' (and not least Burn's 'Tam O'Shanter', which was the beginning of my love of Scots poetry); Shaw's *St Joan* and bits of Sheridan and Pinter. There was also school trips by special train to Stratford to see the RSC in *A Merchant of Venice* and *A Midsummer Night's Dream*, and a very well done Anouilh play at York Rep. And I was listening to a huge range of music. Pretty well everything from the Black and White Minstrels to Schoenberg; and I knew the Beatles' *Help*, *Rubber Soul* and *Revolver* almost by heart.

My obsession with history continued. By myself I read about the Crusades and later (stimulated by Rosemary Sutcliffe's *Lantern Bearers*) I got into the strange mysteries of post Roman Britain. Because of this everyone assumed that I would do History at University and indeed I went to Sussex to do History in 1967. However, the Fates were playing odd games. I did not do English A Level, but threw myself mainly into the Modernist Romantic of MacNeice, Edith Sitwell, Kathleen Raine, Dylan Thomas and above all Eliot. However I dipped into an awful lot of other things and formed lasting contradictory likings for American Poetry (W.C. Williams and Whitman) and the Victorian/

early Twentieth Century rhymed tradition. As a whole this was a liking for a poetry that is equally sound and sense. And I was doing Latin A Level, because it would be useful for history and finding I enjoyed Virgil. Amid all this stuff in my head I was surviving a series of troubling family crises. Said crises, plus usual adolescent traumas started me writing my own poetry. Yet my early poems often emerged in solitary cycling expeditions over wild countryside (e.g. The Pentlands in an early windswept Easter in a trip that took me from Wharfedale to Oban and back in ten days).

At Sussex I did not take to academic history but spent much time devouring Bunting and Kamau Brathwaite and Okigbo and Soyinka and Zukofsky and Roy Fisher and Montgomery's *Circe* and Saint-John Perse's *Amers* and Williams and Pound. I got deep into Waley and A.C. Graham's versions of old Chinese poetry, especially Tu Fu. Having dropped Latin as an academic subject I promptly got into Propertius, Horace, Tibullus and Catullus. Perhaps I should have switched to Literature, but somehow I did not.

In the end I left without a degree, but having acquired a daughter and a young wife. For two years we made do in a cold cottage on the edge of the North York Moors and I wrote a lot and also translated Desnos' *Night of Nightless Loves*, (see Etruscan's *The Bees of the Horizon*). A style emerged that has lasted, however much it has transformed itself. I arguably read less in these North Yorkshire years, but discovered Sorley Maclean, Macdiarmid, Crichton Smith and Mackay Brown.

THE SEVENTIES

The Seventies really began for me in Bath in 1972 and they were hard. First a bookshop job, then unemployment, then bread-van driving.

I joined the Circle in the Square (led by Bill Pickard), that met in Bristol at the Arts Centre in Kings Square. Here at least there was poetic company: two Wednesdays evenings a month we read own work, one week a particular author, the other whatever people wanted to read. And there I met the admirable Charles Hobday, who had links to *Our Time* (the strictly non-Party magazine of the young 1940s Communist writers) but was also to write the life of *Our Time's* editor Edgell

Rickword. Rickword was also important to me for his quasi-surreal poetry (the earliest important such work by an Englishman) and his fine satires (notably *To the Wife of a None Interventionist Statesman*). Partly at least because of Charles I began my obsession with Shelley and the whole Milton to Byron period. This led to my only critical book *The Imaginations of Mr Shelley* (University of Salzburg 1993), but also to satire appearing in my own work.

However, the very low level of so much that went on at the Arts Centre always worried me. Nobody except Charles seemed interested in how sounds and rhythms interact; and yet the failure to redefine our rhythmic practices seemed and seems to me at the root of the essential failure of modern poetry to grow beyond a certain point. The lessons of Eliot, Sitwell, the Thomases (Edward and Dylan), Williams and H.D. have gone unregarded. However Jon Silkin started publishing the odd poem or translation in Stand and Xenia Press produced rather beautiful pamphlets of my *Asides for Quintus* and my Desnos' version. Silkin indeed gave me enormous support till his death in 1997, printing my collection *The Fisher Queen* in 1988 and giving me review work in the Nineties.

Then I joined Chris Hunte's Suspension Poetry. Chris had edited *Perfect Bound* in Cambridge and had J.H. Prynne for a tutor. Through readings he organised I heard Wendy Mulford and through her discovered Doug Oliver's work, but best was an elderly Bunting with a bad cold reading 'Briggflatts' at Clifton College marvellously. Yet the reaction at Clifton College was distressing, with an obvious dislike by the numerous Clifton College part of the audience for this poetic outsider. Chris got me reading Prynne, the most inimitable poet there is, but no less considerable for that! I had found Bill Griffiths' *Cycles* from Jeff Nuttall's *Guardian* column some while before this and was hooked for life. I also came across that considerable Irish outsider Brian Coffey in the late Seventies and the more conservative, but in his way equally adventurous, Edward Boaden Thomas with his fine intricate long poem the *Twelve Parts of Derbyshire*. And there was Heath Stubbs' *Artorius* and Sally Purcell's *Dark of Day* and David Jones' *The Sleeping Lord* to fly the flag for the old Romantic cause. Not a bad lot of poets, but the world was succumbing to the dubious charms of Seamus Heaney etc and I was increasingly conscious I was moving at a tangent to what was officially approved of.

Workshops, Editing and Festivals

The Eighties and Nineties were a difficult time personally. I was a single parent and struggling along on a very inadequate income from jobbing gardening, yet it was also the time I got involved with festivals and editing on a large scale.

The Bath Writers' Workshop began in 1978, when I literally collided with Ian Burton (later a not undistinguished opera producer but then a lecturer at Newton Park College) who was advertising a poetry reading dressed as a dragon. For a couple of years the group was Ian, Ryl Lovell from Bristol (who Bill Pickard strangely misinformed me lived in Bath, but it was a happy error, that led to *The Poet's Voice*, which she partly funded) and myself. Notably Ian and I gave a public reading of 'The Waste Land'.

Then Louis Hawkins contacted us and he brought a lot of vigour and drew in various younger members. Gradually more people joined such as the short story writer, Daniel Richardson from Bristol, Keith Spenser (the editor of the *Green Book* and just before he died founder of *Modern Painters*), Roger Davie Webster (who did much of our printing, including *The Poet's Voice* for some years and was a close personal friend), Linda Saunders (later reviews editor of the *Green Book* and later for many years assistant editor of *Modern Painters*); Douglas Clark of *Lynx* and his own well known website and *The Cat Poems*; and not least Robert/Skip Palmer (later typesetter for Salzburg UP and etruscan).

We ran a large poetry festival in 1981 at the Holbourne Museum as part of the Bath Arts Association fringe, with Logue, Fanthorpe, Wain, Purcell, Tomlinson, Silkin, Dom Sylvester Houédard, Tom Pickard, Frances Horovitz and numerous poets from Bath and Bristol (Hobday, Adams, Chris Hunt, myself, Ryl Lovell, Louis Hawkins, and Les Arnold and Ian Burton, who were colleagues at Newton Park). Inevitably we lost money and Bath Arts Association demanded something much smaller the next year, which was dreary (apart from Wendy Mulford and Libby Houston) and then they dropped us.

Then Bill Duthie (our Treasurer) thought of Walcot Village Hall as a venue for a series of readings. Walcot Village Hall is an old mortuary chapel in an ancient graveyard, which gave a distinctly Gothic tinge to the proceedings. Here we had poets as different as Bill Griffiths,

Roy Fisher, Liz Lochhead, Ken Smith, Anna Adams, Tony Harrison, Douglas Dunn, Ian Crichton Smith and Edwin Morgan. I remember vividly putting on Bill Griffiths and Douglas Dunn. Douglas was my guest. I gave him a meal before. "Who was this Bill Griffiths?" He had never heard of him. I attempted to fill in the blank, but he needed to drink some whiskey with me before proceeding. I don't know if Bill had similar difficulties about appearing with an establishment poet, but certainly they were distinctly wary of one another. However, the air of competition between the poets seemed very conducive and we had a good event. I heard years later Bill was quoting Douglas to a mutual friend after the reading, which is how it should be.

In the aftermath of the two Bath festivals after a gap of a couple of years Bath Writers went on a picnic and wondered how a festival could be run successfully. We came up with the idea of a County of Avon festival with anyone who wanted putting on events. I made the initial proposal to the Avon Arts Officer Roger Bale and a far-reaching organisation was set up, which eventually ran for around a decade. There was a very good initial one month festival with over a hundred events and numerous national poets, though perhaps it was symbolic for the future that my suggestion of Liz Lochhead and Roy Fisher for the opening event at the Arnolfini was rejected in favour of the current circus of poets (Angels of Fire, which included Libby Houston, but little else of any quality). However after that we lost funding for more than minimum staff and the festival had an increasing tendency to be sucked into being an adjunct of Social Services with all too little attention to real poetry. It taught me, who was as chairman for the first two years, that the bad majority will swamp the good minority in poetry and not even realize.

However, what was going on in Bristol and Bath was by no means my only poetic contacts. I got to know William Oxley of *Littack* fame from Brixham and Brian Merrikin Hill (editor of *Pennine Platform* and a fine poet and translator). I attended the Accent on Poetry meetings at Cromford from 1981 and have been Programme Secretary since 1987. Here I met Hugh Mackinley, Edward Boaden Thomas, Doris Corti etc. My knowledge of the scene constantly expanded through the Poetry Library and Alan Halsey's Poetry Bookshop.

At the same time as all this I was editing the Mammon Press: Silkin's *Footsteps on a Downcast Path*, Nicholas Johnson's *Haul Song* and *Land*, Coffey's *Topos*, Hobday's *How Goes the Enemy*, Jenny Johnson's *Becoming*, Michael Ivens *New Divine Comedy*, Merrikin Hill's Saint-Pol-Roux versions etc. I also ran *The Poet's Voice* magazine with help with morale and money from Ryl Lovell (whose blend of the Romantic and Imagist deserves to be much better known) and much unpaid printing by Roger Davie Webster and Skip Palmer. I tried to blend the Avant-garde with the Romantic and to some degree the Mainstream, though it was always difficult to get mainstream contributions for a small press low-circulation magazine. Notable moments included a Bill Griffiths retrospective, the bringing together of Edward Boaden Thomas' later work in a special issue etc.

The Poet's Voice lapsed in 1991. I then got involved with University of Salzburg Press and James Hogg and Wolfgang Görtschacher and the magazine was revived for much of the Nineties. In the end I withdrew because I felt we were getting too far from the original *Poet's Voice*. Görtschacher continued the magazine as *Poetry Salzburg*, with my blessing. In 1992 James Hogg and his University of Salzburg Press kindly published most of my poetry and translations to that date in *The Whiteness of Her Becoming* and followed it up with a book of my Shelley essays and two further volumes of poetry. I persuaded him to publish Jenny Johnson, Steve Sneyd, Edward Boaden Thomas and Brian Merrikin Hill. Not incidentally a vanity press as some have suggested, Hogg paid for his numerous publications in the last resort out of his own pocket, the ideal patron you might say.

James invited me to the 1993 Salzburg Shelley Conference. Here I met Peter Russell, who had to be banned from smoking his very strong cigarettes in the conference room, but gave a good Shelley paper and whom I chatted with about Vaughan Williams and Xenakis (whom he had met). In 1996 there was a memorable retirement conference for Hogg at Salzburg, with participants as different as William and Patricia Oxley, Silkin, Joy Hendry of Chapman, Peter Mortimer of *Iron*, plus various avant-gardists and academics. There was a memorable concluding reading in the University of Salzburg Library, where after three poets plus their Austrian translators had taken the whole first half, it was hurriedly announced everyone else would be limited to three minutes.

Meanwhile back at home there was an effective split in Bath Writers in the later '80s between the determined work-shoppers, who worshipped the Arvon Foundation and had turned their back on the very radical and the rest of us, who had more advanced ideas on the whole. We talk to one another to this day but ceased to meet as a group. At this point the young Nicholas Johnson came on the scene and there were several evenings on the terrace of a house in Larkhall with him and me reading Griffiths, Zukofsky, Rafferty and Maclean. About then *A Mingling of Streams* was published by Salzburg (1989), which gathered in one book the best of *The Poet's Voice* and fascinated Nicholas.

I got Nicholas, and his wife Kate, Ryl Lovell's studio up in Wiltshire for a year. We started *Haul Song* together then, but increasingly Nicholas took it over, with me muttering in the margins. Eventually Nicholas went to Keele University, before getting thrown out for failing the first year and ending up living at Newcastle-under-Lyme in a couple of very cold houses. Yet this disaster led to Nicholas founding the very successful first Six Towns Festival. Because of the disintegration of the Avant-garde in the '80s there was a feeling that this was a new beginning for them. My reading at the first festival was my first outing with *Whiteness of Her Becoming* and I felt it went all wrong. Curiously I talked to Harriet Tarlo years after and found she had liked it. However I was not aware of her that year, but at a later one, when she more or less took on looking after Hamish Henderson in his flapping white shirt.

The later Six Towns Festivals tend to mingle in my head. Alice Notley and Doug Oliver came at least once. Doug was the more reticent. Having read *Whisper Louise* I wish I had talked to him more. Both read well, though I always felt Alice has a star quality as a reader that Doug perhaps lacked. I always remember Alice's story that as a young poet (in San Francisco or maybe New York) the impecunious group she was in used to read cookery books together and carefully plan elaborate menus they could not afford to cook. I had a wonderful talk with Robert Creeley, which was almost entirely about W.C. Williams. He agreed emphatically that Williams in his heart of hearts was a Romantic and not a Realist but a Poet of the Imagination, who turned the Imagination in a wholly new direction. Roy Fisher was always there or thereabouts. I told him when Nicholas moved to Newcastle-under-Lyme to take him seriously and Roy did, to his great credit.

I think the great star of Newcastle under Lyme (other than perhaps Alice Notley) was Sorley Maclean. He gave some quite remarkable readings, which towered over everyone else in their ability to combine sense and communal feeling with extraordinary verbal music. I looked after him and Rene for I think the last occasion. After lunch before the reading he was very edgy and Rene and I took him for a walk. "What am I to read," he said: "The first year I read what I normally read and the second year I read the ones I occasionally read." "Oh read the ones you don't normally read," I said. Rather to my surprise he largely took my advice. The Newcastle-under-Lyme festivals remain quite extraordinary. There was an atmosphere and buzz I have never encountered elsewhere in Poetry in my lifetime.

Through the Millennium

In the Nineties I discovered Classical Greek poetry in the original. It took me back to my first beginnings and reminded me that modern poetry *can* combine sound and sense, without having to be one or the other, (which seems to me to have been the tendency of poetry in my lifetime). The result has been an exploration of both lyric and dramatic monologue in *The Cyclops*, my Shearsman *New and Selected* and the recent *The Old Outlaw*.

After taking a Classics degree at Bristol in the early 2000s I moved to Torquay, where I have been exposed to the very adequate mainstream Torbay Festival run by Patricia Oxley of *Acumen* and Tim Allen's more adventurous Plymouth Language Group with its way-out readings and discussion group, not to mention Torbay Poets run by Crystal Tuckfield. I have also been going to the Callander Festival, run by Sally Evans of Poetry Scotland, and found something different and fresh.

What Lies Behind *Curtains*?
Or What Is Truth When Recounting Memories?

PAUL BUCK

That title arrived as soon as I sat to write a few reminiscences on my magazine *Curtains* that ran with sturdy thighs through the 1970s. A few years ago Iain Sinclair whipped into place an anthology, *London: City of Disappearances*, in which his introduction recounts a remark by Lee Harwood relating to our time in Better Books in the late 1960s. Unfortunately Lee was confusing me with another employee, Paul Selby, though the Penguin paperback edition didn't make the correction, the vagaries of memories being left to run their course. And that is what we live with, waves and weaves of memories that narrate various realities so that myths can become legends. Or, as James Fox said in relation to the Cammell/Roeg film, *Performance*, when asked to clarify or refute any of the myths that had grown up around the film, "When the legend becomes fact, print the legend," a quote lifted from John Ford's *The Man Who Shot Liberty Valance*.

For convenience, let's begin in Better Books, in London, around 1967–68, because that is where I worked, and that is where chance and circumstance collided and developed into that strategic project that was *Curtains*. The bookshop, which was also a meeting place, proffered an extraordinary array of writers on a daily basis. Many left their wares for sale, snapped up eagerly by the staff, "sold out" no sooner had the depositor set off along the Charing Cross Road. Some are mentioned in the Sinclair anthology noted above, the full version of that text online in *Visions of the City*, under the title *Street of Dreams*. Though my interests at that point encompassed theatre, poetry and prose, I was drawn specifically to that oddity often called prose-poetry, or if not that precisely, at least to forms of prose writing that veered away from conventional fiction. I soon realized that my textual research would require places to be published. Dulan Barber at John Calder had called me in to discuss a manuscript I had submitted. On the horizon I saw that there was some exciting writing under way across the Channel. While others were pussyfooting with the *nouveau roman*, I wanted to jump into bed with other writings, many with leanings of a sexual nature.

160

This wasn't too hard to understand as my mother was Italian, and I had been brought up a good Catholic, at least until reason gained the upper hand. And so, when I asked John Calder directly one day if he had plans for further English translations of Georges Bataille and Philippe Sollers, he suggested that if I wanted to read those writers, or similar, I'd have to read them in French. And so I did. And *Curtains* was born in the process, a magazine that became a public research space where I could juxtapose my own writings alongside the work of writers I read, met or corresponded with. As it sparked into life, after a spluttering start with a trial magazine, *Snow* (one edition), that had included Andrew Crozier, David Coxhead, Jeff Nuttall (early *People Show* scripts), Bob Cobbing, Stephen Vincent, Penelope Shuttle, Harold Norse, Christine Bowler…, I moved from London to Maidstone in Kent. My trips back and forth to the metropolis were shaped around part-time work for Fulcrum Press, placing their books (as a "rep") in various shops around London or on sorties to key cities around the country like Oxford, Cambridge, Liverpool, Manchester, Brighton, Birmingham, etc. Reading manuscripts at Fulcrum enabled me to pick up on the prose of Roy Fisher and Larry Eigner, I recall.

Like anything of real interest there is no linear narrative to unravel and plot the course neatly, there is always a weave, a mosaic, a labyrinth… Names too can be strewn left and right. The formidable young English prose writers who intrigued me in those early days included David Coxhead, Doug Oliver, Martin Wright, Paul Selby, Kris Hemensley… names that prove the point today of how hard it is to carve one's way with adventurous prose writing on this little island. And again by naming names I omit names, neglect names… Tomorrow night I might include others.

The French connections expanded rapidly, courtesy of my friendship with Claude Royet-Journoud (whom I met in Better Books), whose generosity knew no bounds, with daily letters and notes telling me about poets and writers, or sending me their texts, or instructing publishers, writers and magazines to send me their work, feeding my voracious appetite through the 1970s, for no sooner had the decade started than we abandoned the sweet-smelling air of Maidstone with its breweries and confectionary factories for a millstone grit house on the

Pennines, next door to Mike Haslam, who had found the property for Glenda and me, and our child.

I wasn't to know that our move from the relative comfort of Southern England to a degree of isolation on the edge of the windy moorland in the North would give me most of a decade to dig in, produce a magazine and set the ground work for the 1980s and beyond after we returned to the South.

What is key in my research, the term that I have always applied to *Curtains*, and indeed my own writings, is that there was never any attempt to edit in terms of gender, age, fame, nationality... or place of living or indeed place of education. This was research that went wherever the needs required. And as the issues took shape, another important development occurred when *Curtains* adopted the form of an essay. I was never interested in producing a magazine that just presented the latest writings of a particular person, or that encouraged unsolicited submissions (often from people who had never seen the magazine in the first place), with intent to market the whole caboodle as a representative product of "contemporary poetry". It was always about juxtapositions of contributors and contributions. The possibility was there because I was selecting from a diversity of French published sources, and then finding links to English and American poets/writers whose work I thought tied in on various levels. In that respect it became easier to produce a magazine that was almost an essay, a work that you could read from start to finish, allowing ideas and issues to evolve, the contributions having another context than their own specific interests. As the magazine progressed some of these writers, including the French, would respond to an edition and send me work that they thought would interest me. I think of Eric Mottram's essay on Derrida, or Allen Fisher's piece on Ulli Freer, or Robert Kelly's poems. Or again, Robert Clark on Soutine. Others too wrote things they said they would not have written otherwise. I'm sure I was also taking my lead from the French magazines I was reading, not only *Change*, Jean Pierre Faye's magazine, that had developed a strong bond with me, to the extent that I ventured to Paris and sat in on "collectif" meetings, forging friendships and strong links with Faye, and indeed Mitsou Ronat, to name two of the group. There were other magazines from *Chemin de Ronde, Dérive, Erres, Exit, Fragment, Gramma, Minuit, Obliques, Tel Quel...* that contributed to and influenced my editing, and indeed invited me into their pursuits.

The fact that many women were taken on board, (Mitsou Ronat, Danielle Collobert, Agnès Rouzier, Michèle Richman, Rosmarie Waldrop, Lydia Davis, Geraldine Monk, Laure, Ulrike Meinhof, Veronica Forrest-Thomson, Wendy Mulford, Carlyle Reedy, Glenda George, artists like Susan Hiller, Gina Pane, Colette Deblé, Cosey Fanni Tutti, Elaine Shemilt, Alison Wilding… and these are the ones who spring to mind without checking the contents pages) at a time when there "appeared" to be few women writing in these fields, had more to do with my interest in the ideas they were pursuing and the sensibilities of their writings and approaches. (I note that Anne-Marie Albiach and Jacqueline Risset were also in my trajectory, and each appeared in work I did away from *Curtains*, and Kathy Acker bounded into my path just as the magazine ended, so became part of a satellite publication *fête,* and later the book *Spread Wide*.) The fact that I took on many more French writers than others was more to do with aspects of their work with language and "writing", and their openness to explore with me and invite me into their research spaces. At that time, Georges Bataille, Maurice Blanchot, Edmond Jabès… were still gaining footholds in France. There was barely any interest here or in America. Instead I received countless unsolicited translations of surrealist writers, which I turned back, as I viewed a slew of magazines that would be receptive to those writings. My interest was unexplored territory. That said, I needed translators. I would regularly write to British poets and ask if they were interested in translating a poet or poem I had found, or a short prose text. Sometimes it worked, most times it didn't. Paul Auster and Lydia Davis however were interested in Bataille and Blanchot, as I was, so they became allies and helped to open up that avenue. And Rosmarie Waldrop was working in a major way through the work of Jabès. That was a real bonus. But, in the main, those asked had other poets they wanted to translate, some of whom were amenable to my interests. So we had to take on the rest. I always thought it would be good to just focus on one or two writers/poets as those above had determined for themselves, good for oneself as a translator (and invariable for one's own writing), and also good for the one translated, putting them on the map in a better way. But that was not the job I had set myself. I wanted to give a breadth to the field I was exploring, to give context to the French as well as to the English-speaking contributors. To have translated more of Roger Laporte's work would have been valuable, to name one who interested, and still interests. And I never got to grips at that time with Matthieu Bénézet, which I regret tremendously. Or... oh dear, the floodgates could be opened. We had too much on our plate.

I say we, for Glenda George, my partner during that decade, was instrumental in taking on board text after text that I found. Her days became cliff-top adventures as I presented her with books and magazines with markers protruding, the results of working through the post, reading the publications sent or asked for. Or others that had journeyed back with us from our expeditions to Paris. One time we went for a six-week trip to Paris, then Mauregny-en-Haye to stay with Bernard Noël, then on to Lausanne to stay with the editor for whom I wrote crime essays (the only paying work I had at that time), to find on return that our neighbour had borrowed a mailbag from our postman to house the daily influx. That bag was full to the brim with letters and packets and took me five months to work through.

And whilst the French exploits were afoot, I was also breaking the boundaries into art, particularly performance art. And the natural progression of those drawn in from a British poetry world continued to link with those often rounded up as Cambridge poets, John James, Peter Riley, Rod Mengham... and others who found themselves in another satellite publication, *Twisted Wrist,* like John Wilkinson and David Trotter. But nothing was simple. All these poets and writers were not members of cliques to me. My affiliations with Allen Fisher, Ulli Freer and others were key to my research. Ulli lived within the echo of a shotgun blast across the valley, outside Sowerby Bridge, before eventually moving to Leeds. Ulli chose to move back to London at the end of the 1970s, at the same time as we moved back to Maidstone, because of various circumstances, but also to distance ourselves from the tensions around the Yorkshire Ripper—we felt vulnerable with a child who walked daily to school along a country road, and Glenda had also picked up the phone to an "I'm Jack" phone call, and decided to engage with the caller, which was ultimately unnerving when it became known not long after that he was suspected of being the Ripper.

I always felt I was an outsider because I was not part of one group or another. And my involvements with those in America veered across their groups, taking in poets like Larry Eigner, Cid Corman, Robert Kelly, George Quasha, Jed Rasula, Jerome Rothenberg and David Antin… or the younger L=A=N=G=U=A=G=E poets, Charles Bernstein and Bruce Andrews, and then others. It was a mosiac, not a jigsaw puzzle that fitted together neatly.

For the final few years *Curtains* received a small regional grant to help with costs. It paid for the basic printing only. I typed the plates and we collated and staple-bound the volumes ourselves on the living-room floor, which was back-breaking once it became a tightly-packed 210-page A4 issue. I was including such large extracts of Bataille, Blanchot, Faye, Jabès, Noël, Laporte, Marcelin Pleynet, Charles Juliet and others alongside the English-language contributions, and the artists' work from Gina Pane, Jean-Luc Parant, Vladimir Velickovic, Ramon Alejandro, Robert Clark, Brian Catling, Paul Neagu, Susan Hiller, Henri Maccheroni, etc, etc. Few of them were barely known at the time. As the printing bill was paid, using the finance from a number of subscriptions enabled me to post further free copies into what I hoped would be good homes. (The time-consuming translation work by all of us was of course done for free.) Today I have almost no copies left as so many were given away. But it seems to have had some influence. Selections from it have been re-edited and appeared in publications here and in America. And offers to do an anthology periodically appear. An anthology is feasible, but not in the way that most construe it. I would need to do an anthology in a far more radical way, re-evaluating the whole notion. I couldn't just gather all the texts together, and agree to play the historical acceptability card, and indeed I'm not sure time is on my side as recent research into copyright and permissions makes the task somewhat daunting. Gone are the days when Blanchot would write to tell me not to bother with official permission from the Gallimard office and just to press on with publishing (on that occasion almost two-thirds of his book *Death Sentence*), and leave it to him to explain to M. Gallimard directly what I was doing. I know many friends who still have cupboards full of their publications because they were afraid to give them away. To me the point was (and still is) that if you believe in your publication you should get it to those readers who seem interested.

And so when *Curtains* blew up, mainly because I was drawing together questions around censorship on various fronts, reflected in my own writings, it ended sharply and I moved my research on to other projects, from my new base outside London. With Roger Ely I staged a week-long event around Bataille, called *Violent Silence*, that included nightly performances of *My Mother*, translated and adapted for the stage, ventured into music worlds (producing a handful of albums in the process), film worlds (making long and short films), and also the art world as a platform to pull the threads together as necessary. It's not that I moved away from the poetry world, but that I allowed the poetry to expand into other ventures. I have never seen that any art-form or discipline should be closed within itself. Not for my interests. Perhaps it would be easier to be a playwright and write plays for the Royal Court (I use that example because that is the first place I was attached to, prior to Better Books, around the time of Edward Bond's *Saved*). It would have made life so much easier. Or to be a painter and explore another language on a canvas. That is one type of "bliss" that I've imagined for myself that will never occur. Instead, I suspect that with hindsight my work has been to focus on particular concerns and to find the disciplines and avenues to venture into for that limited time, with varying degrees of success. But then again what is success? "I don't compose objects but the journey from one object to the other. The route one travels is more important than the vehicle one travels in," as Gérard Grisey, the French composer wrote. I am more interested in being part of a relay team than being the solo sprinter or distance runner. I always relished taking third leg in the house team at school, because I loved running and leaning into that final bend, handing to the anchor man, who was usually not in the lead, so it wasn't a matter of winning, but participating. That seems to set me out of step with what one is supposed to be or do as a writer or artist. And yet I am still working, more than ever, harder than ever, and noticing that besides the concerns that have always been there to explore, there seems to be a very marked way in which I work, something that started with *Curtains*, as I noted, and that involves the constant pulling out of threads from the mass of my notes and resources to weave them into another work. Or, as I said in terms of the book I recently published, *A Public Intimacy*, based on a pile of scrapbooks that I've kept since 1964, I pull out and plant ideas as disturbances on the tracks so that the reader picks them up unconsciously, holding them until triggered later in the text. It is this process that is a feature of my work, and I know that angle took root during that period editing *Curtains*.

So, dear Geraldine, I can see where you are coming from with the notion of London, Cambridge… and "elsewhere", a sense that those outside those two prime locations or "schools" are excluded, or are on the road to exclusion with the climate as perceived. I recall when we first connected in the 1970s, when I was living outside Hebden Bridge, overlooking Mytholmroyd—the birthplace of one Ted Hughes—an irony given my interests which has not escaped me. From that lofty height at Foster Clough (someone called it my "ivory tower", trying to be facetious when they actually wanted me to publish their poetry and not the incomprehensible "stuff" they said I did publish), the *Curtains* caught the breeze, if not something more akin to gusts and gales.

Elsewhere is indeed the place where I am best "categorized" when it comes to just about everything that I'm associated with. Indeed I think that that is the plus side of what I've been about all these years. And whilst I could probably make a good case for neglect of my efforts, I could also say that if I hadn't been elsewhere in every respect I would not have done the various works. In fact I've quite enjoyed the notion of being at a remove.

Some of the fascinations that evolved from *Curtains* and from involvements in Parisian circles, like *Change*, which itself allowed admittance to their circle for Peter Riley, Doug Oliver, Allen Fisher, Ulli Freer, Glenda and myself, was to be in Paris and not to hang out around the English-language depot of Shakespeare & Co, but to attend meetings in back rooms in the Rue de Seine, or various restaurants, bars and apartments around St Germain and the Left Bank. *Change* also generated an Anthology of English poetry, that shifted around a bit before finally shaping as a co-editing with Pierre Joris, an anthology that was chosen to suit the tastes and interests of the contemporary French poetry scene. It was immensely enjoyable to venture to Paris and read in Obliques Bookshop with Ulli and Jerry Rothenberg and to have an assortment of French poets, *Change* writers, Jabès, and others I didn't know jammed into the shop to listen. Or to do a reading at another venue and be approached by a warm and enthusiastic Henri Michaux.

Elsewhere has meant more to me than being tied to anything specific. Elsewhere was where it was happening and still is happening. Today I'm trying to reduce the explorations of all those years where film and music have had their play, or the various transgressive behaviours around criminality and sexuality that have had their fill, or the more recent involvements in Portuguese culture. Since those heady days of *Curtains*, those days in the hills, I've lived whole lives in other fields. But the real nub for me is the use of the term "career". That is an anathema and a misconception. I might well be asked to write songs for someone today, but I have to decline because there is nothing I need to actually explore in that field at this time. I do not wish to take on anything just because I have a track record in that activity. Unless there is a biting need for research, there is no need. I see ahead of me the possibility of some years with art and writing projects. I'm very lucky and privileged, I know, to be able to have enough health and energy to keep up the drive that is necessary to be always exploring, never resting back on possible laurels. And that again is part of the pleasure of being elsewhere. For me being elsewhere is being somewhere.

I think I've stopped teaching/tutoring in the Art School system, bar one or two lectures; I think I have almost come to the end of editing, as I do not keep up with "now" in the broadest sense. That need for dissemination of my passions is now bound into my work, and seems to have taken the form of work/writings that offer possibilities for others to research and take further. The core today seems to be about exploring archives and resources to make something new. One challenge is not to slip into the trap of romanticism and nostalgia, but to find the edge, and to play in the margins. And indeed I still have not properly tackled the idea that my mother was Italian, though I have drafted an essay for a possible book with a couple of others who have not explored their Italian-ness enough either. Perhaps the word "elsewhere" is better served by the word "margins". I live and work in the margins, but treat those margins as the centre, according them my time, energy... and passion. Perhaps if you live your life with passion you make it difficult to be excluded.

The Little Woman at Home

Glenda George

My present home in northern Scotland sits facing southwards from a vantage point 750 feet above sea level; the surrounding landscape is hill farm below and moorland above.

Forty-ish years ago, a similar house in similar surroundings sheltered me and Paul Buck and was the fertile centre of *Curtains* magazine (about which I am sure there is much detail elsewhere). This place was Foster Clough, perched on the hill above Hebden Bridge, West Yorkshire. Even then, this was a place for name-dropping amongst people of a certain age or aspiration. I understand it remains so, continuing to attract the creative, the intellectual, artists and artisans, the world embracing and the world-weary.

Foster Clough was also the venue for the occasional poetry reading and a watering hole for visiting writers and artists from far flung parts, for this was a time when creative English folk were sourcing inspiration from abroad. This was world-writing, when the differing cultures offered something for those tired of English literary tradition. I refuse to name names. In truth the names were never the important thing for me so I have forgotten many; what I have not forgotten are the works, the words and rhythms and the energies that flowed.

The majority of these visitors were male; when women visited (even if they were writers in their own right) it was as part of a couple. Attaching oneself (however loosely) to a respected or, most often, popular male was still one of the ways that a woman could get her work acknowledged. Many of us hung on the coat-tails of our menfolk and oftentimes this was productive, offering additional opportunities to make our voices heard. There were women writers who were forging ahead on their own, drawing from inner strength or that of the sisterhood—perhaps they were right, and I was wrong, for many of those women are still successfully publishing today. And then there were those like myself who saw no virtue in investigating or analysing the current (i.e. 1970) female situation, who looked to bigger horizons and what we thought were more important notions. What were art and literature for? How could they change the world?

Much of the activity at Foster Clough was alien to our surroundings; we were notorious amongst local people. We were incomers; we were young, mostly from cities, bringing radical ideas and possibilities to a rural community. The individual Yorkshire neighbours were forthright, honest, warm and loyal. They were friends. The Corporation saw possible mayhem.

It was a hard time for a young mother; it was without thought (I certainly did not question it, even though, in my writing, I was assertive and inquiring and musing on a woman's place in the world) that I assumed the greatest responsibility for the house and home and what I call the "Daniel factor"—our young son. Paul and I had little opportunity for any sort of conventional, paid work, with no car, no public transport and the nearest large town—Halifax—ten miles distant. There was the "welfare state" which kept body and soul together from time to time—although we managed quite often without it—and ensured that Daniel got fed properly, once a day at school. This was our downfall.

The "Corporation" that I mentioned earlier, in the person of one particular local councillor, took a sudden interest in this "Literary Magazine" that was making the news. *Curtains* had received a small grant from the local arts association, which helped with the production costs, substantially expensive for a couple with no regular income on which to depend. For a period, there were headlines in the newspapers about the "pornographic magazine" (the councillor hadn't read it of course) being published with public money. We lost the minimal state benefit that had paid for our son's school meals and helped with his school uniform costs. Our Yorkshire friends, loyal to the last, refused to believe the picture that was being painted. The important thing about all this was that modern ideas were being attacked in an underhand way and an innocent family—at least our son was truly innocent— was being hounded and vilified. This was the penalty to be paid for trying to widen knowledge and understanding, for attempting to show that literature and art can have some influence in the world. And throughout this, I was the little woman at home, trying to establish my own reputation and protect that of those whose works had been published in a magazine with which I had an association.

During those years at Foster Clough, we were among those who stomped the claggy, furrowed ground with our Wellington boots so that the next generation could cross at a run, barefoot and carefree, bringing yet newer ideas and ways of working. *Curtains* and the associated events that happened at the Clough were not the only forerunners who paved the way for today's renewed interest in poetry or conceptual art but from the standpoint of a little woman at home—writing in isolation (for my work was certainly different from that of Paul Buck—even though we often collaborated on translations)—there is a certain sense of satisfaction that I was a part of that time.

Obstructions for women certainly remain in pockets even today but we have come far. I think that part of my lack of incentive to write or publish over the last 15 years or so is precisely because I have a sense that my job is done.

In any case, I need not write so much now because my whole life is poetry. The little woman has become her words, has opened up her world. Bernard Noël—a writer and a friend, with whom I have had a translating association over time—once told me that if he was forced to choose between Art and Life, he would chose Life. My life is my Poem.

That Spring: 1966–8

John Seed

> "Writers aren't people exactly."
> F. Scott Fitzgerald

I don't know what got me started. Certainly there were books. The first I remember was *The Wind in the Willows* when I was 10. We read it in Miss Widdrington's class at St Cuthbert's R.C. Junior School in Chester-le-Street. I remember the description of hot buttered toast. It made me suddenly hungry—and for hot buttered toast. This was some kind of magic. I have in front of me a faded green hardback copy, last printing 1958, that I asked for, and received on my eleventh birthday—or was it a Christmas present? (Someone had scribbled "4/6" in pencil on the fly-leaf—four shillings and six pence—fifty years ago.)

I'm not sure that it started with books. Nevertheless I became a reader in my teenage years, partly because there wasn't much else to do. Of course I played football in the winter, cricket in the summer. I played cards and *Monopoly* and *Risk* with other kids on endless rainy days. I wandered the woods and fields, climbed trees, lay on my back looking at the sky or kicked a ball against a brick wall a few thousand times. I went to Roker Park regularly on Saturday afternoons between 1962 and 1967—Montgomery, Irwin, Ashurst, Harvey, Hurley, McNab, Usher, Herd, Sharkey, Crosson and Mulhall. Bovril in plastic cups under the Clock Stand and salty vinegary fish and chips at the bus-stop afterwards, and the *Football Pink*. And from 1965 to 1967 there was the greatest, craziest footballer I ever saw at Sunderland—Jim Baxter. I even watched television. But on our 12-inch black-and-white box there were only two—and then three—channels and there wasn't much on any of them that I liked. Black and white movies on Sunday afternoons sometimes held my attention. Watching *The Tender Trap* I fell in love, briefly, with Debbie Reynolds on my 16th birthday, the day I also bought the Beach Boys single 'Sloop John B'.

Watching TV was a family event. I wanted to be elsewhere and on my own. Pretending to be a studious Grammar School boy, I lay on my bed upstairs in an unheated room and read. I read anything that was around at home, which wasn't very much but did include P.G. Wodehouse, Simenon's Inspector Maigret books and a few hundred very dull books by Agatha Christie. I was also reading James Bond novels by the time I was 14 or 15, though I got them from somewhere else. And I'd discovered the treasures of the local branch of the Durham County Library on Chester-le-Street Front Street and my reading had moved on to "Angry Young Men", John Wain and Kingsley Amis, the dismal novels of George Orwell, and the new "northern" working-class novelists like John Braine and Alan Sillitoe. Fortunately I was already a Europhile—or at least a Francophile. While the English football team was winning the World Cup I was reading Sartre's *Nausea* and *Roads to Freedom* trilogy, and Camus. I loved *The Outsider* for its bare prose and its bare world. I think it was the first book I ever bought—a slim grey Penguin paperback—or perhaps that was Sartre's *Nausea*, another dove-grey Penguin paperback, with a painting by Salvador Dalí on the front cover. (Why did Penguin stop being such a brilliant publisher?) The only nineteenth-century novelist I could read at that time with any real engagement was Thomas Hardy. Beautiful doomed heroines, with a more than passing resemblance to Ava Gardner, on windswept heaths under massive starry skies—this was something my imagination could respond to.

And then something happened which left me alone among the ruins of prose: something to do with the Roman Catholic Church and with my severe Catholic Grammar School and with James Joyce—and with being seventeen in 1967. I don't recall much of a devotional atmosphere in the house but we were Catholics and trooped off to the church on Ropery Lane, empty tummy rumbling, every Sunday morning. Then at school one afternoon (in 1957 or 58) Father Johnson—a small, red-nosed, white-haired and very angry priest, who looked like Nikita Khrushchev—took me out of Mrs Coleman's classroom and into the corridor. Here I was handed an elaborate printed card and asked to recite the responses to the opening of the Mass. I then had to take the card home and memorise sections. In subsequent weeks I was tested and given further sections to learn. Fragments remain stored in my memory:

> *Introibo ad altare Dei.*
> *Ad Deum qui laetificat juventutem meam.*
> *Quia tu es Deus fortitude mea quare me repulisti et quare tristis incedo dum affligit me inimicus.*

Of course I had no idea what it all meant. But I liked the sound. And now, at eight years old, I was an altar boy and a Latin scholar, a person of some status. I liked serving mass. I liked wearing the black (occasionally red) cassock and white surplice. I liked my minor role in the strange theatre of the mass. I liked the smell of incense and of wine. But most of all I loved the tranquillity of the church, almost empty on a weekday morning at 7.30—beams of light filtering through high stained-glass windows onto the red-carpeted altar-steps. I served mass regularly and was a choir-boy too at St. Cuthbert's until I was about 14.

But after I accidentally passed the 11-plus I was sent off to the new and dangerous world of St. Joseph's Grammar School at Hebburn—ten miles away on South Tyneside. One of my exact contemporaries there was the actor George Irving and he recalls:

> I was a very good boy but we were beaten for the tiniest misdemeanours—for late homework, for being inside when it was sunny… I was beaten for smudge marks on a piece of drawing paper—I've been put off drawing for life by my experiences in the art class. The beating was random. With one or two exceptions, they truly believed it would do you good.

I too recall a harsh authoritarian regime. I'm not sure I was "a very good boy" but I was no villain. Nevertheless I was caned, strapped and walloped a fair few times during the seven long years I was confined there. The headmaster, incidentally, was called Mr Kane. How we laughed. But here I was also given a rigorous introduction to poetry by two remarkable teachers (I thank them both). Dr James Vincent Curran—icy blue eyes behind rimless spectacles—was my very scary but also very funny English teacher. A select few of us had nicknames. I was Seedy Ben Youssef. "Dark Arabian eyes scan the horizon". Reading the opening lines of 'The Ancient Mariner'— "It is an ancient Mariner, / And he stoppeth one of three…"—he paused and looked my way: "Just like the Sunderland goalkeeper, eh Seedy Ben?"

At A-level we studied intensively the poetry of Donne and the metaphysicals, the Cavalier poets, Marvell and Milton, Browne's *Religio Medici* and Shakespeare. I later began to understand that Curran—"the Doc"—was a Catholic and high Tory disciple of T.S. Eliot and F.R.

Leavis. And maybe "the dissociation of sensibility" that was drummed into us—a few hundred yards from the banks of the Tyne and its shipyards—has lodged deep into the framework of my thinking. We had to keep a "Black Book" in which we wrote about the cultural glories of England under Charles I and the horrors of the civil war and the wickedness of the puritans. I was, of course, on the devil's side and suspicious of this particular party line. But I learned to love the poetry of Donne and Marvell. I can still recite from memory poems by both. My other English teacher could hardly have been more different. Val McLane was in her mid-20s, a tall, confident and attractive woman, passionate about theatre and Shakespeare and up for an argument. And I argued. And I argued. And she, bless her, argued back. In "A-level" English Literature I was in a class of mostly good Catholic girls and took particular pleasure in trying to shock them with declarations of atheism and nihilism. For a while I was the last disciple of Sergey Nechayev, the Russian nihilist. Nothing was sacred—especially the sacred. And I began to find myself opposing every orthodoxy, glorying in finding ways to be an Opposition of one. North-East working-class, labour-voting, Catholic—I wanted out.

I had already discovered James Joyce by this time. *A Portrait of the Artist as a Young Man* seemed to be a portrait of my world. For a while I *was* Stephen Dedalus. His narrow provincial suffocating Catholic Dublin was my narrow provincial suffocating Catholic Tyneside. *Portrait of the Artist* led to *Ulysses* and when my friend James Donnelly brought his own copy of *Ulysses* into school and brazenly read it in the school library, Dr Curran swooped and confiscated it! Eliot yes, Pound yes, but Joyce definitely no! So Joyce, too, was part of the Opposition to Everything. Then there was the prose of Beckett—a further shift towards the dark side and an endless source of laughter. As an old adage of the last years of the Austro-Hungarian Empire put it, the situation was desperate but it was not serious.

At the same time, I began to go to poetry readings at the Morden Tower in Newcastle-upon-Tyne. I only discovered several years later that Ric Caddel had been sitting there similarly isolated and entranced at some of the same readings. How did I find out about them? I don't know. I went there on my own. Perhaps through another discovery: the "Ultima Thule" bookshop in the Handyside Arcade? Here I found nobody willing to talk to me but, browsing there for hours, I did find a wonderful source-book for my hesitant explorations: *The New American Poetry*, edited by Donald Allen. My copy is here on the table, with the wear and burns and stains of numerous journeys over the last 43 years. In its pages I discovered several poets I was to go on to read with enthusiasm, notably Charles Olson, Robert Creeley, Ed Dorn, Gilbert Sorrentino, Gary Snyder and Philip Whalen. As important as the poems was the book's final section: 'Statements on Poetics'. And the most important of these was Olson's essay, 'Projective Verse'. Here at last was a poet writing about the *practice* of writing and telling me how to use my type-writer—how to use line-breaks and indentation and spacing to reproduce the voice and the silence of the poet as he reads and writes his own text. I was also excited by Olson's stress on moving quickly, "despising connectives": "one perception must immediately and directly lead to a further perception". And the whole notion of open form, "composition by field", seemed to describe what writing was beginning to feel like and encouraged me to plunge in further:

> From the moment he ventures into FIELD COMPOSITION— puts himself in the open—he can go by no track other than the one the poem under hand declares, for itself. Thus he has to behave, and be, instant by instant, aware of some several forces just now beginning to be examined.

There was something about Olson's hectoring tone I found off-putting and there was much I didn't and still don't understand. But I think I grasped the gist of 'Projective Verse'. It provided some very practical strategies for experimenting with ways of getting words onto paper. It was also crucial in enabling me to *read* contemporary American writing with growing confidence.

It was around this time too, early in 1968, that I found Basil Bunting's great poem, *Briggflatts*. Maybe I'd already seen the bespectacled old man with the unlikely name at the Tower? As I remember it, I bought *Briggflatts* because I already had that slim Cape paperback of Louis Zukofsky's *Ferdinand*—and that was because of the tiny story at the end of the book with its Beckettian title, 'It Was'. Browsing the shelves in Ultima Thule, I found Zukofsky being thanked in the preface to Bunting's *Collected Poems*. That preface was the first thing I read by Bunting and I was seized by the crispness and wit of his prose. And then, on the bus going back to Chester-le-Street, *Briggflatts* got me too—and not just the beauty of his language. I had begun to explore the wilds of Northumberland, Weardale and the Lake District by this time and *Briggflatts* was (and still is) part of the delights of walking Striding Edge or the bleaker moors above St. John's Chapel or the wide empty windswept beaches below Bambrugh Castle. At that time the attractions of Bunting's writing—and especially of the opening and closing sections of *Briggflatts*—had much to do with its direct and sensual presentation of a material world I knew, presented with clear-eyed objectivity and with minimal reference to subjective feelings. It is a poetry of ice-cold becks, of endless light rain on Cumberland fell-sides, of moonlight on a silent black lake.

Which is why I'm not sure that it started with books: I found the books that found a response in me. Chicken and egg. So books never provided an escape, not for long anyway. They always brought me back to myself and to the people and the material world around me.

Bunting's was also a poetry of the North. Peter Riley recalls no sense of northernness as an aggressive, or at least oppositional stance toward the south in the Stockport of his 1940s childhood and 1950s youth (see his *April Eye* website). "We weren't aware of 'southerners' as a category", he says. I'm not so sure this was the case in the North-East in the 1960s. I should say, first, that I found the term "North" to be an odd category, since much of what was supposed to be "the North"—Manchester, Liverpool, the West Riding of Yorkshire—seemed a very long way south from where I was standing. And Durham and Newcastle-upon-Tyne were the two cities I knew and neither of them looked much like the industrial towns of "the North", as conventionally represented to us at the time. Evidently I lived in some other North which was not "the North". There was also another kind of "south" and this was bound up with class (to rhyme with arse) and especially with the language of authority. In my first year at St. Joseph's we had lessons from Miss Grew in how to speak "properly", which meant "received pronunciation" and "BBC English". I particularly remember having to read aloud, into a large tape recorder, Wordsworth's poem 'The Daffodils'. The situation was excruciatingly embarrassing. For the boys, to try to talk "posh" was somehow a terrible crime against every principle of Geordie manhood. And so I had to endure the public embarrassment of refusing to read aloud in the approved manner. Nelly Grew was a kind teacher, forced to bang her head against this particular brick wall because it was assumed that if working-class grammar-school kids were going "to get on" they had to lose the trappings of region and class and learn to speak "proper English". This was 1962. Everybody in authority spoke "posh". The irony, of course, was that William Wordsworth himself was from just over the other side of the Pennines and spoke with a strong northern accent not so different from ours. (A point made by Bunting in a 1970 BBC radio Broadcast in which he read the whole of Wordsworth's poem 'The Brothers' in his own strange northern accent.)

I don't mean to suggest that there was some widespread and deep hostility towards "southerners'" and "the south". I don't recall that there was. But there was a sense that "they" belonged to some alien and probably privileged world far beyond our southern horizon, some other England of village greens and ancient country churches and "old maids cycling to communion through the early morning mist", which I had only glimpsed in books, films and television programmes. I didn't feel excluded and I didn't see that poetry or art or music was confined to that other England. But it is striking that it was modern Irish and American literature that had such a powerful impact on me.

I suppose there is no way back into those moments when, briefly, a door opened in prose and I walked or fell through it into another kind of space. My memory retains vivid details of that long spring of the late '60s. I can *see* specific places and faces, remember names, occasional moments, scraps of conversation, odd jokes. I can still navigate the corridors of St. Joseph's over forty years after I was last in them. Hours of staring from the classroom window have imprinted the image of the Jarrow coke works at Monckton on the back of my skull—it is always late afternoon, a painting by Charles Sheeler. I can accumulate further details of John Seed and the world—the many worlds—around him in 1967 and 1968, too many and not enough to make any kind of coherent narrative. And I'm not sure if I've telescoped key events and confused the chronology in this cursory sketch. Any image of that eighteen-month spring would have to include moments of Sibelius's Fifth Symphony, the Kinks and 'Sunny Afternoon' or Cream and

'Badge', the view from Scafell on a golden September afternoon, Wensleydale cheese eaten with fresh bread and a sharp green apple outside a pub in Stanhope, Newcastle spread out along the river as the bus descended through Gateshead down to the Tyne Bridge… and the faces and voices of many people, many of them long gone.

Perhaps this story, my story of how I found my way to poetry, could find some coherence as a tiny and unimportant strand of a much bigger social and political and cultural history? Certainly the several massive transformations which I was experiencing were more broadly shared. Passing the 11-plus was the start of a process of separation from my family and their world, a long exile into a social no-man's land from which there was no way back home for many thousands of us. I've always read *Great Expectations* as a kind of allegory of the working-class grammar-school boy. Pip's relations to Joe and home I found—and find—particularly poignant. Perhaps the Labour Party could play the role of Miss Havisham? Then, there was the loss between 16 and 18, of most of the coordinates provided by my familial Catholicism. These experiences in turn were framed by a wider political moment of crisis and transformation. 1967 was, after all, the summer of love—though that was definitely happening somewhere else. And this was a time when a few of the human consequences of the current vicious imperial project of the United States were broadcast nightly on television. Within a year I was rampaging outside the American Embassy in Grosvenor Square and chanting "Ho, Ho, Ho Chi Minh". But I don't know how these experiences and wider processes fit together. And perhaps that is the point—they don't. "There are many truths, / But they are not parts of a truth",—lines from a poem by Wallace Stevens, 'On the Road Home', that I've argued with, and against, for at least forty years. What began as a narrative of how I came to write poems at the age of 17 or 18 is turning into a reflection on the difficulty of writing a history…

Sartre is unfashionable these days, air-brushed out of intellectual history by many of the French post-structuralists. In *What is Literature* he suggests a way of engaging with these questions which brings us back to writing and to poetry:

> When the instruments are broken and unusable, when plans are blasted and effort is useless, the world appears with a childlike and terrible freshness, without supports, without paths.

That sounds familiar. Perhaps poetry originates in this kind of breakdown of communication and crisis of meaning? In Sartre's words, "poetic language rises out of the ruins of prose". There is an important political point here about the relations of poetry to the dominant prose of the world—one that converges with the argument that philosophy originates in the ruins of "common sense". But rather than set off across that particular windswept moor I'll point to a poem by George Oppen instead. It opens with a description of a busy highway, cars full of people talking to each other.

> Imagine a man in the ditch,
> The wheels of the overturned wreck
> Still spinning—
>
> I don't mean he despairs, I mean if he does not
> He sees in the manner of poetry

Continuing the metaphor, he has to find a way to resume the journey, whether on that or another road. Or, better, perhaps he (and/or she) has to continue on foot across difficult terrain with no clear path ahead? So it's not just a matter of "seeing". It is also a matter of *work*. Poetry is not a state of mind or a way of seeing, it's an activity, a practice. "Writing a book is a horrible, exhausting struggle, like a long bout of some painful illness," George Orwell comments in his 1946 essay 'Why I Write', "One would never undertake such a thing if one were not driven on by some demon whom one can neither resist nor understand." I wouldn't want to disagree with this, except for its gloomy tone which underplays the sheer joy of writing—the moments of exhilaration when everything seems to come together into a new coherence. I think of those lines by Shelley: "A tone / Of some world far from ours, / Where music and moonlight and feeling / Are one."

I never wanted to be "a poet". I've never thought of myself as "a poet" and I don't think I've ever called myself "a poet"—not even to myself. On odd occasions when other people have called me "a poet", I feel awkward and embarrassed and look out of the nearest window and I don't know what to say, except to change the subject as quickly as possible, preferably with a witty riposte. I do write poems though, from time to time. And somehow this is a very important fact of my life, for me. But as this short account should have demonstrated, I was able to find my way to poetry because, even as a working-class kid in the North-East of England, I was surrounded by a rich literary and cultural infrastructure—some good schoolteachers, a good free local library, a brilliant poetry bookshop and a venue where international poets read their work. And so writing this I find I am nostalgic for long-ago sunny Saturday afternoons in Newcastle and feel lucky that I happened to be, in 1967 and 1968, in a situation where poetry seemed for a while to be just about the most important thing in the world.

A Working Class Elitist Is Something to Be

Geraldine Monk

The Dandy. The Beano. The Beezer. There were three of them and three of us. My two elder brothers and me. One comic each weekly. I don't remember any consultation on this choice. As the youngest *and* a god-forbid-girl, I had very little say in anything that concerned me. So the comics came with existence every Monday and Wednesday. Choice or not I devoured them with a relish. Desperate Dan. The Bash Street Kids. Dennis the Menace. Minnie the Minx…

During the summer holiday or *Wakes Week* as it was still known in the Northern mill towns of the 1950's, we got *The Topper* as a special treat. Inside was Beryl the Peril. I *adored* Beryl more than Minnie. Her pigtailed rebellion. Gangly-gait. Gawky strips. Bendy boy body. Daft as a brush. Mischief maker. And then there was this:

> Nymph, nymph, what are your beads?
> Green glass, goblin. Why do you stare at them?
> Give them me. No!
> Then I shall howl all night in the reeds…

Lines recited by my mother rare, howling the "howl". Head thrown back. Auburn-autumn-haired cascading. Small. Dumpy. Athletic. Voice full-on in deep gestural mode, ending in doubled up belly laugh. The words she recited were from 'Overheard on a Salt Marsh' by Harold Monro, shamefully neglected poet and founder of the fabled Poetry Bookshop. One day I would marry Alan Halsey, another poet who ran another fabled Poetry Bookshop in Hay-on-Wye.

Mary Monk's/Harold Monro's words would find their way into my poetry one day—they became Pendle Witch words in 'Interregnum' "They are better than stars or water/Better than voices of winds that sing" but it would be a long and bumpy road to get to that point. I didn't know it then but as a working class girl I was born and bred *factory fodder* and that particular futility would hit me hard at the age of 14. The only respite was to become a *Good Catholic Mother* but in Lancashire the respite was short-lived as most women dropped their sprogs and went back to work before the ink had dried on the birth certificate. My mother breast-fed me, then went off to the cotton mill to do the 6-10 pm "housewives' shift". Back in time for my top-up.

I was brought up in the 1950s in a spectacularly drab decade in a spectacularly draughty terraced house in Blackburn, Lancashire. Winters were a trial. Curtains billowed at the least ghostly breeze. The outdoor bog would freeze and the pan would fill up profoundly. When it thawed all the pipes burst—umbrella on the bog time—an impossible manoeuvre. As was avoiding smogs, packs of dogs and recalcitrant snow, whooping cough, oil cloth, bedrooms colder than the planet Pluto. We all crammed into the living room around the hypnotic coal fire, faces burning, backs frozen. But summers were bliss as we kids took to the streets till dark, shinning walls, playing in the "catacombs" (air-raid shelters), French cricket frustrated on cobbled streets, us girls doing our handstands and crab walking and our endless reciting of rhymes & chants for our two-ball wall games and skipping. Political satirical rhymes turned nonsense playground chant and recounted by the street kids centuries later:

Farmer farmer may we cross your golden river…

That would form the refrain for my 'Manufractured Moon' decades later.

I was the only daughter of a Roman Catholic mother and a father who didn't much like Catholics and drank a lot. It was a home bereft of art & culture except "pub culture". A dartboard hung on the living room wall, a miniature snooker table was ensconced in the attic and everyone played cards. One day my brother threw a dart as I was crossing the room and instead of sticking in the dartboard it stuck in my temple— blood everywhere; courtesy of a neighbour, my first outing in a car was to Blackburn Royal Infirmary.

Apart from dad we all trotted off to mass every Sunday. The sumptuous Tridentine mass with its ritual, incense, gold and Latin was pure theatre and I awaited with anticipation my favourite Latin, *Et cum spiritu tuo*. I also had a passion for *Saecula saeculorum*. It felt good. Words without meaning were never a problem. Although I lived in a culture-free house it wasn't a culture-free existence. My maternal grandmother had been a keen amateur singer and had sung a duet with Dame Isobel Baillie who in turn had sung with local legend Kathleen Ferrier (our one claim to fame as a family). No one owned books, public libraries had queues. The radio was a constant and I was a member of the first "Telly generation", albeit in a very crude and rudimentary stage of development. B & W. Very low tech. Very well spoken. Very moral. Later, the Vietnam War would enter our lives and living-rooms, shockingly.

Sometime around the 1960s television's stiff moral lip began to slip thrillingly and it was to prove my gateway to intellectual and artistic freedom. This small box of tricks with such delightful silliness as Stanley Unwin forming Stanley bookends with Mr Holloway and his monologues on the radio. Beautiful & exotic women flickered across the screen like Maria Callas, Margot Fontaine & Princess Margaret and a host of screen goddesses. In 1959 the weirdest looking bird-like creature turned up on *Face to Face*: it was Edith Sitwell. It would be years before I encountered this mesmerising creature again through her mesmerising poetry. Her image haunted me. Still does. Females like that didn't exist in my world of worried women working their bones to weariness. I failed the Eleven Plus and was set to join the ranks of the weary-women.

On the heels of the glamorous women came the hairy men. In the early '60s a regional North West news & arts magazine programme hit our screen: *Scene at Six Thirty*. Its effect on me was to be profound. The "pop" explosion spearheaded by The Beatles was emanating from Liverpool, just down the road. The obscure North West of England with all its funny accents and love of black pudding was suddenly the centre of the world. Concurrent with The Beatles was a resident troupe of poets called the Liverpool Scene (McGough, Patten and Henri). This was my first substantial encounter with poetry and it drew me in. The Beatles were still penning adolescent love songs and the genius of 'A Day in the Life' and 'Eleanor Rigby' had yet to be realised. By comparison the Liverpool Scene were doing grown-up stuff and the moment of revelation came with Adrian Henri's 'The Entry of Christ into Liverpool' which referenced an advertising hoarding making a splash at the time. As Christ enters Liverpool the hoarding comes into focus circa 1964:

GUIN/ GUINN/ GUINNESS IS/ GUINNESS IS GOOD/
GUINNESS IS GOOD FOR /GUINNESS IS GOOD FOR YOU

We all thought it a scream. Me and dad would chant it for months. Eh? Me and Dad? Chant poetry? Parents rarely spoke to you in those days let alone chanted poetry with you (apart from mum and her Monro). Dad could identify with Guinness but it wasn't just that, it was fun and funny. So, my dad, the most philistine person ever to tread the planet was "reciting" poetry! Pretty impressive, Mr Henri.

I now had my career sorted: I was going to be a beatnik when I grew up. What's more I could wear a beret and stripy jumper like Beryl the Peril (is the dress code a coincidence?). Some time afterwards there was a feature on the television about a place called Morden Tower in Newcastle. A place full of poets. It sounded wonderful. My 13-year-old brain made a mental note of it and to my aspiration to be a beatnik I added poet. At the age of fourteen I left St Joseph's Secondary Modern School for Girls and went to work in a handbag factory. My life as a beatnik/poet was on hold.

I "turned" pockets. Tall, dark, handsome Ishmael sprayed them with latex and a group of 4 women turned the pockets with bone. Real bone. It made your fingers blister but that was the least of it. OMG it was boring! Weepingly so. Catastrophically so. Like a chained elephant in a zoo. Not really knowing how to cope with this I went a bit off the rails. One day, aged 15, I ran away to Liverpool. I'd chucked in my job without telling anyone and was bumming around town, I bummed down Dandy Walk and bumped into my mum! "Wait till yer dad… etc". I was as good as mincemeat—so: I ran away from home.

As this was on the spur of the moment I had virtually no money and nothing but the clothes on my back. I decided to go and find the Liverpool poets, I rather fancied the fabled Morden Tower in Newcastle but I'd no more idea how to get to Newcastle than to get to Outer Mongolia. So, I hitched the 30 miles to Liverpool. It was a "learning curve" as they say now. The first guy that picked me up thought I was a prostitute and threw me out his car when he realised I hadn't a clue what he was talking about. "Stop wasting my time", he said. Me? Wasting his time? The silly bugger. Man number two was a young lorry driver with his cab plastered with pics of naked ladies. I'd never seen pics of naked ladies before. I was deeply shocked. He asked if I wanted to spend the night with him. I was deeply shocked. Blimey. Getting to a poetry reading was a bit tricky. Still, it was better than "death by dad". He was a nice lorry driver though. He sussed I was a runaway and as he dropped me off he told me to take care. I remember him with fondness for that kind thought. And for not raping and murdering me. Cheers mate.

It was getting dark. I'd never been to Liverpool before. It was big and I was clueless. In the centre of town people queued outside dance halls or bingo halls. I went down the queues of people asking where the poets read. No one knew. I got some very amused looks. After many an adventure, mainly of a deeply depressing kind and too long to recount here, I ended up in a police cell in Preston. My incandescent dad came to collect me and returned me to my not amused mum. My dad didn't quite kill me but poetry had proved a perilously hard substance to obtain. My life as a beatnik/poet was yet again put on hold.

Fast forward. I went into voluntary isolation. I'd finally got a job I liked at a wholesale newsagents. Surrounded with newsprint and books I taught myself to read. Properly. Brought up on a diet of comics was no preparation for complex paragraphs and involved thoughts. Armed with a copy of D.H. Lawrence's *The White Peacock* and a dictionary I ploughed through to the end. It was hard, laborious work but I got there and it did the trick. My second book was Dostoevsky's *The Idiot*!

In 1969 at the age of 17, after what seemed a dozen lifetimes and several jobs I enrolled at Accrington College of Further Education (as a mature student!) and began the education the R.C. Church had singularly denied me. I was hungry for knowledge and it was there for the taking. And it was there that Frank Welch, my brilliant English teacher brought in a recording of Gertrude Stein reading 'If I Told Him'. I went delirious with bewildered joy. Seriously. The hypnotic rush of it. The sheer bloody cheek of it. And it was there that I met the painter Robert Clark (a.k.a Bob Clark a.k.a. Robert Casselton Clark) with whom I would spend the next 24 years.

Amidst this immense and intense flood of artistic and intellectual stimulus I discovered the Surrealist and Dadaist but also home-grown poets like Sitwell and Hopkins, Blake and Swinburne, Dylan Thomas and Ted Hughes. There was also a flourish of underground magazines and *International Times* regularly featured articles by Jeff Nuttall who would eventually play such a big role in my life. Another magazine, whose predecessor, *Poetmeat*, had, a few years earlier, fallen prey to the stringent obscenity laws, was *Global Tapestry*. *Global Tapestry* was a poetry/prose/visual arts magazine published by Dave Cunliffe and Dave Cunliffe lived in Blackburn. It would be with the glorious symmetry of irony that the first poetry reading I attended was not in Liverpool or Newcastle but in my own little town at one of Dave's poetry and music events in the Borough Arms, Blackburn (a pub that my family had been proprietors of more than a century before). It was a lively and amusing evening as Dave gambolled about being Dave. And the Beatles were also maturing and had now put Blackburn on the map for its 4,000 holes. Life was bucking up!

LEEDS, WEST YORKSHIRE

In 1969/70 Robert moved to Leeds to take a Fine Art degree at the Polytechnic. I moved to Leeds shortly after. He had applied there because Jeff Nuttall was there. It is difficult to explain what an influential figure Nuttall was at the time; his best selling book, *Bomb Culture,* had exploded (sorry) on the world a couple of years earlier and he was a force to be reckoned with; a small, dumpy man, tousle-haired à la Dylan Thomas, with his ill-fitting, pink check suit and blustery walk. A cheeky chappy with a mustard-keen mind that you could never second-guess. A man of many talents sprinkled with genius. He inhabited opposites and profound contradictions, he was as at home in the drear urban sprawl of Northern towns and cities as he was in the pantheistic countryside. Gillian Whiteley sums up this contradiction nicely: "he saw no paradox in bringing together the ideas of French essayist and philosopher Georges Bataille and the Blackpool comedian Frank Randall." (from 'The Life and Works of Jeff Nuttall' web tribute site). The first time I heard Jeff read was another key moment for my own, future, poetic development. His delivery was riveting. So gleefully irreverent and full of unbridled energy shot through with pathos. But I

187

was having a bad time in Leeds. My parents had stopped talking to me because I was "living in sin" and I began having nightmares. Terrified of sleeping. Terrified of waking. In retrospect I had a mini-breakdown. We had to leave Leeds.

Before I move out of West Yorkshire *we have to talk about Ted* because no visit to West Yorkshire is complete without a sideways glance at the quiffed and brooding shadow which was Ted Hughes. Hughes was massive in the craggy old mill towns of East Lancs & West Yorks. He was famous and he was "ours". A poet employing slowly tortured Northern vowels, evoking the genius loci of the Northern landscape, burrowing into the dank heart of a dark landscape and darker psyche. Profound. Ludicrous. Compulsive. Repulsive. Bloody marvellous.

STAITHES, NORTH YORKSHIRE

1974. Oneholme Farm was cut into a hill. We rented half of it. After Leeds this was dreamtime. It was exquisite. Between the North Yorkshire Moors and the North Sea I finally started to write poetry...& write & write & write. All night. Whole chunks of junk experience surfaced and turned to words. Some of it still disturbs me. I didn't set out to write in any particular style. It just arrived, almost fully formed, in the middle of the night, as if it was prewritten, out it poured in a kind of gothic surreal stream of consciousness. I showed them to Robert and then put them in a drawer. It never occurred to me to show them to anyone else let alone get them published. I wasn't interested in that. Robert was though. He asked me if he could send some to Jeff Nuttall, whom he was in regular correspondence with. I said no. But Robert was nothing if not persistent and finally, for a quiet life, I let him. Nuttall wrote directly back to me and his response took me by surprise. He loved them. Send them to Faber he enthused! I never did. But encouraged I began to send them to magazines. They all came back to me. It was a bit crushing. Maybe I *should* have tried Faber.

Later that year I entered my first and last poetry competition. It was a *Yorkshire Post* competition for young poets, judged by Brian Patten, Alan Sillitoe and Ted Hughes. My poem was amongst the chosen few and published in the newspaper. Fame at last. Shortly afterwards I received my first "anti-fan" letter. It was from a woman telling me to kill myself. She wrote, "I have visited Staithes, throw yourself into the sea at high tide". Oh dear. That was one of the nicer things she wrote. On top of the death threat I was packed off with the other young hopefuls to Lumb Bank's Arvon Centre to spend one of the craziest weeks of my life with Ken Smith and Angela Carter. Ken, moody and aggressive. Angela. Ah. We danced and smoked and smoked and danced and she said my writing was "blood-bolted" and we both dissolved into laughter. She said she wanted to "mother" me and we both dissolved into laughter. I was a little in love with her.

More important than a competition was Jeff putting me in contact with Bill Griffiths. Bill became my very first "poet friend". He was a total original. A complete one-off. He stayed with us often. Bill introduced me to Bob Cobbing. Bob became a very close friend. I was gradually being drawn into the "avant-garde" or "experimental" poetry scene and I would find myself being tagged with those labels even though I thought, and still think, my work is rooted in tradition. I was called an "elitist"—a working class elitist? Brilliant! Not sure what's elitist in writing about North Yorkshire Moors and East Lancashire but there you have it. That's tags for you.

So a million miles from nowhere I was now on the edge of in the thick of it. The flurry of indecipherable mimeo magazines became an avalanche. Peter Hodgkiss' *Poetry Information* and *PALPI* kept me up to date with publications and developments and in 1977, Jeff wrote my first ever review, it was of *Invasion*, in the magazine *Aquarius*. After Griffiths and Cobbing published my *Long Wake* in 1979, I received another "fan letter", a real one, full of sticky stars and high praise from a young woman called Maggie O'Sullivan. She would become my first female poet friend and she also began regular visits to Staithes. Another visitor was David Tipton of Rivelin Press who in 1982 published my first "posh" book, *Tiger Lilies*. It was printed by Tony Ward in Todmorden and Tony deserves a mention. His Arc & Throstle press enabled us all to publish beautiful books, professionally printed, by someone who specialised in poetry. His book designs and printing were exquisite in contrast to the cut & paste, splodge & patch method most of us employed at the time. So much was starting to happen in Yorkshire with its indigenous poets and refugees from elsewhere contributing to the milieu that Yorkshire became one of the most exciting places for poetry in the country.

SHEFFIELD, SOUTH YORKSHIRE

After 10 years of splendid isolation we re-entered civilisation by moving to Sheffield. Margaret Thatcher was starting to utter threats against student grants and I seized the opportunity to get a degree. In 1985 I enrolled for an English and American Studies course at Sheffield Polytechnic. I graduated in '88 but my dad had died in '84 and my mum was now suffering terribly from Alzheimers. If only…

And now technology was breaking into a canter and my electronic typewriter was quickly traded in for a Starwriter word processor which had those dodgy memory plates called floppy discs which corrupted in the middle of the night for no reason whatsoever. Every word you wrote disappeared in a puff of trust. Computers were just around the corner and a whole new universe would soon be revealed. But before that happened I sat down at my Starwriter in my spooky room in Nether Edge and began to write *Interregnum*. My mother's voice reciting the lines from Monro filled the room:

> They are better than stars and water
> Better than voices of winds that sing

Odyssey

Tilla Brading

convention to contraflow

yo-yo a dominant perspective   between places   stretching the
gambolling fleece   walking crocodile drunk at the shearing
party   hand in hand with the director's daughter bi-lingual
juxtaposing registers *question the opposition*   "Why should I?"
gaps   gape   gathering answers   in the margins

Contraflow was the forerunner of *Odyssey*. It was published circa 1985–9
before we all had easy access to the internet or had even heard of it. This
was the era of the smudged and stapled magazines (do you have some
magazines with rusting staples?), designed, typed, sliced and spliced by
hand from variously organised and disorganised studies, kitchens and
spare-rooms. *Contraflow* was edited by Steve Davies and Richard Tabor
of Lobby Press lurking somewhere in Somerset (Yeovil to be precise).
There's an example issue ("collectable") with Richard Tabor, Paul
Buck, P.C. Fencott, Ulli Freer, Peter Larkin, Michael O'Higgins, Steve
Davies; quite a line-up. It includes several names who continue in an
authentic exploration, excavation and creativity of text often extending
the differently formed, visual and acoustic aspects. This amorphous
waterbed became my exploration and experimentation. Previously, I
had subscribed to such as *second aeon* (Peter Finch), *Anglo-Welsh Review*
(Roland Mathias), *Phoenix* (Harry Chambers), *Outposts* (before Roland
John), *Workshop* (Norman Hidden) and had attended any and every
poetry reading as a student in London but these were few and far
between in the South West.

At the same time, Derrick Woolf, a retired architect living in
Somerset, began producing a magazine, *Quorum*, for the Dillington
Poets who met monthly to read and discuss their own writing. The
group included Elma Mitchell who:

"first came to public attention in middle life, when her devastatingly original poem, 'Thoughts After Ruskin', appeared in the 1967 PEN anthology." (*The Guardian*, 05.12.2000).

With several collections from Peterloo Poets (Harry Chambers), she was always supportive and non-judgmental but astute to others including me, Julie Sampson, Chris Banks, Derek Power, Genista Lewes, and many who are continuing to write. Derrick and Steve, who also attended these meetings, evolved *Odyssey*.

This evolution was against a background of ALP (the Association of Little Presses). This was set up in 1966 by Bob Cobbing of Writers Forum and Stuart Montgomery of Fulcrum Press. Among other things, it ran regular bookfairs at which members could sell their books and magazines. It published an annual catalogue until about 1997. The bookfairs were hosted by different small presses; Odyssey Poets press attended at least half a dozen; Norwich, Newcastle (twice, hosted by Iron Press—Pete Mortimer), Middlesbrough (Scratch—Mark Robinson), Birmingham (Headlock—Tony Charles), West Bromwich (Purple Patch—Geoff Stevens), London, and hosted one itself (or was it two?) at Exeter.

Somewhere I've got a set of *Odyssey* magazines; probably stored in a box in a case under another trunk behind the lawnmower in the garage of memory; I'm relying on that for this meander... aaah; the creative inaccuracy of serendipity versus authoritative scholarship... The issues began as saddle-stitched—and graduated to perfect bound. David Rose was prose editor but became disillusioned with the caprices of publishing. At some point, Steve Davies drew back, sloping off into music and a collection from Arc, *Flowers from the Slaghills*. Derrick Woolf became custodian of Coleridge Cottage, Nether Stowey. While opening to the public he re-located his office downstairs because he was also co-ordinating an appeal to raise money to open the erstwhile up-stairs office as a display room with a bedroom.

Days became a round of *typing, cutting, collating, pasting, typing, cutting, collating, posting,* not to mention reading submissions and accepting, returning or binning them. Typing began as inkjet on a Canon "Starwriter" and master copies were photocopied. I began assisting on an ad-hoc basis. Derrick Woolf had an eye for recognising genuine and stimulating work, often from emerging poets; Michael Ayres, Elisabeth Bletsoe, Giles Goodland, Gordon Wardman to name a few. Bletsoe edited a special issue called *Unanchored in Ecumenopolis* and other special issues included *Poets in their Twenties* and *Featuring the Experimental.*

We exchanged the magazine with many others; names like *Joe Soap's Canoe* (Martin Stannard), *Terrible Work* (Tim Allen), *Tears in the Fence* (Dave Caddy), *Stride* (Rupert Loydell), *Iron* (Pete Mortimer), *Oasis* (Ian Robinson), *Westwords* (David Woolley) and the more quirky survivors; *Krax* (Andy Robson), *New Hope International* (Gerald England), *Purple Patch* (Geoff Stevens).

Producing the magazine led to publishing pamphlets, initially for some of the members of the Dillington poets named above. These were followed by collections which were always designed with professionalism. Launches were memorable parties in Coleridge Cottage, poets and editors visited and *Odyssey* began to be recognised in the small press poetry world. There are stories of a certain visiting editor asleep on the desk, romances blossoming, someone nursing Coleridge's death mask and a spoon flying up to meet Barry MacSweeney's magnetic glasses. As the review section of the magazine grew, Derrick Woolf decided to develop this aspect into an A4 folded and stapled quarterly *PQR (Poetry Quarterly Review).* This included a centre page spread featuring a guest poet who was paid (£20), rare in the small press world; Caroline Bergvall, Frances Presley, Sheila Murphy, Keith Jebb, John Hall were some of these. We graduated to a Mac and I became reviews editor.

Meanwhile, there were exciting developments at Dartington, then College of the Arts, which had a thriving Creative Writing scene with cris cheek, Caroline Bergvall, Alaric Sumner, John Hall. Nearby, too, was Tony Lopez and colleagues developing the poetry module of the MA for Plymouth University. Nicholas Johnson was developing etruscan books in Totnes, Tim Allen was producing *Terrible Work* mag and running regular reading events in Plymouth. I set up an annual Poetry Picnic at Dillington where local groups could meet, read and picnic and host a guest reader. Maggie O'Sullivan was one.

Sometimes I escaped family commitments or work; there was the first "Kicking Daffodils" conference of women's poetry at Oxford Brookes (somehow I missed the recent one). Others included a conference of

Innovative Women Poets at Leeds, and an Arvon (Totleigh Barton, Devon) course hosted by *Stride*, featuring Sheila Murphy.

We've moved on but I'd like to highlight the influences of Alaric Sumner (*Wordsworth* magazine), Bill Griffiths, Barry MacSweeney, Ian Robinson, Elma Mitchell et al., who paved the way for us.

Personally, already this is history and herstory and now we're into the 21st internet and electronic explosion… and more… and more… breaking through the frontiers; to be content and complacent spells textual stagnation.

The Difference Is Still the Same Plymouth 1990 /2010

TIM ALLEN

As a child I lived on Portland, Dorset. After college years in London I came to Plymouth in 1973 to work as a teacher. Twenty years later I started the magazine *Terrible Work* and the Poetry Exchange and in 2000 started the Language Club. All of these things I've done with others that chance brought together, because there is nothing particular about Plymouth; it just happens to be where we are. If anything it's quite ironic that we have done it here in a city that is far from being conducive to the arts, let alone poetry, let alone innovative poetry. The human core of this activity was six: Plymothians Norman Jope, Kenny Knight and Alexis Kirke, plus incomers Steve Spence and myself, and latterly Philip Kuhn.

A selected list of guest readers of the Poetry Exchange and the Language Club might surprise some people: Chris Torrance, Lloyd Robson (twice), Andrew Duncan, Alice Notley, Aaron Williamson, Tom Raworth (twice), Maggie O'Sullivan (twice), Lee Harwood (twice), Jeremy Hilton, Helen Macdonald, Geraldine Monk, Alan Halsey, Robert Sheppard, Iain Sinclair, Ben Watson, Sean Bonney, Ken Edwards, John James, Vahni Capildeo, Barry MacSweeney, Simon Smith, Drew Milne, Tony Lopez, Kelvin Corcoran, Jeff Hilson, Gavin Selerie, Erin Moure, Nicholas Johnson, Hannah Silva, Frances Presley, Tilla Brading, Giles Goodland, Chris McCabe, Scott Thurston, John Hall and Elisabeth Bletsoe (twice).

What story lies behind such a list, why these names instead of those you would normally find guesting at provincial art centres? Is it some tweak of personality or background or is it simply chance (e.g. one day we just happen to pick up a certain book) that determines such choices? I developed a knack for imaginative writing in my early teens and had always told myself stories and created inner worlds but why does that lead to writing poetry and not novels and then why the kind of poetry that still elicits negative reactions from some sections of the literati? After all, I'm not the only one to have their head turned by Bob Dylan or to discover Rimbaud or surrealism in their teens. All I can say is that

I found a match, when I read the French symbolists and modernists something rang deep and true which, when compared to other things I read and liked, (whether Ted Hughes or Adrian Henri) resonated in a far more complex and mysterious way. The first poetry in English to do something similar for me was Eliot's, followed very soon after by the young Lee Harwood and Tom Raworth; the difference was that the tone, texture and material focus of Harwood and Raworth etc came across as modern, as versions of myself.

The others who have played their part in the Language Club and its satellite activities have all been singularly unimpressed by the mainstream while being drawn towards some aspect of the alternative poetries, Norman Jope, for example, like me, found his early inspirations to be European. Kenny Knight had roots in free-form psychedelia. Alexis Kirke was into cyberpunk and slipstream. Steve Spence was as much influenced by visual artforms as by literature and was still overcoming a strong attachment to the poetry of Tony Harrison. Philip Kuhn came with a highly developed part dialectic and part hermetic open-field poetic. You could say we were all lucky to find each other because without that mutuality I don't think anything of interest would have happened here. Nevertheless, we are all quite different, both as people and writers—we never resembled anything like a school and if anything our work diverged even further.

THE POET TRAP

Mid '70s, punk on the horizon, with my brother-in-law Sid and two of his cool mates, we set up the Poet Trap at Plymouth Arts Centre. It produced two performances (during one a poet was sick over the audience) and one issue of a mag. It wasn't very good but it did have a kind of seedy charm. We did it because a few weeks before I'd been walking back from the pub with Brian Patten, following a reading he'd given, when he told me I should start a poetry group. I said, "It's not in my nature", and Brian replied, "Sometimes we have to do things that are against our nature, otherwise nothing happens." And actually I was right, it wasn't in my nature, but Brian was right as well.

On one occasion there I picked up a magazine someone had left on a windowsill: *Poetry Review,* 40p, a few years old, *Spring 1973.* The jacket featured a concrete poem so I opened it up. There was a simultaneous double flash of the strange and the familiar as I browsed through with a growing warm feeling in heart and head—this was the first time I read any Roy Fisher, Ulli McCarthy or Kenneth Koch. Little did I know then of the shenanigans that went on at the Poetry Society to produce such a thing.

Around the same time I made a half-hearted attempt to make contact and get published by sending for Ken Edwards' *Alembic* and a fascinating sounding *Spectacular Diseases.* I wasn't ready though, I lacked confidence in my own work and didn't know where it fitted, most of it having been written in my teens. I went back into my shell for another decade and a half.

THE SWARTHMORE POETS

It's an autumn evening in 1990 and a small, tired, middle-aged primary school teacher looking a lot like me takes the fifteen-minute walk from his house to the Swarthmore Centre in Mutley Plain. Tight in his grip, wrapped in a plastic supermarket bag, is a notebook crammed with ink-black, tiny, squashed, almost indecipherable handwriting. It is some 15 years since last sharing his writing with strangers but he has noticed a local poetry group advertised in a brochure along with evening classes for life drawing and macramé. On getting there he finds 12 people squashed on hard chairs against the walls in a little room. They take it in turns to read their poems and get encouraging comments back from the moon-faced girl who seems to be running the show.

This was the first link in a chain of events that would see this unlikely city being referred to as a healthy outpost of the alternative poetry scene—not that anyone in Plymouth itself, beyond a small band of individuals, would ever know this, not even twenty years later.

The Swarthmore Poets—a mixed bunch of ordinary people who happen to write poetry and feel motivated enough to test it in public. They even do performances, which tend to be highly rehearsed dramatic affairs, as a leading member is a drama teacher. I don't really like that side of it but do my bit and love the weekly meetings because of the different characters that come and go, not all of them so "ordinary"—a lad dressed in leather who comes pretending that Jim Morrison lyrics are his own, an ex-inmate from Dartmoor with poems on a weird little computer he carries in a case (just a gimmick, surely?) and a tall, thin, long-haired, well-weathered looking hippy with a striking face that could be Alice Cooper without makeup. This is Kenny Knight. The two of us realise our work is bouncing off the same wall, even though years later, when it gets caught, it is two very different balls.

A highlight: I'm reading my 'Land of a Thousand Dances' and Phil, the drama teacher, is laughing so much (it was meant to be funny) he nearly chokes. However, the group's good will towards "weird poetry" doesn't last, and Kenny and myself grow restless. The outline of an all too familiar opposition begins to show, it doesn't matter at what level, the difference is still the same, the old versus the new, the safe versus the experimental, the formal versus the expansive. The strain finally breaks the group and in 1993 Kenny and myself take the rump with us to start a new group based at Plymouth Art Centre. We call the new meetings The Poetry Exchange.

The Poetry Exchange

The new group is not avant-garde (this is Plymouth, not Bloomsbury), however, its eclectic span definitely leans to the left. It doesn't concern itself with fostering the publishable poem but allows people time to develop by encouraging them to take what they are doing seriously. It isn't a workshop but a forum of equal exchange. It works. Over a period of 8 years with average attendances of around 12 it provides a rewarding and relaxed atmosphere. Important long-term members include Helen Foster, Dee Marshall, Viv Grant, (those three along with Alexis Kirke and myself also performed as The Terrible Workers, at Glastonbury etc) Margaret Kirke, Rosie Smith, Jean Symons, John Daniel, Jane Spiro, Susie Shelley, Frank Luce, Jason Hirons, Wendy McBride and Chris Deakin, the last two both painters.

It was never a planned programme, it ran on instinct and enthusiasms. Those who did well out of it were the open-minded who wanted to learn and read the modern poetry of others, while those who came pre-conditioned with notions about what poetry should be didn't last long. For some it was primarily a social event and we didn't mind that as long as the social event was the vehicle for the poetry, not the other way round. So, it had a social function but was ignored by the organs of society, e.g. a local arts reporter came and sat in taking notes then said to me sneeringly, "Our readers won't be interested in this—it's all too arty and intellectual"—and sure enough nothing appeared in the paper. We kept trying with the press over the years but they didn't want to know—they put in their articles about am-dram productions and classical concerts and the latest grunge band to hit town but the only poetry stories were those featuring someone who'd had a poem in a BOOK (always a vanity press). The City Council weren't interested in us because we weren't a jazz club. These problems of conservative provincialism and parochialism continued to plague us in our further mutations—we remained invisible.

In the mid '90s the Exchange went through a crisis when a new enlightened regime at the Arts Centre (including a well-known children's author) evicted us because we were not a "core activity". This was accompanied by personality clashes followed by an attempt to reconcile the differences under a broader umbrella, The Wordshop, but it was too ambitious and stalled. We finally managed to restore the Exchange at its home base where it continued in an even stronger form. By the late '90s we had started putting on events too: Paul Violi and Martin Stannard, Andrew Duncan and Alice Notley at the Arts Centre, Barry MacSweeney and Nick Johnson at Plymouth Museum and Tom Raworth and Maggie O'Sullivan in Robert Lenkiewicz's studio, where the poets read from a dais behind which was hung a huge portrait of a naked man. Now I'm shorter than everyone else so when I read it looked as though a penis was resting on my head.

TERRIBLE WORK

The vehicle which brought this poetry world to us, though, was not the Exchange, it was the magazine *Terrible Work*, whose history as a hard-copy runs parallel to the Poetry Exchange through the '90s. In '92 I was still teaching at a Primary School in Devonport and I was sat outside a Barbican pub one summer evening with my teaching colleague Steve Soames when he asked me if I'd ever thought of editing a poetry magazine, as he was interested in doing some tabletop publishing. And yes, I had thought about it, always imagining a magazine called *Terrible Work* (after Rimbaud's description of what future poets would be involved in), and so it started, the first two issues in 1993 being produced on his Acorn computer and the school photocopier. That's really what changed things. Suddenly I was in contact with all these people who shared my enthusiasm for a different sort of modern poetry than that being written by Heaney and Motion. The first issue for example included work by Peter Redgrove, Sean Bonney, Elisabeth Bletsoe, Rupert Loydell, Chris Torrance and Jay Ramsay and the second included Roy Fisher and Giles Goodland. I'd been helped immensely in finding these people in the first place by Norman Jope, who gave me names and addresses of poets who had contributed to his magazine *Memes*, and almost overnight the mad vista of the small press poetry scene opened up. As a fundraiser for *TW* we organised the largest poetry bash the city had ever seen—the Terrible Workers' Party—over a dozen poets from all over the country came and read for free.

That scene was on a high due to desk-topping and *TW* found itself in a niche along with other new mags like *10th Muse* and *Ramraid Extraordinaire*. We were engaging with a wide spread of alternative poetries, following in the footsteps of Rupert Loydell's *Stride* etc., but found ourselves in opposition to the domestic realism which was finding success under the banner of the Northern School. I also became aware of the more focused *avant* mags, particularly *Angel Exhaust* and *Parataxis*, but wasn't so interested in following their line at the time, despite my own taste, because I was into exploring the scene in its variety and soon became interested (far too interested some would say) in the fracture lines between the different poetries: what aesthetic, generational, social, political and philosophical differences lay behind the fault lines? This is what fed directly into the reviewing, which became more and more polemical. I was becoming militant.

My assistant editors were first Steve Soames, who had much to do with the design, then Alexis Kirke and finally Steve Spence. Alexis is a sort of restless genius who excels at everything he touches—now he's into experimental music. Steve Spence had a history of putting on events at the Cambridge Poetry Festival fringe and a period in Swindon organising outreach poetry gigs. We became great friends—his more tolerant tastes the foil to my growing wish to push *TW* closer to the post-modernists. I had caught up with what the Americans had been up to and discovered Language Poetry.

As the millennium approached internal contradictions finally did for *TW* as a poetry magazine. The final issue was #10 in 2000. It ended partly because of the workload caused by extensive reviewing but also because I felt that its project, the juxtaposition of styles and foregrounding of difference, had gone as far as it could—it wasn't the kind of thing that could go on indefinitely. And the web was beckoning, the possibility of doing it in an easier way while at the same time reaching far more people. The gap was also partly filled by Kenny Knight's magazine *Tremblestone*, which ran to 5 issues between '99 and '06. My aim was to transfer *TW* to the web as an ongoing reviews e-zine and start a new poetry-only magazine of the linguistically innovative, which I was going to call *a very rare magazine upon the Earth*. The former happened in 2002 but the latter never got started. *TW* had a good four years as a website before it closed down, due largely to illness (which made me think it was time I concentrated on my own work instead of other people's), but also because production values were moving very fast then and the site soon seemed clunky. The blogs were also appearing, with ones such as *Intercapillary Space* doing what we'd been doing, but never with such a range.

The Language Club

The Poetry Exchange lingered into the new millennium but differing needs were making it increasingly difficult to handle and once again a gap was widening between different poetic inclinations—the difference was still the same. We set up a new organisation to put on regular events with guest poets and open-mike sessions and called it the Language Club, while the Exchange's round-table format went underground to become the Language Club Discussion Group.

For over a decade the Language Club succeeded, far beyond our expectations. We got a grant in 2004—thanks to Philip Kuhn—which we used prudently, enabling us to actually pay guest readers. These weren't exclusively from *avant* circles but represented the span of our poetic tastes; for example, in addition to those mentioned earlier, it also put on people like Fred Beake, Joolz, Penelope Shuttle, W.N. Herbert, Andy Brown, Daljit Nagra, John Hartley Williams, Harry Guest, Luke Kennard, Philip Gross, Richard Berengarten and even Attila the Stockbroker and the famous poetry boy-band, Aisle 16. We also collaborated with other organisations such as Apples and Snakes and the BBC, and put on improvised Jazz and poetry events with Sam Richards. We also networked across the west country, had close ties with David Caddy's annual festivals in Blandford, Tilla Brading's poetry picnics in Somerset and of course with the Exeter crowd. At one point both *Stride* and *Shearsman* were coming out of Exeter and Nick Johnson's etruscan books and Anderson Festivals were just up the road in Buckfastleigh. So while it lasted it was quite a rich little scene.

Sometimes though the tension between different poetries was a tad too much—the night we put on a double-bill of Ken Edwards and Joolz Denby for example—it was one of our best attended events but the contrast was startling and uncomfortable. When Ken was reading the look of total bewilderment on the face of the New Model Army's Justin Sullivan (Joolz' partner) was hilarious. And Drew Milne didn't go down too well with some of our audience—you have to remember that the Language Club audiences were not specialists with an appetite for the innovative but a cross-section of poetry fans, something which some of our guests were not used to facing. The Language Club was never about preaching to the converted but in giving people the opportunity to hear stuff which they would otherwise never have encountered, probably. It meant taking chances, and most of the time those chances paid off, but rarely 100%. It always amused me to watch faces in the audience while our guest poets were reading and see the different play of responses. But in all that time I can only remember two people walking out, though I have to admit sometimes there would be empty seats following the mid session break.

It could work the other way as well—Attila the Stockbroker gave us the biggest audience we ever had—all these ageing punks and crusties came up from Cornwall to invade our sacred space, and one of the strangest evenings was with Daljit Nagra, not because his poetry was strange but because it was so unstrange. I'd published Daljit in *TW* not realising that the voice in the poems was a "voice". I was really looking forward to it but his reading turned out to be just about the most mainstream we ever put on. But you could never tell how someone was going to go down—our audience loved it when Maggie O'Sullivan lay her drawings on the floor and got everyone up out of their seats to look at them closely, when Geraldine Monk stomped to-and-fro, when Robert Sheppard's voice bellowed through the room with such aggressive volume, and of course few of them had ever experienced anything like Tom Raworth's speed of delivery. If nothing else, it demonstrated that poetry was a many-faced beast, the surprise factor alone often making it worthwhile.

There were disasters too—Lee Harwood and Helen Macdonald trying to read to an audience in the upper room of a pub on a traffic island on bonfire night; Erín Moure, the brilliant Canadian innovative poet, getting serious anaphylactic shock after eating a peanut curry in the Art Centre restaurant before her reading and ending up in Casualty instead; Andrew Brewerton trying to read over the noise of the industrial fridge in his own Art College. But these were anomalies, the majority of the readings were memorable for all the right reasons and among those that stand out I would have to mention those by John James, Elisabeth Bletsoe, Vahni Capildeo, John Hartley Williams and Chris McCabe, who through the fug of the worst cold ever and broad scouse still managed to impress everyone. His poem 'The Barry MacSweeney Guest Room' (see p.206), was written in the same spare room where nearly all of the Language Club guests have had to spend the night.

The Language Club was also a forum for the local poets, our open-mike sessions giving countless people the opportunity to read to an audience for the first time, as well as being a regular vehicle for more experienced performers from around the south-west. There were no restrictions—anybody could get up there and own the floor for five minutes. Some could be funny to the point of tears (hi there, Michael Dax) and some could hit the ground running, Will Morris for example, whose reading style was as unexpected as his brilliant poems. We never knew what we were going to get—you sit back and enjoy the flow and marvel at the sound of the human voice. The only ones to get my goat were the well-rehearsed performance poets, but we never got many of those—someone must have tipped them off that over-confidence and rhymed cliché wouldn't impress us. Nothing wrong with attitude though—we always got plenty of that.

In all this time too, behind the scenes, the Language Club Discussion Group has been meeting—an intense exploration of poetics, wine and cheeses where the focus is on poetry as an art form and not just a transparent means of personal expression. In addition to the Plymouth contingent other regulars such as Fred Beake, Sarah Hopkins, John Hall, Susan Taylor, Simon Williams, Roselle Angwin and Philip Kuhn all live in the Dartmoor/South Hams area. philip kuhn, who publishes beautiful limited editions of "artist's books" (itinerant press), also holds his 'occasional reading series' at his studio on Dartmoor. This gives poets a wonderful opportunity to read long pieces and extended sequences that might be difficult to deliver in other forums.

Poets connected with the Language Club featured in an anthology edited by Norman Jope and Ian Robinson, *In the Presence of Sharks* (2006) but most of the main players have had books published now and been recognised further afield. Nevertheless, locally, the poet most recognised is Kenny Knight, down to his book about his youth on a council estate in the city, *The Honicknowle Book of the Dead*. Steve Spence's *A Curious Shipwreck* even made it to the Forward Prize first-book shortlist, which made us all laugh.

Wondering what effect all of this activity has had on others is a bit like trying to gauge how much influence I ever had when I was teaching—I just don't know. Would I do it again? Probably! Would I do it differently? Probably not!

The Barry MacSweeney Guest Room

CHRIS McCABE

for Tim Allen & The Language Club

Wolftongue there's polar bears above my head.
Twenty-four polar bears in a scrapbook montage.
Above my head are two portraits of the Bard—
one the dot-matrix state-embossed folio shot.

After your reading did Tim drive you back via
Union St., his homicidal sling-shot side-door insecure
after the ritual elixirs of dancing liquids had done their trick
as anti-ageing remedials for the turbot-white teenagers

spewed back on a stomach surf of Kronenbergs,
on a tide of bravado & fizz, masquerading above
the clamp of the newly pink, the fuck-you flotsam
of the heart's (—as trickster, as pump—) first seaflower?

Steve & Norman in the back, I had no appetite for the diluvian
drink, the crashpad catch-up of a cold & the cache of the trains
was pushing me on for the polar bears & bards. Shit joke
at the junction : *Exit pursued by a polar bear.*

First we lost Norman through the gates of The Fin-de-Siècle
Hotel, then Steve at Krushchev Holiday Hill. Earlier,
when we'd met at the Station, Tim had filled up on petrol
now I couldn't see the point : de-crank the handbreak

and a city of hills drops me down to the arctic sleep.
As we drove he said, Wolftongue, that you'd read
at The Language Club—Il Duce of the lexicon—
and you'd slept under the same Bard's sexless sidepart

where the white clip-on cubs flower—sweating out
the clinics with *The Book of Demons*—not stones but in the gutter—
face up to the gulls, feet down to the velveteen cactus,
as good a place as any to get yourself clean, in Tim's

upside-down house where you walk in upstairs to look
down on the birds. The peewits rang shrill but you'd
already committed to death-by-stereo. Your Gunslinger-
Dylan boots collapsed at the bed's end like chess-pieces

danced too long across disco-squares of boredom. Looking
up at the crocheted mask that once craved the selfsame froth
—apocryphally dead after a pissup with an alchemist—
you knew the peewits only wallock in flight. This mortal coil

that rings itself out in the peel of each peeled ring-pull.

Hidden Lines

Frances Presley

1960s: From Field to Image

I've been thinking about my childhood in Lincolnshire recently, while writing an alphabet sequence with drawings by Peterjon Skelt. It has to do with landscape and language, including the songs and nursery rhymes that we learnt. The letter "c", for example, makes use of the folk song 'John Barleycorn', a tale of birth, death and rebirth in the eternal round of the harvest. In our songbook there were darkly etched drawings of the planting of John, his growth, and the three men who came from the west to cut him down and bind him as the reapers would once have bound the sheaves. It is graphic violence, in which John Barleycorn is cut off at the knee, rolled and tied, and pricked to the heart with sharp pitchforks. I was at an age when I could simultaneously understand that this was a song about the harvest and be equally convinced that it was actual murder:

> They ploughed, they sowed, they harrowed him in,
> > throwed clods upon his head,
> And these three men made a solemn vow, John Barleycorn
> > was dead.

'John Barleycorn' bore no relation to my experience of the planting or harvest of corn. Our house was at the edge of a council estate, bounded on two sides by immense corn fields, and large combine harvesters would appear in August. I don't know who did the work, or whose fields they were, and it was a bloodless, disembodied murder, which eliminated most of the wild life.

In "i", there is a nursery rhyme which begins:

> If all the world were paper,
> and all the sea were ink

I was in the school playground, and I was jumping between the areas in shadow and those in light. These were my continents and oceans. They were uninhabitable with nothing to eat or to drink, no life at all. I could taste this strange world, hold it on my tongue, as if I was forced to eat paper, like communion wafers, and drink ink. The school playground was my first experience of a man made desert. This nursery rhyme began as a sophisticated satire for adults in the 17th century: the *Oxford Dictionary of Nursery Rhymes* believes it is a parody of the extravagant language of ancient Jewish and Mediaeval scholarly adoration of the deity. Its other verses, not included in the children's version, satirise financial get rich quick schemes, as Noel Malcolm argues in *The Origins of English Nonsense*. Like 'John Barleycorn', it is a dark adult lyric handed to children, as if it were childish nonsense.

Grantham Grammar school was an hour's bus ride from the village. My first English teacher made us enact Tennyson's 'The Lady of Shalott' and I found her and the poem ridiculous. It didn't help that she was bent on changing my speech, from the short Northern vowels to a more elongated received pronunciation. I remember a girl reciting W.B. Yeats' 'The Fiddler of Dooney' with correct vowel sounds: "and dahnced like the wa-aves of the sea". All that you had to know was the regularity of the waves and all that you had to fear was the stammer, the hesitation, the sense. A new English teacher introduced us to the First World War poets and soon I would be writing anti-Vietnam-War poetry. I was also in the school choir and sang the Middle English lyrics of Benjamin Britten's 'Ceremony of Carols'. My favourite text, which ricochets with multi-layered dissonance in Britten's setting, is 'This Little Babe' from Robert Southwell's 'Newe Heaven, New Warre'.

In 1967 we moved to Minehead, a small seaside town in Somerset. I studied Chaucer, Milton, Pope, and Yeats. I discovered Emily Dickinson and Gertrude Stein. I recited Manley Hopkins with my best friend. We also wrote poems in alternate hidden lines, a game of poetic consequences. Our first lines were often the best, such as one of hers: "It was snowing in the cellar onto dissipated lard", which it probably was.

Then I heard about Ezra Pound, ordered some books from the public library, and was transfixed by the poems of *Lustra* and *Cathay*, their wit and their epigrammatic and Imagist techniques. It was my first experience of free verse which mattered. The 'Dos and Don't of

Imagism' and the *ABC of Reading* would dominate my reading and writing for years to come. Both in the landscape of Somerset and in the new affluence of the '60s in southern England there was also plenty of scope for epigrammatic and Imagist poems.

1970S:
THE NEW AMERICAN POETRY, SURREALISM AND LEE HARWOOD

I studied American and English literature and history at the new University of East Anglia. My first collection of poems, *The Sex of Art* (1988) begins in America, when I had a scholarship at Franklin and Marshall College from 1973–4. I spent as much time as I could on the road, and my poetry was often a response to political and cultural tensions post-Vietnam in the conservative Nixon era. F&M did teach me an American lack of embarrassment about career and publication. I was also researching and writing about the "new American poetry" and the heirs of Pound and Carlos Williams: Charles Olson's projective verse, Robert Duncan and Robert Creeley. There were also the West Coast poets: I was influenced by Gary Snyder and his "nonhuman, nonverbal world, which is nature as nature is itself". In 'Riprap' the construction of a mountain trail combines language and things, as a poem could:

> Lay down these words
> Before your mind like rocks.
>   placed solid, by hands

Snyder was fine for crossing the Rockies, where I chanted the *Cold Mountain* poems, but more often I was in the city. There was Ginsberg, of course, who, in his assumption of Whitman's cloak, made my journeys through the American nightmare more bearable, and I also turned to the New York poets.

In 1972, on a poetry course at Totleigh Barton Manor in Devon, I met Peterjon Skelt who, as well as writing poetry, was making strange and exquisite drawings. It was Peterjon who introduced me to Lee Harwood's poetry, as well as sharing his interest in the work of the New York poets Ashbery and O'Hara. As we both lived in Somerset we would meet during the long vacations. In the summer of 1975 we hitched around France, visiting the Max Ernst exhibition in Paris and carrying with us a copy of Lee Harwood's newly published translations of Tristan Tzara.

It took living and studying in America to make me realise how European I was, and to see the importance of Surrealism for much of what had happened in contemporary American poetry. Back at UEA I took European literature seminars in my final year. I studied Futurism and Expressionism, and their relationship to modern technology. My disillusionment with the American dream and technology was expressed in a poem about my visit to the John F. Kennedy Space Center and the gloom expressed by the engineers: "we're all stopping/ to take account/ and play back".

From 1975–76 I did an MA in Comparative Literature at Sussex University and my dissertation was a comparative study of Pound, Apollinaire and the visual arts. I got involved with the student arts magazine at Sussex, both editing and contributing. There was a power struggle with a student who propounded anarchist politics. His language was generally that of '60s counterculture, but with a new element of (male) intolerance and aggression which was disturbing. We agreed to do an issue on 'Liberation' and I published an essay I'd written for a feminist seminar in the States, underpinned by Simone de Beauvoir's theory. The shifting of genders and roles became a theme in my poetry.

In 1976 I went to a conference on Ezra Pound at the University of Keele. It brought me face to face with the full extent of Pound's fascist politics, which I could no longer ignore, and which I responded to in 'The Pound Papers'.

I got a scholarship to study French poetry and the visual arts, especially post Surrealism, in Switzerland, as part of my PhD, and I wrote about Artaud, Breton, Eluard, and Reverdy. My poetry was influenced by Reverdy, who had learnt a new syntax from Mallarmé, as well as responding to the Cubism. Ultimately I found him too ascetic and hermetic, as he withdrew from the world. I also wrote about the contemporary poet, Yves Bonnefoy, but I became increasingly uncomfortable with his poetics—their essentialist and quasi-metaphysical use of language. Rexroth had called him the "cul de sac of modern French poetry". Studying the Surrealists inevitably encouraged me to attempt automatic writing, although it was a technique that I would not seriously practice until much later. I did write a version of Breton's 'L'Union libre' (Free Union) with the male as object of desire rather than the female. It's an unedited version, as my lover objected to any deletions or revisions.

The good thing about returning to Brighton was that I could go to Lee Harwood's readings at the Public House bookshop. Lee has given me "such rare moments of being where one is", especially in the hills of the West Country and Wales. Peterjon, by this time, was studying Lee Harwood's poetry with Eric Mottram at King's College, and doing some of his research with Lee in Brighton.

I also did other courses at Totleigh Barton, which were fairly unstructured, a contrast to the later excess of programming and "value for money". One was for poets and painters, and all we had was the theme of "face in the landscape" and the opportunity to collaborate. We made an unfolding image/text called 'North Face'.

1980s: New British Poetry, Feminism and Publishing

In 1980 I moved to London to work in a library, and got to know much more about contemporary British poetry, especially in its radical manifestations at Sub-Voicive readings. The London poetry scene is not the subject of this book, but it is a history which still needs to be recounted in its full complexity and multipli(city). The history of Sub-Voicive alone needs to be told fully and more accurately. The role of women poets has been neglected, which is a common occurrence and not confined to that venue or to London. As Robert Sheppard has recently suggested, it has something to do with the male group operating in a way that was intimidating to women; but it also has to do with male critics, whether consciously or unconsciously, writing women out of the history of performance spaces and small presses.

There was a new wave of feminism in the '80s and it was a time of discovering important women modernist poets such as H.D. and Mina Loy, as well as the work of Surrealist women writers and artists, who had been marginalised or ignored in the university curriculum and the literary canon, and whose works were being reprinted and discussed at last.

I became involved in small press activity in the late '80s, partly as a continuation of my creative friendship with Peterjon Skelt. He had always wanted to be a publisher and in 1986 began North and South press with his wife Yasmin, his friend from Aberystwyth University, the poet David Annwn, and me. North and South was so named because it was based at the Skelts' in London and with David in Wakefield, and was intended to publish poets from Britain and the States. I got to know David well, often through his letters, a late night gift after a day at work, full of wit and insight. As well as publishing our own poetry and art, North and South authors included Lee Harwood, Elaine Randell, Ric Caddel, Eric Mottram, Geraldine Monk, Kelvin Corcoran and Catherine Walsh. We read and discussed the manuscripts as they came in, and it was a wonderful opportunity for me to gain a deeper understanding of the work of some of the best contemporary British poets. I was excited by Elaine Randell's work; her selected poems had recently been published by Pig Press. We published her collection of prose texts, *Gut Reaction*, which were not afraid of social realities and recorded the voices of the people that she worked with. Randell compared these pieces to Barry MacSweeney's texts about journalism. There is nothing lyrical about them. I was working on community projects, so I understood the subject matter as well as the desire to break with the consoling patterns that poetry could provide. We became friends, I visited her in Kent, and we exchanged letters and poems.

We also took North and South to bookfairs, the first and possibly most memorable being the Oriel Book Fair in Cardiff in 1987, hosted by Peter Finch, where I also met Chris Broadribb (now Ozzard), publisher of *Kite* magazine, and the poet Graham Hartill. Cardiff was also where I met Elisabeth Bletsoe a few years later, when I performed at the 'Deadlier than the Male' cabaret.

1990–94: Other Collaborations, Outside

In the early '90s North & South published Kelvin Corcoran who became a friend and correspondent, and his book *Next Wave*, mirrored my outrage with a country dying from the political centre. I was also keen for North and South to publish Geraldine Monk. Her use of the grotesque, menacing nursery rhymes and innovative, but often constricting layout, seemed to me to offer another route to surviving the Thatcher era. I contacted her about a possible book, and we entered into a long and enjoyable correspondence, which eventually resulted in her selected poems, *The Sway of Precious Demons* (1992). (Both David and Geraldine were given to satirising letterheads, including one from a creative writing course, "Starting to Write?", to which Geraldine has penned "Don't. See a doctor."). In 1991 we also published *Prospect into Breath: interviews with North and South writers*, which is an important source reference and full account of many of the writers mentioned here from the 1960s to the '80s. However, North & South was hit hard by the recession and financial commitments, and ceased publishing a few years later.

After North & South, I started a very small low-budget press of my own, The Other Press. The first publication in 1993 was *Climbing through Fire*, an anthology of work by various poets and artists. This was followed by my book, *Hula Hoop* in 1993, which includes poems written in response to some of the poets already mentioned. The Other Press has focused primarily on women poets, as one of the things I noticed at North and South was how few women poets submitted their work, feeling inhibited in a way that did not seem to affect their male contemporaries.

Although based in London, I continued to spend time in Somerset, and *Somerset letters* (Oasis, 2002) consists of 10 prose "letters" and 10 poems which were written on occasional visits over a seven-year period, combined with drawings by Ian Robinson. *Somerset letters* began in the early '90s as an exchange of letters and poems with Elaine Randell: I was attracted by her exploration of both rural landscape and fractured rural communities. Another poet whose poetry and correspondence became part of that sequence was Harriet Tarlo, whom I met at a feminist poetry conference in the early '90s. Living in Northumberland and researching H.D., she was finding new ways to write about landscape, as well as co-organising the H.D. reading week in Cornwall. Later I would publish her first book, *Brancepeth Beck*, with drawings by Julia Ball.

SUM

This has been a rapid and highly condensed account of aspects of my life as a British poet up to 1995. Significant themes, such as landscape, gender and politics, had emerged and would continue in my later work, such as *Stone settings*. Before the internet, there were meetings, readings, conferences and small press publications which enabled me to find new developments in poetic form, as well as publishing and performing opportunities. Collaborative methods of working would lead to a series of projects with other poets and artists, such as *Neither the One nor the Other*, with Elizabeth James, which encouraged experimentation and mutual support. All of these things were essential for any poet marginalised by the conservative British poetry establishment, or by a male-dominated avant-garde.

Selected References

'The convergence of art and poetry in the work of Guillaume Apollinaire and Ezra Pound' (MA, University of Sussex, 1976)

'Yves Bonnefoy and the poetics of unity' (MPhil, University of East Anglia, 1986)

The Sex of Art: selected poems and prose 1973–1986, London & Wakefield: North and South, 1988

Prospect into Breath: interviews with North and South writers, edited by Peterjon Skelt, ibid. 1991

Hula Hoop, London: Other Press, 1993

Climbing through Fire: a collection of texts and images from a performance and correspondence, in August 1992, edited by Frances Presley, ibid. 1993

'*Surrealism and Women*, edited by Mary Ann Caws', *Word & Image*, 9(1), 1993, pp. 90–92

'Collaboration: *Neither the One nor the Other*, by Elizabeth James and Frances Presley, with an introduction on working practice', in *How2*, Fall 2001

Somerset letters, London: Oasis, 2002

'Common pink metaphor: from "The Landscape Room" to *Somerset Letters*', in *How2*, 2008

'Half of Goodbye'

Ian Davidson

Poetry and the University of Essex 1975–82

This essay is made up of personal memories of a particular period in Essex from the mid 1970s to the early 1980s. It makes no attempt to give a comprehensive history. It also makes no attempt to summarise the very important work currently taking place in Essex in relation to poetry, and the symposium on the work of Douglas Oliver and the recent work on dreams are only two examples. And of those who were there but I've not mentioned, I apologise.

Poetry was big at Essex University when I was there. I could give you a list of names and will later, but it will be a sample, without any pretence of being a complete list. Nor will it claim to be representative. There is no core group of poets that make up an Essex School of Poetry. I could try to say something general about the poetics of an Essex School of Poetry but I'd fail in that, resorting to the specifics of examples that are also exceptions, and end up telling you something about the kind of poetry some of them wrote, or at least what was important to me in their poetry. There was no Essex School, and therefore there can be no representative or example.

There was no vanguard of poets on the eastern edge of England who all wrote about similar things in similar ways, or poets fulfilling a manifesto, or a movement that has now become exhausted and must be recorded for history. Perhaps the only thing the poets I talk about would have in common is that they wouldn't want to be part of an Essex School of Poetry even if there was one. So this essay is not a strategic attempt to mark out an institutional or national space, to give Essex Poetry a place of authority in the histories of British poetry, nor is it even tactically trying to insert the work into narratives of experimentalism.

If there is no "who or what" of Essex Poetry there may be little left to say and I should let the histories dwindle away, or remain within the very vibrant activity that happens there now. Maybe the enduring memory of Essex University from the early decades of its life (it didn't exist until the mid-1960s) is of its radical politics, of the sit-ins, the Angry Brigade down the road at Wivenhoe, the repeated attempts of the anarchists to blow up Barclays Bank in Square 4.

There is, however, something to say, and the evidence of its importance is in the number and variety of people who attended Essex as undergraduates and postgraduates and who, thirty or forty years later in some cases, are still writing, publishing and performing poetry, and perhaps even more importantly, persisting in publishing the work of others through books, chapbooks, pamphlets and magazines. The connections back to Essex might be gossamer thin and some writers are completely independent of others who were at Essex, with no contact, while others form small partnerships or constellations of activity that might appear occasionally. The journal *Active in Airtime* is one example, appearing in the 1990s and edited out of Brightlingsea by Ralph Hawkins and John Muckle, both of whom were in Essex in the 1970s and '80s. If this essay is, in any ways, part of a history, it is not the history of a period with start and end dates, but moments, and moments that might have significant duration, that might keep going but are all out of time with each other.

Alongside the list of names, and I will get to that, there were certain other characteristics of life at Essex University. The degree to which these characteristics were significant is difficult to assess, but they form a part of the overall context. The first is the curriculum. At Essex you studied Literature, not English. In the first-year 18th-Century module you studied Voltaire as well as Richardson and Defoe. In the second and third years you studied English and European Literature or US literature, mixing George Eliot and Elizabeth Gaskell with Emile Zola and Nathaniel Hawthorne. In Renaissance prose you would study Bocaccio and Rabelais as well as Bacon and there was strong interest in Latin American literature. And these period and area studies were supported by Practical Criticism classes where you learnt the formal art of reading literature without the historical context. More importantly the Practical Criticism classes allowed PhD students the chance to earn some money, and to introduce thrill-seeking undergraduates to stuff that sat outside the curriculum, literature that was too hot for a cool academic examination. In Ralph Hawkins' class we looked at Prynne, Zukofsky, Niedecker, Oppen, Berrigan, among others, Ralph claiming that he knew nothing of the poems before the class but simply opening the book at random before making the photocopies. I took his class alongside Kelvin Corcoran. In Doug Oliver's class I can remember looking at a section of *Naked Lunch*, and one of the anarchists had scrawled across the board "Storm the Reality Studios". Anthony Barnett used to come to those classes (he was taking an MA in Translation). I was a Prac Crit slut, often two-timing and going to more classes than I should. And all this took place in a University with only 2,000 students in total. There can't have been more than 200 studying literature, maybe far less. We all knew each other, and I also knew mathematicians, sociologists and computer scientists.

Essex University was famous for being a place of radical politics, occupations and demonstrations. In the language at the time it was a "hotbed" of left-wing political activity. Anna Mendelssohn, who was jailed for her alleged activity with the Angry Brigade, dropped out of her literature course at Essex in the 1960s but went on to write and publish under the name of Grace Lake. The poetry and the politics were, for some, inextricably linked through their subject matter, through the use of poetic form to expose those truths British Imperialism and the capitalist system sought to conceal in a manipulated and manipulative mass media, and the use of home-made methods of producing and distributing political and poetic material. There was a strong sense of urgency in the political agenda and a desire to expose the workings of the "justice" system and government and the ways that the capitalist system lied and cheated to normalise prejudice and inequality. Part of the political activism produced a steady flow of home printed news-sheets, pamphlets and broadsheet publications, distributed by hand at rallies and meetings. For some, poetry followed this model. It was work that had to be got out, work that the more mainstream poetic establishment would suppress simply by ignoring it. It was poetry that exposed or critiqued the way that social power was produced and sustained. Poetry wasn't just a calling, it was absolutely necessary, and a strong interest in the sociology of literature, in formalism, structuralism and poststructuralism, meant that the poetry challenged social structures, not just by creating new meanings but by challenging the process of making meaning itself.

There was another, less obvious, benefit to this political activism—a diverse student body. Most of the students I knew at Essex would be classified as "non-traditional"; mature students, overseas students, political refugees, self-educators through the trade-union movement, and with a high proportion from working class backgrounds. It was unremittingly and entirely international and internationalist, linking individual to individual without the barriers of national formations. In retrospect it was probably the result of a recruitment and financial crisis rather than policy to widen access, as the university was shunned by the more aware middle-class families. The result was that many of the student body were wide-eyed at the possibility of a university education for which there was no family precedent. All things seemed possible. In retrospect, and this wasn't obvious at the time, or certainly wasn't a particular topic of discussion, there was little overlap or connection between a very active feminist movement at Essex and the poetry. The poets were nearly all male, although the ones I knew did read the work of many women poets, particularly from the US. This didn't mean a lack of awareness or contact in other ways, and I remember accompanying John Muckle on "Reclaim the Night" marches as a pre-ecologically-conscious feminist movement demanded more and better street lights, but the link never transpired through the poetry. This was a loss, but was also only one manifestation of the tension between a populist politics and a poetry that promoted a populism in work that was often very difficult to understand and distributed outside of the normal commercial channels. I'll return to this.

Essex University always had poets around in a variety of roles. Long before Creative Writing was a glint of precious metal in a Head of Department's budget line, Donald Davie, as the first Professor of Literature at Essex, established a department which subsequently brought in Robert Lowell, Ed Dorn, Tom Raworth and Ted Berrigan. They had all finished their stints as visiting writers by the time I got there, but their influence continued. But as I said at the start of this essay I'm less interested in giving a documented history, although there might well be a place for that, but more interested in looking at the writing and publishing activities of those who went there, and the different parts that Essex play in their trajectory. I can only give examples. Of my immediate peers Kelvin Corcoran and John Muckle are both still writing, although John's focus is now more on novels. John Muckle, through his work at Paladin in the 1980s took British experimental poetry into mainstream publishing, as general editor of *New British Poetry* and a range of collections of work by Allen Fisher, Bill Griffiths, Doug Oliver, Brian Catling and many others through Paladin. Kelvin Corcoran has engaged in a range of small-scale publishing ventures through Short Run Press and Gratton Street Irregulars, publishing writers from across the experimental range, as well as sustaining a run of book publications. Ralph Hawkins, a PhD student while we were undergraduates, is still writing as much as ever, and edited *The Human Handkerchief, Ochre* and *Active in Airtime*. Doug Oliver's commitment to publishing continued and he began editing the magazine *Gare du Nord* from Paris with Alice Notley in the 1990s, and Allen Fisher continues to write and publish through his Spanner press. Tony Frazer is now the major specialist publisher of experimental poetry in the UK through his Shearsman press, and has brought into print many of the most important figures in contemporary British poetry. The list of names continues: Tony Lopez, Paul Brown, Jeremy Reed, Andrew Crozier and Ken Smith. Who have I missed out?

But this is no homogenous group of figures. While the dominant poetic might lie somewhere between Black Mountain, New York, London and Cambridge, one characteristic of this list of names is that so many of them didn't formally study poetry, or chose to study other things as well. Allen Fisher and Tony Frazer both studied History of Art, Doug Oliver's MA was in Linguistics, Anthony Barnett and Pierre Joris took MAs in Literary Translation. So the characteristic of Essex is that the focus of the work was not on one country, and the early interest in Essex in the work of O'Hara and Ashbery could as well have stemmed from their links with French writing as their status as Americans or New Yorkers. Nor was it in one discipline, spreading across Comparative Literature and the arts, humanities and social sciences. The lack of ability and desire to mark out a place for itself in a culturally or socially determined space is a principal characteristic and the reason for its enduring influence, and an influence determined as much by doing things as by talking about them. The concrete structures of early Essex University provided no shelter for a poetic that isolated itself from cultural and material consequences and responsibilities in a writing life that could remain intramural. The buildings at Essex never kept out the East wind that blew straight down from the Urals but only served to strengthen it as it was funnelled between the towers and into the concrete squares. The result has been poetry that has often sat uneasily between an experimentation that can remain within the walls of the institution, in intense conversation with the English lyric tradition, and a poetry that has to, however imperfectly, prove itself within a world of real material consequences for ordinary people living everyday lives.

You Need an Urn

Nicholas Johnson

Early auspices for the 6 Towns Poetry Festival 1992–1997,
Stoke-on-Trent

for Roger Brown of Hartshill

*I would sit high up on the rocks and listen to the sounds of the night:
the water birds over at Tittesworth Reservoir and nocturnal and domestic
animals all adding to the sounds of movement and calling, shrieking and
squealing, making their contributions to the sounds of the night. There are
different noises for different things, all adding up to life and death and
Mother Nature in her different moods. No one can beat her, as she is always
the winner in the long run.*

King Doug, Lord of the Roaches

1

In 1990, aged twenty-seven, I moved from the West Country to live
in Stoke-on-Trent in the Potteries. There I was to hear an accent that
was strong and bewildering. People talked at a rapid, emphatic pace,
and appeared to go off at a tangent, when really they'd communicated
something quite clear to you. There were streets of two-up two-downs,
parlours with ornaments and photographs where nobody sat. Foyers
to vibrant *backs*. Streets were often on hills, the city existed in a bowl;
inebriated by spume from factories and scuzzy cars; the potbanks of
Spode Wedgwood Doulton. The speech I listened to was warm and
vibrant, sing-song, stuffed with strange sounds and phrases.

Everywhere you went was *oop*. Stoke-on-Trent was its kingdom.
Now you could buy it. Stoke was skint. It had the worst diet in
England. The hospital had been investigated for forged paperwork and
irregularities regarding neonatal ventilatory and bronchiolitis support
over three years. Many potbanks had shut down. Etruria Station would
too.

Near the canal, opposite Stoke-on-Trent station, stood the North Staffordshire hotel where the American poet Edward Dorn would, six years later, leave his cowboy boots, ready for the fleet foot transit to Colorado. Here stood the Polytechnic (now Staffordshire University), that evolved from Burslem Art College. This housed The Flaxman Gallery, and Film Theatre. I saw Geoffrey Soar's and David Miller's exhibition *The Story of Little Presses and How They Got That Way* (1991). Value was given pamphlets, letraset, photocopying on different colour papers, threads running like sutures through four folded sheets was a revelation.

The painter and writer Arthur Berry had taught at Burslem. Andrew Crozier included a poem, 'The Life Class', dedicated to him in *A Various Art*. Barry MacSweeney read with Berry to a large audience at Burslem Town Hall in the 1970s. Arthur Berry's rendition of a Mrs Potter who began to grow feathers while hanging out washing, perched on the clothesline was priceless. Learning to gauge historical affiliation between poets became crucial in the shaping of the 6 Towns Poetry Festival. Determining the interstices.

The history of any set-up is dependent on layers of the previous occupants. Which artists had already resided in Stoke-on-Trent? What artistic medium were its citizens most proud of? In the 1970s, Peter Riley recalls; "The attempts to set up free-jazz and poetry events… grants were available through the *Quality of Life* schemes… mostly attendance was very poor, there was no continuity…" Andrew Crozier occasionally put on something at Keele including, 'The unveiling of Peter Riley'.

Riley was writing his thesis on Jack Spicer at Keele under Roy Fisher. Riley writes, "In Macclesfield we began to relate more strongly to Manchester, where there was a lot more happening, but there was never a poetry event there of the scope of your enterprises in Stoke… what the 6 Towns Poetry Festivals meant to me was mainly an instance of what one person can do with energy and devotion in an unpromising environment."

The University of Keele was five miles from Stoke[1]. I should have liked Keele better; for it had an American Studies department, where Crozier and Fisher had taught, and Keele was also home to Pound and Beckett scholars. Few academics were to attend the festival.

Stoke-on-Trent stood on the crossroads of Derbyshire, Shropshire, Cheshire and its own Staffordshire. It was two hours from Yorkshire and the Welsh Marches. I was able to create a poetry festival, possessing neither rival nor precedent because nobody ran one. Stoke-on-Trent possessed civic pride in the arts, the tiling in Burslem library proves that. So does the Havergal Brian festival, whose posters I saw in *Tostevins*, the Hartshill piano dealers.

I hadn't given logical thought as to why I was there; uprooting my wife and sons from what was familiar and encompassed friendships, family. Impulse? Instinct? Ideals of perpetuating poetry, by studying Anglo Saxon? Or French, which I never comprehended the grammar of?

That summer I bought an undergraduate magazine (20p) containing an interview with Roy Fisher, who had left Keele in 1982 to complete *A Furnace*. The interview, by Jonathan Roper, contained a description of a surprise visit made to his Devon home while he was out teaching, in the 1950s, by the American poet Louis Zukofsky, his wife Celia, their son Paul and Paul's cello teacher. Roy's wife served them tea. Roy was never to meet the Zukofskys.

The immediacy of Fisher's speech and his perceptions on location and writing intrigued me. Roy Fisher: no longer visible at Keele, but in the aether, named on an out-of-date poster for his jazz combo in the New Victoria Theatre, Newcastle-under-Lyme, a foyer performance one Sunday spent and past, the persona of his poem 'Paraphrases'.

Then I got a letter from another American poet, Jonathan Williams, from Cumbria. The postscript intrigued me: "Gael Turnbull crossing the Potteries now". This should have alerted me that Turnbull divided his week between Edinburgh and the colliery village of Silverdale, where his wife studied Ceramics at the Poly. Roy's wife, Joyce Halliday, had her play *Go See Fanny Deakin!* performed at the New Victoria Theatre, celebrating a Silverdale pioneer for healthcare and children's nutrition.

If you knew Gael Turnbull, which three years later I did, you could never say he divided his time. How could he, once an anaesthetist and GP, have at any point divided his time? This was simply not possible. Gael was a daily writer of poems, of letters, who began each day with melancholia, and pushed this incrementally aside. He saw equal value in hiking miles *and* gathering sheep's wool, or keeping vigil at Carlton Hill round the brazier and morris dancing.

Turnbull read border ballads from memory and was fluent in French. He showed poetry was a craft, but also trade, transmitting a joy in creation. He would staple together homemade £1 *Selected Poems*, and bulletins—*Minimal Missives* he called these. He busked with a kinetic sculpture each year at the Edinburgh festival, wearing top hat and tails. He forged friendships by letter and in person all over the world. In the early, lonely Stoke years I'd have revelled in his friendship.

Gael was not one to say, "look who I am being", but would sign his poems using alternative persona, filtering in poems about his father into *Migrant*, signed Thomas Lundin. In one sense this was a bit of frivolity, just as his writing as C.B. Rutley was. As Fisher would say, "Gael had a strange set of shutters and opening bits; and was not wont to hang about to describe his motives."

Roy Fisher would become an ally. In 1993 I gave him his blue-inked stamp, ROY FISHER, PATRON. To see him publicly at his most happy was to see a raconteur; weaving in his knobbled synonyms, a note-perfect mimic. His sons, Ben and Joe, possessed a similar elation in mimicry, the absurd. Ben Fisher wrote a book on Alfred Jarry. They ran a Moore Marriott Appreciation Society, and concocted a campaign to erect a statue of this actor, born Norman Hedges, as Bognor Regis' most famous son. Fisher *senior* wrote letters of support, posing as a Vicar. Marriott played toothless Harbottle, near to death, reciting a bad, short poem 'The 'Eadless Horseman' with Will Hay, and Graham Moffat who "died of being fat", in Marcel Vernel's *Ask a Policeman* (1939).

As a poet, still young in practice, I needed to find writers to hear, read, and write to. I revered John Riley and Seán Rafferty, their poetry barely in print. And Sorley MacLean, whom I'd travelled twice to hear read. After a long book-signing queue he recited me from memory undergraduate verses by J.D.K Rafferty, 'The Road To Wittenberg' (1931).

That same week (October 1991) I'd travelled to The Poetry Bookshop in Hay-on-Wye, and bought on tick a large batch of booklets broadsheets and folded ephemera by Bill Griffiths, and, with a screen window onto the title, *Prior* by Maurice Scully, (Staple Diet). I'd failed the Keele foundation year exams that summer and spent a night before one exam reading *David Jones: The Long Conversation* by William Blissett, that exemplifies the heart of friendship between a poet still in his observations and a young novice.

By Easter 1992 I was working at The Cactus Community Bookshop in Hope Street, Hanley, near Jehovah's chapel, the guitar shop, shops for toys or prams, the shut Six Towns Café, jutting out like a vein in a neck. This thinly stocked threadbare shop with an outdoor latrine was where I began threading in a poetry stock, from Writers Forum, Equofinality, Galloping Dog, Pig Press; Paladin Re/active, and distributing Seán Rafferty's *Poems 1940–1982*, a strange brown book nameless on the spine, resembling a Latin primer, anonymously paid for.

To promote our stock, I began a reading series over the shop. They included a celebration of the poetry of Giorgio Verrechia, which Tom Lowenstein hosted. James Keery read with John Welch, Fred Beake with Jenny Johnson. Kris Hemensley wrote aerogrammes from Melbourne, as if he were nearby. Elizabeth Burns read (and sometimes worked) at Cactus too. She was to bear quiet witness to the trajectory of events. Bill Griffiths read poems about carrots with his Doc Martens tapping on the ridge of the latrine wall, and 'The Bowmen'. There was a sharp, clear reading by Jim Burns. He read for his fares from Stockport. His movements were always geared to the train timetable. "We're in the same boat", Burns said, "all baling out".

His encouragement was calmer than Griffiths'. Both were important. Griffiths had tattoos on each hand. LOVE. HATE. And saffron fingers. When I introduced myself after a London reading he ground his foot into mine; a kind of dominance dog game. He took me that Stoke night to the pub in Hope Street; happened to be frequented by bikers, due up to the Roaches and onto Ashbourne towards Sheffield. He asked if I know the Anglo Saxon scholar Barbara Raw up at Keele—and maybe you should do a poetry festival, he said. Mebbe you should.

The spine of 6 Towns Poetry Festival would be grant and sponsorship: incrementally increased West Midland Arts grants under the wise auspices of David Hart and practical help from people who liked a festival, and an endorsement of the festival, their name (Sentinel Newspapers, North Staffordshire Hotel, Webberleys Books). Local guest houses, a health food shop, Scarthin Books of Cromford, and more assumingly, The Poetry Bookshop, all pitched in money or sponsorship.

One result was (apart from Alan Halsey meeting Geraldine Monk at a 1996 reading honouring David Jones, resulting in his essay *Stalking Within Yer Chamber* and her wedding ring) from the cheerful print department of Staffordshire University, was the annual series of festival anthologies, *Peacocks Was Really Great*, (a Seán Rafferty phrase), *Peacocks Two* (a Many Press chapbook typeset by Wellsweep, Bob Cobbing cover), *Peacock Blue, Ink Feathers* (Bill Griffiths title and cover) and *Etruscan Jetty*.

I bought an electronic typewriter, and a second disc with a font I liked. With two fonts and hand-drawn author names, I typed each poem representing each poet in order of appearance. I included work by writers pleased to be invited, but unable to participate, like David Gascoyne, William Bronk and Brian Coffey (1994–96). Coffey's letters were a pleasure to receive, the handwriting miniscule. He invited me to Southampton to spend an afternoon, and the Gascoynes to stay.

As well as instilling early editing practice, it also formed the origin of the Etruscan Readers, 3-in-1 volumes, with a series of covers of feathers by Brigid McLeer in a finite series of 9. In 1996, I reasoned that instead of a 300-photocopy run for an anthology, Staffordshire could print six thin readers in 75-print-runs, and 125 copies of *Etruscan Jetty*. They barely had a spine, or two staples but they laid the ground for the material I would use in the series *proper*. Martin Grant at GTI Print became printer of the Etruscan brochures, and one of my trusted four, the two Roberts (typographers), the two Martins (brochures), Martyn Young who ran Budget Books.[2]

The objective was: gather writers at the festival, whom I felt would sound their work, give them an armchair, or a bonkers lamp, a draw leaf table but have an acoustic where sound could be aimed at the far wall to peal off. Brian Catling was to say "You know an audience's energy with your back to them." No. 19 Barracks Square provided this. They were former barracks, 19th century, with a cobbled square, housing 24 businesses. The audience passed through a doorway and up a flight of stairs and turned right into a room with a black rubber floor with the chairs in a horseshoe, the writer against one wall the pitch was rich and vibrant. The sound had strata.

At Leek three weeks before the festival, set up at Cactus and the Hassell phonebox, I had a *grand mal* epileptic seizure, sticking up posters. My landlord Peter Wilshaw came by. He said you need an urn. Plenty of chairs, and folks to put up poets. He chose John Seed and Barry MacSweeney, found lodgings for other poets, and hired 50 chairs from Hassell primary school. Maurice Scully had told me his wife Mary was a pyromaniac, so Peter put a rickety caravan in our garden, where the Scullys could have bonfires. Peter and Susan Clarke enabled the festival to occur and flourish, by their generosity, wit and common sense.[3] They steered and shaped practical corners of the festival. We revelled in reliving the antics and presence of the poets every year.

2

Once the train passed Wolverhampton, you fell into a reverie—as you headed for Birmingham's tunnels, beside sliding windows of a silent film poem compatriot to reading and memorised recall of Roy Fisher's voice. "Roy Fisher", he said, quizzically viewing the photocopied programme two teenagers had done for the 6 Towns Poetry Festival, *A Guide To 13 Hard Working Poets*, "Writes prose poems. He reads them too." His reading had begun. He didn't share the complexity of *The Ship's Orchestra* or *The Cut Pages* with the audience. No, Fisher read jagged squibs about Zoggists, Edwin Morgan, Ianists. This line got a laugh. "The spirit of Queen Geraldine, Borne on a Cloud, Encourages Flagging Zoggists during a Skirmish near Burnley." The chairs creaked in rows down one end of The Barracks. The acoustic rising like a spent kit. Geraldine Monk had read first, premiering *Interregnum*, ripper poems like the music hall skirl 'Jennet Device.'

On the second day, with a radical rethink of seating, John Seed read. He said it was like a Beckett set. He remembers: "A courtyard, a door, stairs up to a kind of loft with bits of second-hand furniture distributed around rather like a charity furniture shop. A sofa and an old lamp standard? It was in that doorway I first got to know Bill Griffiths as we both tugged on our cigarettes. I'd seen and heard him read a couple of times and been in his company together with others at *Writers Forum* events and elsewhere. But this was first time we'd talked one to one and from it came our regular meetings in South West London for the remainder of his life—and a few meetings in the North East and dozens of letters and emails and a real friendship... I remember Barry MacSweeney's powerful reading and how he mysteriously disappeared from the house where I was staying in the middle of the night. We were all worried about where a drunken stranger and poet might end up at 4 or 5 am on a Sunday morning somewhere in the Potteries! Was [Peter Wilshaw's] house on a hill, looking over a valley? I remember sitting in a narrow bar later that Sunday morning—Peter Riley was there—and had arrived from Cambridge with Helen Macdonald—and Bill was there and seemed to have no money and I had to insist very strongly that he let me buy him a pint (maybe he didn't want a pint) and our esteemed editor Geraldine was there too."

During the miner's strike of 1972, in a chilly candle-lit pub in the Potteries, Seed first met Andrew Crozier. He then got to know John Riley in Leeds. That afternoon Seed sat tall in the armchair and gave a strongly accented, lyrical reading from *Interior in the Open Air*. Each sheet dropped on the floor when he'd finished.

Allen Fisher showed slides from *Blood Bone Brain* an earlier Fluxus work, and read various poems in working form, and at my request, 'Gripping The Rail, for Fritz Lang'. His wife, poet Paige Mitchell was with him, and she was very enthusiastic that the festival continue. Many people asked that weekend, when the next festival would be.

The festival, established the format it would use until 1997. Friday to Sunday night, with two matinees over the weekend. Generally, a trio of writers read at each session. The most unusual trio was Lee Harwood, Bill Griffiths and King Doug, Lord of the Roaches, a.k.a. Doug Moller, had fought and lost a battle against the Peak Authorities, who forced him to leave his home built into the rock of The Roaches. A Derbyshire folk devil to climbers and bureaucrats.

King Doug had booked himself into the station hotel, and loped in, with an eye patch. He read a couple of the 'War Correspondence', then began a monologue, scratched by one idea, which sputtered and coalesced a further 20 minutes. All he needed to do was read his vibrant, anarchic letters and some *Autobiography*. Doug sat aside while Griffiths read, fists jangling coins in his shell suit. Allen Fisher had just published Griffiths' *Calendar Contents* at Spanner. I asked Bill what he thought of the King. I thought he needed an injection, he replied. I often found, that, prison campaigns aside, other people's conflict disturbed Bill deeply. I thought his King Doug the Ranter would contrast with Griffiths, and with Harwood, a climber. Harwood read poems from *In The Mists*, grieving the recent death of Paul Evans, killed when in the mountains together. Lee's reading was quiet and brave, modulated by his speech rhythms. His hands as he read indicated the quotation[s] melded into his lines.

The double bill of Barry MacSweeney and Maggie O'Sullivan kicked up a few sparks. MacSweeney's first reading since 1988, his only writing a column on the *South Shields Gazette*, 'The Mouth of the Tyne'. Of poetry, he said, "I have been laid by in a corner". He'd heard a man say to BBC reporters about the death of his grandson in the Meadow Well riots in September 1991, "but our lad was the greatest hotter in Newcastle". That nudged MacSweeney to write again. He opened with 'Finnbar's Lament', formerly known as *Glad Battle Wolf Gosling*, about "a man who has made some bad mistakes". Then he read many *Hell Hound Memos*, and a few squibs by his French pen pal, Edith Cresson.

Following O'Sullivan, who'd dedicated *States of Emergency* to him years before, he said "To continue the lament tone, to read alongside Maggie O'Sullivan, who has swallowed the OED whole and caught some of the best words in any language". Her sound was accumulatory. The splicing, fusing of words built up as an incantatory quilt in front of your ears and eyes.

Maurice Scully opened his reading with the poem I'd asked for, "Sell everything then hope for the best: these are the basic instructions." He'd given a workshop that Friday at a 6th form school. Content, form and style. He travelled from Ennis, Co. Clare, for the reading. Seán Rafferty paid for all the posters that year. He was drawn particularly to Griffiths' hand-made, hand-drawn covered books, and his evocation of Delvan B. McIntosh, who was in prison, Tom Leonard's *Ghostie Men* and to Scully's pamphlet *Over and Through*, with lines like "In kikuyu there is no word for Thankyou".

Rajiv C. Krishnan and Fred Beake read with Maurice Scully. Fred was raising his two children alone, and gardening for old ladies. He had Jonathan Williams' photograph of Basil Bunting looking at a bull on his mantelpiece. I liked his poetry, (and still remember the poem he read that night at Bath workshop, 'Mind Ride'), surreal, lyrical, colloquial, and domestic. His *The Whiteness of Becoming* had just been published. I liked his open view of poetry and the way his editorials emphasised neglect. And exhortation. He'd published an edition of Saint-Pol-Roux, translated Desnos' *The Night of Dreadful Nights,* and edited a valuable anthology *A Mingling of Streams.* His grandfather had run Fred Hill Books in Leek. Now I would ask him as he read Spenser in my bedroom the day before, is that accent how Spenser wrote? "*That* is the accent of my North Staffordshire great grandmothers", Fred declared. "The tendency of Spenser to sound like North West English, tho' he's a South Easterner is curious."

Rajiv C. Krishnan was a devout Hindu who had done a PhD on Pound at Cambridge. J.H. Prynne was his tutor. He enjoyed life in England, but he was returning to India. Over the long, exhilarating weekend, many poets streamed through the parlour to gather in the kitchen. Rajiv chased my sons upstairs, over excited them, then read a story to them. Sunday matinees were made for him. Barefoot, he read his lone three poems *The Watches*[4], and sang a raga. Perhaps he almost danced. And soon, he was back in the house, eating pizza, and once again the house seemed imbued with the social spirit of Kerala. Kerala. We were almost there.

Notes

1. Crewe & Alsager College was 12 miles from Keele. Allen Fisher was Professor of Poetry & Art. It is now part of Manchester Metropolitan University. Nancy Reilley-McVitie who used to be with Wooster Group in New York has lectured there since the early 1990s.

2. Young co-founded Athenaeum, which meant his becoming *Intimate Voices* printer twice. He'd done Galloping Dog and Pig Press. Bill Griffiths recommended him. We went to Bill Griffiths' funeral together.

3. Through their community arts projects with Beavers Arts and collaboration with Welfare State.

4 "Rajiv lived in Cambridge for about three years, and brought a refreshing sense of a socially welcome poetry, sometimes improvised, which has not been seen since." *Peter Riley.*

Courtesy Winter

Anthony Mellors

I've always been slow to cotton-on. I shan't rule out the reason for this being an innate, conservative dullness, but generally attribute it to my abiding hatred of authority which, schooled at forepangs, is sometimes so irrational that it blinds me to my own self-interest and the interest of those closest to me. I was hurting deep inside from the sad business of trying to deny what was. In any case it was a tender little drama in the Sunday countryside. It's comic, therefore, that I became notorious at the crummy, disrupted school in the East of England I (almost) attended for being the first "punk". Another excuse for my troglodyte peers to jeer and kick, though with the changing cultural climate the tag backfired on them, and I went from zero to anti-hero faster than you could play 'Rockaway Beach' by The Ramones. Not that this could prevent the downward spiral of my school career; it just meant I no longer needed to bite the health inspector or slash my legs with a razor blade. I was but a slim, loose-jointed boy at that time, fond of the pretty intangibilities of romance, and of dreaming when broad awake. Strangely, I was still listening to Genesis and Yes and Van der Graaf Generator, but had bought a copy of 'Anarchy in the UK'—news of which formed the legend of my infame—just to see if it was as woefully bad as I was convinced it must be. (It wasn't.)

Simon Reynolds argues in his book *Rip It Up and Start Again* that progressive rock resurfaced after the first flush of punk as a serious if unacknowledged influence on experimental bands. To some extent, then, punk was a momentary repression of a larger tradition of anti-pop, anti-establishment sound invention that retained an "underground" essence even though its better-known exponents had turned into stadium-filling dinosaurs. For the post-punks, punk proper was too much of a step back, too formally conservative; instead, "radical content demands radical form" was the watchword for a generation dedicated to the overthrow of what was to become the Thatcherite consensus. I read Gramsci and Adorno at Sussex University in much the same spirit: it was only a matter of time before the scumbags who told me at school that all that mattered was jobs and money and status and family, keeping your nose to the grindstone, not offending people who mattered, etc., got their tickets punched as the power of the dialectic overcame all the grubby nonsense that went before and still threatened to wreck the lives of enlightened people like me. That revolution is still to come. Today, the likes of Mandelson and Willetts have succeeded in infecting the universities with the old life-denying cant: aspire to conformity, serve the economy, don't ask questions. You might not need a credit card to ride this train, but you sure as hell need one to get off it.

History was to repeat itself. I was contemplating the posters on a wall of Reynolds' rooms in Brasenose College which read "If voting changed anything they'd ban it" and "X X X X X X X X X X X X X : Here's Your Lifetime's Democracy" when the man himself said "You've got to hear this. And hear it again." It was Scritti Politti's 'The Sweetest Girl', a catchy deconstructed pop song, replete with its contextualizing sleeve image of a dreamy girl in military uniform. Scritti seemed to have it all going on at the level of the signifier; a year later, their debut album even included a paean to Jacques Derrida (although they could only get the name to rhyme by mispronouncing it). A year or so after that, lead singer Green Gartside had changed his image from that of revolutionary poster-boy to androgynous neo-romantic. He looked like Lady Di and sounded like The Chipmunks. It was tragic. Any element of political consciousness in the songs was now at best residual. The lesson: the most ambitiously radical may be the most prone to their own subversion.

Even so, the new wave—for want of a better inclusive term— had changed something. In 1977 Pink Floyd came up with their own "punk" diatribe on the state of the nation: *Animals*. In the monumental *Dark Side of the Moon*, lyricist Roger Waters had crisply voiced existential dissatisfaction with the options available in the capitalist lifeworld, offering no political solution or carpe diem motif against the mood of despair for which hippiedom's "softly-spoken magic spells" were as illusory as the promise of a Learjet. But by the time Floyd made the frightful *The Wall* (1979), this lyrical discontent could find no other object than the woes of rock-star success, at which point Prog disappeared so far up its own backside that it was doomed to generate a vast audience of losers forever mourning the demise of a non-existent organic community and the "real music" that was its religion. Just before that moment, however, *Animals* tried to achieve a formal terseness and critical anger quite out of kilter with Prog's growing irrelevance. The album is composed of three movements, each an Orwellian satire on broad class positions in contemporary Britain, and is bookended by plaintive acoustic metacommentaries. 'Dogs' represents middle-class business-led aspirational culture, 'Sheep' dumb though potentially revolutionary workers, and 'Pigs' an amorphous group of fat-cats, busybodies, and moral reformers such as Mary Whitehouse. What emerges as a tripartite class division is played out as a classic bourgeois / proletariat them-and-us opposition, with the others configured as parasites. The dogs are people trained against their better natures to adopt the killer-instinct; they are alienated from themselves and strive pointlessly to achieve worldly success in the face of melancholy death, "dragged down by the stone", as the chief metaphor has it. The sheep, meanwhile, spend their time at pasture, dimly aware of something terrible on the horizon beyond their ken. They are fated to become prey to the dogs. A quick narrative shift has the sheep rise up against their oppressors only to find themselves ensnared by a new regime—their own. So much so Orwell.

The Who expressed the sense of political deadlock more succinctly in 1971 when they declared that the new boss is a repackaged version of the old boss. The framing narrative provided by the Floyd's acoustic vignettes offers token redemption from this grammar-school nihilism: only by caring for one another will people escape their class / animal programming. Yet, with some irony (one hopes), the vocalist acknowledges that he doesn't simply stand outside class identification; caring, he believes, might release him from "the weight of the stone". Ironic or not, this declaration sets the terms of identification as fundamentally petit-bourgeois. The dogs, "trained not to spit in the fan" and "told what to do by the man", remain under the thumb of the pigs, though—crucially—the pigs lack any coherent identity, being merely selected objects of hysterical contempt (the rat-bag at the bus stop arguably having nothing in common with the fatcat in the pig-bin). The narrative can't decide where authority and the critique of authority lies, and so plumps for unfocused them-and-us clichés. And, finally, it has to side with the dogs, splenetically mourning the loss to politics of human decency.

Compared with the bombast of other Prog lyrics, such as the purpled ramblings of Jon Anderson, who branched out from Yes to create the insipid epic *Olias of Sunhillow* (1976), Floyd's are notably free from

Jungian residua. Like good Cambridge puritans, the band eschewed the Celtic fringe for the long view across the fens, a prospect offering no transcendence. This is its virtue, but also its bleakness; when reduced to the cod-modernism of the rock genre, there is nowhere to go. Formally, the lyrics remain tied to simple rhyming schemes, narrative coherence, and stock metaphors. But what grated with me then—even as I lapped-up the concept-album platitudes—and seems to me the first stirrings of my critical sensibility—were the joyless "literary" constructions, as far removed from punk's strident plainness as from the careful attention to register of a Ralph Hawkins or John James. Even as a stripling I hated the imprecision of rock and pop lyrics: their routine, clumsy rhymes, their mismanaged metaphors, their wrenched accents, skewed tenses, and dumb elisions made to fit the music, which you try to read as poetic license but know to be thoughtless expediency. At the very least, there should be a moratorium on songs that include any mention of "dancing in the moonlight" or loving "all night long". Perhaps only Bob Dylan (particularly on his 1978 album *Street Legal*) manages to use rhymes with such unremitting crassness that they sound like genius, e.g., "vacant lot / forget-me-not". Waters' "radiate cold shafts of broken glass", for example, is a ghastly overblown metaphor, which gains nothing from conferring oxymoronic status on "radiate cold", of which its author is almost certainly oblivious. 'Pigs' works hard to generate punk venom, yet calling Mrs Whitehouse a "fucked-up old hag" sounds merely churlish when the refrain is "Ha ha, charade you are". The use of inversion is chronically inept; not only would it not feature in a punk song (instead, perhaps, "you fucking charade") but the wordy word "charade" would not be included in the first place ("you fucking con"). One might as well write a song about toilets and serviettes.

Prog achieved its finest moments by getting rid of lyrics altogether, as in most of Soft Machine's *Third* and all of *Fourth*. Ironically, perhaps only Robert Wyatt had the offbeat flair to come close to the kind of writing made possible by the destruction of the "serious" rock aesthetic. When Morrissey sings about love not being possible until one has seen the stars "reflect" in reservoirs or until dawn has come up behind a Home for the Blind, it's possible to imagine Syd Barrett having a go at the effect, but never the later Floyd or even quirkier Prog outfits such as Caravan and Genesis, whose forays into British whimsy are little more than schoolboy silliness tinged with psychedelic surrealism and literary posturing. In this song, 'The First of the Gang to Die', Morrissey is of course indulging his trademark conceit, the skewed perspective of the boy with a hearing-aid and a thorn in his side. It might all be a little arch, but it can move effortlessly from a Wordsworthian simplicity of image to surprising parodic pathos. 'Reflect' is beautifully placed in the line, and precise, so that if you think for a moment that it ought to be "reflected", you think again; and the rhyming of "stars" with "reservoirs" is both ingenious and funny. As soon as you've taken in this mundane pastoral, you're presented with a pathetic fallacy, calculated to upset the romantic idea of love: if the Home for the Blind is a pathos against which the revelation of dawn appears, it's also clear that the blind themselves cannot share the sentiment. Since the song as a whole concerns the mock-heroic demise of one Hector, who steals from rich and poor alike, as well as from those not so rich and not so poor, and yet "stole all hearts away", this insensitivity is entirely appropriate. Morrissey can deploy the word "sod" in much the same way as Keats in 'Ode to a Nightingale', but he uses it in the knowledge of a colloquial charge that for the modern reader imbues Keats's line with unintended bathos.

"The most undefinable of all kinds of poetical inspiration are surely songs. They seem to start up indeed from the dew-sprinkled soil of a poet's soul like flowers", writes Edwin Paxton Hood in an 1852 study of peasant poetry. More interesting to me than the carefully-fashioned lyric, although I didn't conceptualize it at the time, was the New Wave's abandonment of songwriter sincerity in favour of a semi-random facture that invites contextualization and listener gestalt but doesn't join up the dots. Politically, this radical form had the potential to move away from both finger-pointing protest and quietist soul-searching. As Reynolds argues, "Gang of Four's songs implicated listeners in the very processes being critiqued, rather than cosily dividing the world into a righteous 'us' versus a corrupt 'them'." As with supposedly committed paratactically-organized poetry today, what remains at issue is the question of praxis: does the reflexive, implicative lyric mode really have more power than the agitprop of the chant? Hasn't reflexivity more to do with a romantic version of the poetic as spiritual discipline? Nevertheless, the valuable thing here, and beyond, is the voiding of what J.H. Prynne terms the greasy sureties of our proper selves, a consolatory subjectivity that longs to wallow in the false unities of the rock idiom. The Fall are exemplary in this respect, rarely allowing mere consciousness to get in the way of a train of thought. In 'Winter' (I'm listening to the 1981 Peel Session version here), repetition (e.g., "back from the backward kids party" echoes "cans of barbican" and "side... on the inside") and chance half-rhymes allow for striking images and conjunctions that suggest some kind of symbolic resolution without bothering to go there: the image is all, comic yet disturbing. We never find out why entrances and enquiries are uncovered by winter itself, nor why they are "delivered"; nor who the "both of you" are. "Street signs you never saw" again suggests a symbolic level, as if the song is all about misdirection, but Mark E. Smith is too wise or too stupid to allow for a message to gel. The words catch on the mind; the mind attempts to process, is left with the bizarre beauty of the images. At least that's how it seemed to me when I first heard the song on John Peel's wireless show and revisited it from time to time in the relative safety of student flats, derelict hospitals, caves, and shotgun shacks. There's something there that's essentially poetic to my taste, just as I like Spike Hawkins (sometimes) and Lynette Roberts and John James. But then Milton is my favourite poet. I don't believe a dissociation of sensibility set in.

But that may be because my mind is dissociated, certainly from place. Much as I've tried to be at home in various parts of England— Herefordshire, Devon, Sussex, Oxford, Manchester, Yorkshire, London, Norfolk—and tend to present myself as an East Anglian poet—my experience has been generally of exile. Perhaps because growing up doltish and lonely in an isolated seaside town, with the grey expanse of the Wash in one direction and miles of uninterrupted fen in the other, leaves an empty space inside you that is impossible to fill. You consider other zones as possible utopias but quickly see though the mythic structures other people seem all too happy to feed themselves into. Everything is provisional, everywhere has a cold ditch at its heart; there is only nomadism, moving on, looking for somewhere rich and strange and unencumbered by clichés, stereotypes, meanness and double-glazing salesmen. Since the alternative to poetic parochialism in Britain seems to be just this kind of rootless fatalism, which in one direction leads paradoxically to the depressive provincialism of Philip Larkin, I can see why people choose to cling to myths of poetic place—

London, Cambridge, Newcastle, and all that—which at least throw up the promise of community. "This is the life fantastic / Where a promise is the same as a guarantee." Thus, David Rees, a similarly disenchanted communitarian, a snowman made of frozen chicken, malingering in Hampton Wick. I truly long for those locales where poets feel at home enough to want to belong to a tendency or movement, but reject their attendant coteries, which blur the distinction between the necessary objectivity of poetry and self-advertisement.

When Andrew Lawson and I set up *fragmente: a magazine of contemporary poetics*, we wanted to celebrate radical poetry and critique while cutting out all the "are you one of us or against us?" downside sentiments of the communities. It worked quite well, though the Cambridge lot showed their old school colours by insisting, as Mr. A. Barnett of Lewes, East Sussex, put it, "no decent poetry comes out of Oxford." Unfortunately for us, they were right—at least up to a point. Plenty of good poetry comes out of Oxford, it just doesn't happen in Oxford. The University was sustaining only as something to kick against. I'm not saying the place is poetically conservative, but I recently overheard an undergraduate say "I've just discovered Rupert Brooke—he really is awfully good"; and, apart from Mike Weaver and (maybe) Terry Eagleton, I've never met anyone there, student or faculty, who's heard of Lorine Niedecker. There were a few interesting people lurking about. I met Bill Herbert at readings by Edwin Morgan and Robert Creeley. He insisted we read Frank O'Hara together wearing fezs. I liked him immensely, but he didn't write *fragmente* poetry. One day, while my visiting father was enjoying the spectacle of a house burning down, I popped round the corner from Iffley Fields into Iffley Road to meet up with a fledgling poet called Simon Smith. We've tormented each other ever since, but he did write the sort of stuff both Lawson and I went for. We were both fans of Tom Raworth and John Wilkinson, and managed to get them together for a reading at Exeter College. The audience of one was highly attentive, though it was at this point we realized that *fragmente* had to range as far out of Oxford as possible.

So I suppose what I'm saying is that a poet needs ideally to be balanced between the inside and the outside of community. The weight easily falls too much on the "out" side to provide a home: too much void and not enough construction. With Pound, I feel the want of what cannot be got in Britain, the "effect of a decent climate where a man leaves his nerve-set open, or allows it to tune into its ambience". But this may be little more than the mid-winter fantasy of "a sudden consistency between incompatibles / as the sun seizes you by the hair / on a terraced path of steps / lined with asphodel and stinking inula." You have to realize that outsideness is largely an imposition of your own dislocated sense of place, the autism of an essential solitude that enfolds the subject into itself even as it begs to be overcome.

Bibliography

Jon Anderson, *Olias of Sunhillow.* Atlantic Records, 1976.

Bob Dylan, *Street Legal.* Columbia, 1978.

The Fall, *The Complete Peel Sessions, 1978–2004.* BBC, 2005.

Edwin Paxton Hood, *The Literature of Labour: Illustrious Instances of the Education of Poetry in Poverty.* 2nd edn. London: Partridge and Oakey, 1852.

Jack Kerouac, *The Dharma Bums.* New York: Viking, 1958.

Morrissey, *You Are the Quarry.* Attack / Sanctuary, 2004.

Pink Floyd, *Animals.* EMI, 1977.

Pink Floyd, *The Wall,* EMI, 1979.

Ezra Pound, 'Cavalcanti', *Literary Essays of Ezra Pound,* ed. T.S. Eliot. London: Faber and Faber, 1954.

J. H. Prynne, *Kitchen Poems.* London: Cape Goliard, 1968.

The Ramones, *Rocket to Russia.* Sire Records, 1977.

David Rees, *david rees enjoys the life fantastic.* London: Simple Vice, 2011.

Scritti Politti, *Songs to Remember.* Virgin Records, 1982.

Simon Reynolds, *Rip It Up and Start Again: Post-punk 1978–1984.* London: Faber, 2005.

The Who, *Who's Next?* Track, 1971.

Biographical Notes

Tim Allen: Poet, polemicist, editor and poetry promoter, though he has spent most of his life as a primary school teacher. Latest publications: *incidental harvest (*Oystercatcher 2011), *Anabranch with Slug*—a robotic pastoral in honor of Raymond Roussel (Knives Forks & Spoons 2011) and *The Voice Thrower* (Shearsman 2012).

David Annwn: Congleton, (Cheshire), Abercynon, (Glam.), Trentham, (Staffs), Nefyn, (Gwynedd), Newton-le-Willows, (Lancs.), Aberystwyth, (Dyfed), Bronant, (Dyfed), Bath, (Avon), Abermad, (Dyfed), Borth, (Dyfed), Ossett, (West Yorks.), Kellington, (North Yorks.), Wakefield, (West Yorks.). Most recent publications include, *Bela Fawr's Cabaret* (2008), *Thel-Time* (2010), (ed.) *Dracula's Precursors*, (2011), *Gothic Machine*, (2011). Lectures for the Open University. www.davidannwn.co.uk/

Tony Baker is a musician and poet who has lived for 15 years in France, to which he is rumoured to have emigrated by mistake. These things happen. In another life he completed a PhD on William Carlos Williams and edited the magazine *FIGS*, thus handsomely equipping himself for an existence of economic insecurity and happy encounters with interesting people without whom the world would be much, much duller. A lucky soul, *quoi*?

Fred Beake has been involved in poetry since 1970. Most recent books are *The Old Outlaw (*Shoestring Press) and *New and Selected Poems* (Shearsman). Edited Mammon Press and *The Poet's Voice*. Was first chair of Avon Poetry Festival. Birmingham University Library Special Collections hold a wide-ranging collection of his papers.

Tilla Brading, poet, performer and textual artist was brought up in Ystradfellte, Powys. Poetry publications: *Possibility of Inferno* (Odyssey Poets 1997), *AUTUMnal Jour* (Maquette Press 1998), *Notes in a Manor: of Speaking* (Leafe Press 2002), *Stone Settings*, with Frances Presley (Odyssey Books & Other Press 2010); *Grid* (Dusie Kollektiv 2012).

Paul Buck: Recent activity includes A *Public Intimacy* (BookWorks, 2011), and *Performance* (Omnibus Press 2012)… and the next translation from Catherine and I in 2012 will be Raúl Ruiz's final novel, *The Wit of the Staircase*.

Jim Burns: Born 1936 in Preston, Lancashire and now lives near Stockport. Recent poetry collections: *Laying Something Down: Poems 1962-2007* (Shoestring Press, 2007); *Streetsinger* (Shoestring Press, 2010). Recent prose: *Radicals, Beats and Beboppers* (Penniless Press, 2011); *Brits, Beats & Outsiders* (Penniless Press, 2012).

Ian Davidson's recent publications include a collection of poems, *Partly in Riga* (Shearsman 2010), and a critical book, *Radical Spaces of Poetry* (Palgrave 2010). After living much of his life in Wales he now works in the English Department at Northumbria University in Newcastle.

Peter Finch is a poet, psychogeographer and literary entrepreneur living in Cardiff. He has been a publisher, bookseller, event organiser, literary agent and literary promoter. Until recently he was Chief Executive of Academi and its successor body, Literature Wales. He finished in 2011 in order to write full time.

Roy Fisher spent half his life in Birmingham, where he was born in 1930, before moving north in stages to the Peak District. His poems are published by Bloodaxe; his interviews and a forthcoming *Collected Prose* by Shearsman.

John Freeman's latest collection is *A Suite for Summer* (Tonbridge: Worple Press 2007). Stride published *The Light Is of Love, I Think: New and Selected Poems* in 1997, and a collection of essays, *The Less Received: Neglected Modern Poets,* in 2000. He teaches at Cardiff University.

Glenda George was born in 1951. She was an active member of the poetry community in England in the 1970s and '80s co-producing *Curtains* with Paul Buck and guest-editing *Reality Studios Vol 7, 'The Inseam'.* She lives in Northern Scotland and is a songwriter and a member of the all-female, world music group MoZaiC.

Alan Halsey: Born in Croydon, 1949. *Marginalien* (Five Seasons 2005) collects his poems, prose and graphics 1988-2004. *Not Everything Remotely* (Salt Publishing 2006) is a selected poems 1978-2005. His recent books are *Term as in Aftermath* (Ahadada 2009), *Lives of the Poets* (Five Seasons 2009), *Even if only out of* (Veer 2011) and the text-graphic *In White Writing* (Xexoxial 2012). With Ken Edwards he edited Bill Griffiths' *Collected Earlier Poems* (Reality Street 2010). He co-directs the Sheffield-based antichoir, Juxtavoices, with Martin Archer.

Kris Hemensley: Born in the UK in 1946. He emigrated to Melbourne in 1966, returning to England for periods throughout these decades. Active in both the New Australian & New British poetry scenes, he manages the poetry bookshop, Collected Works, and publishes his blog www.collectedworks-poetryideas.blogspot.com

Peter Hodgkiss: Born 1944, Belper, Derbyshire. Editor *Poetry Information* 1970-1980. Editor *Not Poetry* 1980-1985. Publisher Galloping Dog Press 1974-1991. Member of Poetry Society General Council 1975-1977. Publisher's Rep for Yale University Press (and others) 1985-2012.

Nicholas Johnson was born and raised in North Devon. His works include *Loup, Haul Song, Land* and *Cleave* (Writers Forum, Mammon Press, and Waterloo Press). He read Performance Writing and Visual Performance at Dartington College, and was Writer-in-Residence at the Arnolfini, Bristol, for *Starting at Zero, Black Mountain College*. He has run For The Locker And The Steerer in London since 1999. He curated B.M. Bottomley's exhibition at *Salthouse*, St Ives, in 2009.

Chris McCabe is a widely-published poet and joint librarian of the Poetry Library in London. His latest publication is *The Restructure* (Salt Publishing 2012).

Anthony Mellors has recently completed 'Autopsia: Olson, Themis, Pausanias', which will appear in the journal *Modernism / Modernity*, 'Disabled Poetry' for *Textual Practice*, and an introduction to the aesthetics of economic crisis. He is the author of *Late Modernist Poetics from Pound to Prynne* (Manchester University Press 2005). His poetry includes *A Pastoral* (Oxford 1992; reprinted in *Exact Change Yearbook* (Exact Change / Carcanet 1995)) and *The Gordon Brown Sonnets* (Verisimilitude 2009). He is currently working on *Bent Out of Shape*.

Geraldine Monk is a Lancastrian who lives in Yorkshire. Her book *Interregnum* (Creation Books 1995) centred around East Lancashire and the Pendle witches, her book *Escafeld Hangings* (West House Books 2005) centred around South Yorkshire and Mary Queen of Scots. Her latest book *Lobe Scarps & Finials* (Leafe Press 2011) centres around the moon and raccoons.

Hannah Neate is a cultural and historical geographer who works at the University of Central Lancashire. She carried out her doctoral research (completed 2010) on the cultural life of Nottingham in the 1960s. It was during her research into creative and artistic offerings emanating from the East Midlands that she came across the Tarasque Press and Trent Book Shop. Her other interests include the history of regional arts centres in Britain and twentieth century architecture.

Connie Pickard was born on Tyneside and educated at King's College, Dunelm, in the 1950s. She co-founded Morden Tower poetry-reading centre in 1964 with Tom Pickard and still takes an active interest in its activities. She now lives in Gateshead.

Tom Pickard's last three books of poetry published in Chicago by Flood Editions: *Hole in the Wall* (2002); *Dark Months of May* (2004); *Ballad of Jamie Allan* (2008). His part-memoir, *More Pricks Than Prizes* was published in 20011 by Pressed Wafer in Boston.

Frances Presley was born in Derbyshire and lives in London and Somerset. Recent publications include *Paravane: new and selected poems, 1996-2003* (Salt Publishing 2004), *Myne: new and selected poems and prose, 1976-2005* (Shearsman 2006), *Lines of sight* (Shearsman 2009), and *Stone settings*, with Tilla Brading (Odyssey Books & Other Press 2010).

Peter Riley has had some fifteen books of poetry published, of which the most recent is *The Glacial Stairway* (Carcanet 2011). Following the adventures related herein, he studied at Cambridge and Sussex universities, lived in Denmark and the Peak District, and after a long and varied lack of career took to poetry bookselling. He now lives in retirement in Cambridge.

John Seed is the author of several collections of verse, including *History Labour Night* (Pig Press, Durham 1984), *Interior in the Open Air* (Reality Studios, London 1993), *Divided into One* (Poetical Histories, Cambridge 2003), and *New and Collected Poems* and *Pictures from Mayhew* (both Shearsman 2005). He has also written a lot of history, a book on Marx, and essays on the poetry of Basil Bunting, George Oppen and Bill Griffiths.

Chris Torrance continues to live & write in the Welsh uplands. His work with Heatpoets (with musician Chris Vine) has resulted in the CD and booklet *RORI*, which has also been performed live at several venues. His book *PATH*, containing poems from the last 25 years, is due out from Skysill Press in 2012.

Gillian Whiteley is an artist-curator-writer based at Loughborough University. She also operates as bricolagekitchen, a multifaceted project space for creative-critical practice, emerging from preoccupations with the art and politics of bricolage, assemblage and trash. Publications include *Junk: Art and the Politics of Trash* (I.B.Tauris, 2011). She is co-organiser of *RadicalAesthetics-RadicalArt* (RaRa). See www.bricolagekitchen.com

Index